LINKING THEORY AND PRACTICE

SAFEGUARDING AND CHILD PROTECTION

FIFTH EDITION

Jennie Lindon
Janet Webb

HODDER
EDUCATION
AN HACHETTE UK COMPANY

Hachette UK's policy is to use papers that are natural, renewable and recyclable products and made from wood grown in sustainable forests. The logging and manufacturing processes are expected to conform to the environmental regulations of the country of origin.

Orders: please contact Bookpoint Ltd, 130 Park Drive, Milton Park, Abingdon, Oxon OX14 4SE. Telephone: (44) 01235 827720. Fax: (44) 01235 400454. Email education@bookpoint.co.uk Lines are open from 9 a.m. to 5 p.m., Monday to Saturday, with a 24-hour message answering service. You can also order through our website: www.hoddereducation.co.uk

ISBN: 978 1471 86605 0

© Jennie Lindon and Janet Webb 2016
First published in 1998
Second edition published in 2003
Third edition published in 2008
Fourth edition published in 2012

This edition published in 2016 by
Hodder Education,
An Hachette UK Company
Carmelite House
50 Victoria Embankment
London EC4Y 0DZ

www.hoddereducation.co.uk
Impression number   10 9 8 7 6 5 4 3 2 1
Year   2020 2019 2018 2017 2016

Cover photo © Ralf Hettler/Vetta/Getty Images. This photo is used for illustrative purposes only. The child depicted is a model.
Typeset in ITC Garamond Std 10.5/13pt by Aptara inc.
Printed in Italy
A catalogue record for this title is available from the British Library.

Contents

Introduction

This is now the fifth edition of a book that started life in 1998. The landscape of safeguarding work continues to evolve, as do the legislative and policy frameworks that guide practice. It is now embedded in national policy that safeguarding is everyone's responsibility and while local authorities play a lead role, everyone who comes into contact with a child and their families has a role to play both in preventative work and interventions to protect children from harm. As identified in previous editions, local authorities have overarching responsibility for safeguarding and promoting the welfare of all children in their area (HM Government, 2015). However, while social workers are the leads in inter-agency and inter-professional working, when child protection interventions are required safeguarding and child protection are issues of multi-agency responsibility. This is in terms of inter-agency and professional working, information sharing across sectors and working with local communities, families and children themselves (Laming, 2009; Munro, 2011; HM Government, 2015). Laming (2009) highlights that in order to safeguard children from harm, relationships between practitioners are crucial: 'it's not about structures, it's about making it work out there for children'. Social services cannot work in isolation from other agencies. All service providers in touch with children have a role in prevention, recognising and responding to concerns about a child. Those working in universal services, education as well as health, are in a prime position to identify situations that may fall outside the 'norm' and threaten the safety and well being of children.

In recent years there has been increasing emphasis on prevention and early intervention. Child abuse itself can only be prevented if vulnerable children are identified early – before abuse takes place. However, as Powell (2011) notes, good safeguarding practice across all agencies remains largely hidden and unannounced. It is difficult to capture evidence of success in preventing harm. However, anyone whose work brings them into contact with children and or their families may come across situations that present a significant risk to children. This book starts with the premise that safeguarding the welfare of children is a public health issue for all sectors not just social care or those specifically working in public health.

As Powell (2011) notes, the core skills for safeguarding include the ability to assess need, to work in partnership with children, their families and multi-disciplinary teams in order to promote physical and emotional well being and to ensure safety. If outcomes for vulnerable children are to be improved, practice itself must also take account of and reflect the changes that relate to wider society as well as practice itself, such as the ever increasing use of technologies. Best practice must be based on best evidence and be in accordance with contemporary policy and legislation so as to reflect the current safeguarding agendas across all sectors. Children are best protected from harm when practitioners are clear about what is required of them individually and how they need to work together. This book is primarily aimed at those working in childcare settings and the early years. It is also relevant for students on undergraduate childcare/childhood studies and early-years programmes and primary teacher training programmes. However, the book is also relevant to a wider professional audience than is initially evident, including that of healthcare and social care. Safeguarding is an inter-professional responsibility and, while each profession and practice area may have specific responsibilities related to individual roles, each sector cannot work in isolation from each other if vulnerable children are to be protected from harm.

The previous four editions of this book were written by Jennie Lindon, a respected expert in the field of early years, education and play who has extensive experience of working with professionals to safeguard vulnerable children. I am privileged to update this edition, the aims of which remain philosophically the same as the previous editions in showing active respect for the needs of children and their families. This book seeks to retain the uniqueness of Jennie's approach while providing contemporary perspectives on safeguarding. This edition focuses on how those working with children should respond to concerns about a child's vulnerability and work together with others to effectively address the needs of vulnerable children and those children who need protecting from harm. This focus is set within current legislative and policy frameworks. It will take account of the 'early help' and children's rights agendas in order that practitioners might contribute to the prevention of abuse to children and intervene early to improve outcomes for vulnerable children within an inter-professional context and to help ensure that the child's needs are at the centre of all decisions and interventions.

However, what is important to remember is that the core of safe practice when working with and for children remains unaltered. At root, as identified in the previous editions, children are kept safe, or put at risk, through the behaviour of other adults or other children but largely by people they know. Additionally, children and young people steadily need to share in the responsibility to keep themselves safe although they are inevitably influenced by their previous experience, including the extent to which familiar adults have taken seriously their responsibility to enable older children and adolescents to take good care of themselves.

The authors are committed to the Children's Rights agendas and continue to promote the importance of listening to and hearing the child's voice. They support the notion that learning and knowledge is generated from conversations with, and listening to the voice of, children and young people. This book, therefore, has as its premise that children's rights and child-centredness are essential to effective safeguarding. A wide range of practitioners make up the children's workforce across the sectors and it therefore remains imperative that an inter-professional disciplinary approach be taken and that practitioners, within and across all sectors, work together to protect vulnerable children. Additionally, safeguarding can only work if practitioners have the opportunity to understand about safeguarding in action, to reflect, to explain (hopefully more clearly) and to double-check. Furthermore, all practitioners need to understand their own role within safeguarding – what they do as well as those parts of the process that are the direct responsibility of another professional service (Lindon, 2008). Practitioners can, however, only understand their involvement by understanding the larger picture, including historical influences and how the broad framework for safeguarding and child protection developed in the UK, as well as the key issues needed for the system to work effectively.

'Ultimately, effective safeguarding of children can only be achieved by putting children at the centre of the system, and by every individual and agency playing their full part, working together to meet the needs of our most vulnerable children' (HM Government, 2015). The structure of this book has been adjusted slightly to address contemporary approaches. It discusses the principles, definitions and how to recognise abuse and neglect before discussing the steps to take within the legislative and policy framework. It is important to note that this edition of the book draws on contemporary legislation and uses the current government guidelines as a framework and makes reference to these guidelines for formal definitions of abuse and neglect.

It is recognised that policy for practice may change during the lifetime of this edition and it is the reader's individual responsibility to ensure that they are cognizant with contemporary legislation and policy for practice.

An introductory first chapter has been included in this edition to consider the underpinning principles and frameworks for safeguarding and child–protection practice and to provide a contextual background. This includes a brief overview of contemporary policy and introduces the roles of others, including health and statutory lead agencies (children's social care and the police). It will discuss contemporary perspectives, and define key terms.

Chapter 2 explains and describes the main types of abuse and neglect, as they are covered within the child-protection policy guidance in the UK. It therefore looks at what constitutes abuse and neglect and presents policy definitions of abuse and neglect and the historical influences on these. Definitions are important as they influence contemporary perspectives and inform understandings for the recognition and response to abuse and neglect. Definitions are inextricably linked to incidence and prevalence. Consideration is given to extrafamilial abuse as well as intrafamilial abuse. The chapter acknowledges that the scope of child protection has increased with contemporary concerns that include: child abuse and neglect in an international context, child asylum seekers, unaccompanied minors, trafficking of children, the abuse of children online, 'fabricated' or 'induced' illness, child sexual exploitation and the impact of extremism.

Chapter 3 provides an overview of the legislative and policy context from a historical and contemporary perspective. It addresses how practitioners should respond to concerns within the legislative and policy frameworks. While practitioners are working within the present, it is useful to have an understanding of how historical perspectives have influenced the development of legislation and policy in the UK before addressing contemporary perspectives.

Chapter 4 is concerned with 'child protection in action': how practitioners recognise and respond to concerns and the steps they should take to deal with them. It considers the notion of the vulnerable child and signs of vulnerability before discussing steps and interventions that should be taken to address concerns. It discusses signs of abuse or neglect in light of the definitions provided in Chapter 2, and also factors that might influence whether or not a child discloses abuse.

Chapter 5 considers equality practice and safeguarding. This chapter identifies key issues related to gender and disability, as well as cultural background, faith and cultural traditions that challenge safeguarding and child protection.

Chapter 6 reviews policy, procedures and what constitutes best practice. The implications for safety and security are identified and the chapter emphasises the importance of documentation and record keeping, information sharing and why an inter-professional integrated approach is required.

Chapter 7 is concerned with how practitioners promote the well being and welfare of children and the principles that underpin 'good' care of children. It considers physical care and nurture, keeping children safe and the impact of troubled relationships between peers.

Chapter 8 aims to bring together the main principles of good practice that support children and families in order to empower them. It considers how practitioners should work for and with families. It also provides perspectives for child protection and the courts, and, drawing on previous discussions about the vulnerable child, gives attention to families and children under stress.

Chapter 9 discusses the importance of early help and aims to summarise key issues and reflect on the implications for future safeguarding practice.

As with previous editions, the authors have had to make some decisions about terminology and the following definitions are used within this book:

- Child: A child is defined as anyone who had not yet reached their eighteenth birthday (HM Government, 2015a). However, this book is concerned with children 0–8 years of age. Therefore, unless stated otherwise, 'children' means this age group. Older children will be referred to as young people.
- Parent: anyone who takes the main family responsibility for children and acts in a parental role, whether or not that person is a birth parent. Please assume the word always includes 'and other family carers'.
- Practitioner: anyone whose work brings them into face-to-face contact with children on a regular basis. I have been specific about the profession whenever the information is relevant.
- Practice area: any group situation, attended by children, where services are delivered to children and their families.

- Designated safeguarding professional lead: Contemporary safeguarding–children policy requires 'a designated professional lead' (or, for health provider organisations, named professionals) for safeguarding. Their role is to support other professionals in their agencies to recognise the needs of children, including rescue from possible abuse or neglect. Designated professional roles should always be explicitly defined in job descriptions. 'Professionals should be given sufficient time, funding, supervision and support to fulfil their child welfare and safeguarding responsibilities effectively' (HM Government, 2015).

  In educational settings this lead is referred to as the 'designated safeguarding lead' and so throughout this book, that term will be used. However, in healthcare the terms 'named professional' and 'safeguarding adviser' will be used.

The scenarios were developed from real people and places, but in every case details have been changed to provide anonymity and confidentiality. Readers can use these examples to explore aspects of practice – either on their own or in discussion with colleagues or fellow students. Throughout the book there are key messages for practice that help to link theory to practice and 'reflection points' that provides the reader with opportunities to consider some of the issues discussed and the implications for their own and others' practice and or practice experiences. Additionally, the reader is signposted to further resources at the end of each chapter. Any references to websites were correct at the time the book went to press.

The information in *Safeguarding and Child Protection* is accurate to the best of our knowledge, at the time of writing in 2015. As with every other edition of this book, reviews of safeguarding and proposals for change may occur after the book has gone to press. It is the individual responsibility of all readers to check and to update themselves. This responsibility is especially sharp if you or your colleagues are seeking to reach a difficult decision that is dependent on interpretation of the law, or a precise understanding of guidance or local guidelines. No section of this book claims to offer legal advice.

Otherwise, we take the usual responsibility for the content of the book, the ideas within it and any errors we have failed to recognise. Please let Hodder Education know if you identify mistakes or misunderstandings and we will correct them as soon as possible.

Dedications and acknowledgements

Jennie Lindon
To my parents, from whom I experienced respect and such very good care. To my son and daughter, who taught me a great deal about being a parent.

Janet Webb
I would like to thank my husband and sons for their patience and support. I also thank Jennie Lindon for allowing me the privilege of updating her book.

The Publishers would like to thank the following for permission to reproduce copyright material.

Open University Press for Table 3.2 from B. Corby, D. Shemmings and D. Wilkins *Child Abuse: An Evidence Base for Confident Practice, 4th edition*, © 2012.

Research in Practice for Figure 4.1 from J. Webb and D. Holmes (2015) *Working Effectively to Address Child Sexual Exploitation: Evidence Scope.*

This book also contains public sector information licensed under the Open Government Licence v3.0.

Every effort has been made to trace all copyright holders, but if any have been inadvertently overlooked, the Publishers will be pleased to make the necessary arrangements at the first opportunity.

1 Safeguarding children: principles for practice

Introduction

The aim of this book is to prepare and support those students and practitioners working within, or studying, early years or childcare settings for school-aged children, and to confirm the importance of safeguarding for practitioners in these and other practice settings. It is about promoting best outcomes for children and to help determine that the actions and interventions of practitioners ensure the welfare and well being of vulnerable children. This chapter provides a contextual background.

This book starts with the premise that safeguarding children is the responsibility of all practitioners whose work brings them into contact with children, young people and their families. It is acknowledged that 'Local authorities have overarching responsibility for safeguarding and promoting the welfare of all children and young people in their area. They have a number of statutory functions under the 1989 and 2004 Children Acts which make this clear, and ... This includes specific duties in relation to children in need and children suffering, or likely to suffer, significant harm, regardless of where they are found, under sections 17 and 47 of the Children Act 1989. The Director of Children's Services and Lead Member for Children's Services in local authorities are the key points of professional and political accountability, with responsibility for the effective delivery of these functions' (HM Government, 2015a).

Section 17 of the Children Act pertains to 'children in need' who would benefit from additional statutory support and Section 47 pertains to those children who have suffered or are likely to suffer significant harm and require more urgent interventions.

However, local authorities do not have *sole* responsibility for safeguarding and as HM Government (2015a: 5) states: 'safeguarding children and protecting them from harm is everyone's responsibility. Everyone who comes into contact with children and families has a role to play' and that 'Local agencies, including the police and health services, also have a duty under section 11 of the Children Act 2004 to ensure that they consider the need to safeguard and promote the welfare of children when carrying out their functions. Under section 10 of the same Act, a similar range of agencies are required to co-operate with local authorities to promote the well being of children in each local authority area. This co-operation should exist and be effective at all levels of the organisation, from strategic level through to operational delivery' and 'Professionals working in agencies →

with these duties are responsible for ensuring that they fulfil their role and responsibilities in a manner consistent with the statutory duties of their employer'.

All practitioners, therefore, need to understand their own role within safeguarding: what they do, as well as those parts of the process that are the direct responsibility of another professional or service. Children are best protected when all professionals understand their individual and others' roles (HM Government, 2015a). You can only make sense of your involvement by understanding the larger picture: how the broad framework for child protection developed in the UK and key issues for the system to work effectively. This opening chapter outlines the principles for safeguarding practice and provides a context from a historical and contemporary perspective. The legislative and policy frameworks are introduced, as are the roles of different professionals across the sectors.

This chapter therefore covers the current context of safeguarding in the UK, providing an overview of contemporary perspectives. It considers children's rights, parenting and 'parental responsibility' and what this means. It defines the key terms used in current policy and highlights the implications for multi-agency practice.

The current context of safeguarding in the UK

In recent years, the scope of safeguarding work has increased and developed. When the Children Act 1989 (Great Britain 1989) was implemented in 1991 the main concerns for child protection workers were with intrafamilial neglect and abuse, and the main forms of abuse were physical, sexual, emotional and neglect. However, as Corby *et al.* (2012) note, the early 1990s saw increased attention given to organised abuse and both a rise and fall in concerns about ritual abuse. By 2000, the abuse of children in institutional settings was on the agenda, and remains a concern, particularly in light of historical child abuse cases. Bullying is now contextualised as peer abuse and it is recognised that children may abuse other children, although it has to be recognised that the 'bully' may also be a victim in light of their own unmet needs or that their behaviour is a maladaptation to previous harm. Since 2000, it has also been highlighted that parental drug and alcohol misuse, parental mental health and domestic abuse have adverse effects on children and often coexist as 'the toxic trio' (Brandon *et al.* 2009, 2011, 2012). Other concerns have also emerged such as child abuse and neglect in an international context, child trafficking, child asylum seekers, as well as 'fabricated' or 'induced illness' and female genital mutilation. There is now a focus on extrafamilial abuse as well as intrafamilial abuse, with increased understandings of the extent and nature of Child Sexual Exploitation both on and off line (Webb and Holmes, 2015). The perpetrators, however, are still usually known to their victims.

In recent years, the concept of safeguarding children has taken on a higher profile than in the past. However, promoting the welfare of children and ensuring that they are protected from harm is challenging. It does, though, (as Powell (2011) notes) cut across all sectors within a context of multi-professional and inter-agency working and requires that all partners from education, health, children's social care, and the police work together. It is everyone's responsibility and a key public-health issue that encompasses a wide range of activities including:

- preventative work
- holistic assessment of need
- early identification of vulnerability and prevention of harm or further harm
- referral to appropriate agencies who can provide family and parenting support
- recognition and referral of children who are at risk of, or who are suffering from significant harm
- working within a multi-agency team to provide additional support, on-going assessment and interventions as part of a 'child in need' or 'child protection plan'
- reviews of child deaths and serious cases.

It is also worth noting, as highlighted by Powell (2011), that successful safeguarding practice across all agencies remains largely hidden. Examples of success are rarely captured. However, anyone whose work brings them into contact with children and their families may come across situations that present a significant risk to children but rarely the serious injury or death of a child from abuse or neglect. Reviews of such cases, along with opportunity to reflect on practice through supervision, can offer insight into good practice and opportunities for improvement on an individual and organisational level.

The next section will briefly review the underpinning knowledge for practice and key terms, before discussing some of the contemporary considerations for practice.

Keep the child in mind

In light of the above, a key message for those working with children is that successful safeguarding practice is based on the willingness to work in partnership with other colleagues as well as children and families, and on the promotion of physical and emotional well being through actions that promote early intervention and prevention of harm or further harm.

Children: the wider context

As noted in the introduction, the UK has adopted the legal definition of a child as being an individual who has not yet reached the age of 18 years. This is in line with the United Nation (UN) Convention on the Rights of the Child 1989 (UN, 1989) and is the definition used within safeguarding policy. The definition applies to all children and young people, including those who are living independently, are in the armed forces, are in secure custodial accommodation or are in further or higher education. The definition also applies to those in hospital (HM Government, 2015a). It also means that young people over the age of 16 years are entitled to statutory child-protection interventions, including teenage parents who might be vulnerable themselves.

It is also important to note that childhood itself is a period of rapid maturity. Development is, however, multifaceted, and sometimes uneven, and includes physical, psychological, cognitive, emotional and social development. It is worth noting that from a health perspective, the National Institute for Health and Clinical Excellence (NICE) offer the definitions as follows:

- Infant: aged under one year
- Child: aged under 13 years
- Young person: aged 13–17 years.

Take another perspective

It is also important to consider unborn infants. While unborn infants are not legally defined as children, their need for protection from harm must still be considered in cases where there is concern that the expectant parents may not have the capacity to meet the baby's needs following birth. This would primarily be the responsibility of the midwife and other professionals providing care in the antenatal period. However, practitioners working in all sectors need to be aware of the specific factors that may affect the welfare of the unborn child and recognise and respond to concerns. This may include such factors as substance misuse and/or adult mental-health problems. It is also pertinent to reiterate that a young parent may still be a child themselves. Those working with infants and children may well come across parents who are pregnant and give cause for concern, hence the need to consider the unborn on the age spectrum.

This book is focusing on the infant and younger child but, whatever age the child, it is important to acknowledge that children at different points on the age spectrum have different and individual needs.

Pause for reflection

What do you think are the particular developmental needs of infants and children under the age of eight years?

Children's rights: rights for all children

Each individual child has the right to provision for welfare and protection from harm as contained within the United Nations Convention on the Rights of the Child (UNCRC), which provides a basis for practice to ensure that actions are taken to ensure a child's welfare (Powell, 2011). The UNCRC details the responsibilities of governments to provide the best possible services to support children to achieve their full potential and make a successful transition to adulthood as they grow and develop. This includes all sectors, i.e. education and health as well as social care.

The UNCRC has four core principles:

- non-discrimination
- devotion to the best interests of the child
- the right to life, survival and development
- respect for the views of the child.

The UNCRC provides the principles for a rights-based approach to the safeguarding of children – an approach that is enshrined in safeguarding and child protection legislation, policy and practice guidance within the UK and that should therefore be embedded within practice.

The UNCRC articulates the need for children to be both seen and heard. It is an international agreement that protects the rights of children and provides a framework that enables children to be put at the centre of service delivery. The UK Government ratified the UNCRC in 1991 and, in doing so, upholds children's rights to expression and also the receiving of information (HM Government, 2015a).

Keep the child in mind

Children's rights, child-centredness and listening to the voice of the child are essential for effective safeguarding practice across all agencies and sectors (HM Government, 2015a; Powell, 2011) and, as Laming (2009) points out, this approach is essential for the achievement of best outcomes for children.

Notably the child's best interests must be the top priority at all times and the paramountcy principle of the Children Act 1989 (see page 55) must be adhered to where applicable and children's rights under the UNCRC, Article 3 be fully honoured (Webb and Holmes, 2015).

Pause for reflection

How would you describe your approach to practice?

How will you ensure that you will uphold a 'rights based' approach to your work with children?

Parents, parenting and parental responsibility

It has been reiterated above that safeguarding is everyone's responsibility. However, as Powell (2011) notes, it is important to point out that the care and protection of children is primarily the role and responsibility of parents, or those who have been granted, through the courts, parental responsibility for a child. Parental responsibility can be held by more than one person other than the biological mother with or without the biological father. This could be the local authority if the child is in care or another member of the family through, for example, a 'child arrangement order'.

What does it mean?

In April 2015, 'residence' and 'contact' orders were abolished and replaced by **child arrangement orders**. Previously it was a *residence order* that settled the arrangements as to the person with whom a child was to live. It was a *contact order* that previously required the person with whom a child lives, or is going to live, to allow that child to visit or stay with the person named in the order, or for that person and the child otherwise to have contact with each other.

The new 'child arrangement orders' determine:

a. **With whom** a child is to live, spend time or otherwise have contact, and
b. **When** a child is to live, spend time or otherwise have contact with any person.

As such, a child arrangement order therefore decides:

- Where a child lives
- When a child spends time with each parent
- When and what other types of contact (like phone calls) take place

The legislation of Children Act 1989 has therefore been amended.

(Alternative Family Law, 2015)

Parental responsibility

This is defined as 'all the rights, duties, powers, responsibilities and authority which by law a parent of a child has'. The mother always has parental responsibility but others can acquire it. It is important to note that with regard to fathers, the child's father has parental responsibility if:

- he **is married** to the mother at the time of the birth;
- under English law also, **if he marries** the mother later on;
- he **is on the birth certificate** for births registered in England or Wales after 1 December 2003;

- he and the mother have signed a parental responsibility agreement which is a prescribed form, and lodged it with the court; or
- the court has made a parental responsibility order in the father's favour.

Find out more

For further information regarding this, please access the following resources:

www.legislation.gov.uk/ukpga/1989/41/contents

www.gov.uk/looking-after-children-divorce/types-of-court-order

www.alternativefamilylaw.co.uk/en/children/child-arrangements-orders.htm

www.netmums.com/coffeehouse/advice-support-40/single-parents-support-45/418066-residence-order-advice-all.html

Whoever has parental responsibility it is important that a child's basic needs are met, that they are kept safe and protected and are shown warmth and love. If a reciprocal bond develops between the carer and their child it is more likely to impact positively on a child's development. However, it's worth mentioning here that bonding and attachment are not the same. As Wilkins *et al.* (2015) discuss, bonding is a general term relating to the many different kind of relationships people have. Attachment, however, is about another human being providing a secure base and a focus for proximity seeking and safe-haven behaviours at times of heightened anxiety. Within attachment relationships there is a sense of turning to someone else for safety and security, whereas the reciprocal bond that an 'adult attachment' figure develops with their child is known in attachment theory as a caregiving bond. As the infant develops, an attachment relationship is formed with their parent, and so the parent develops a caregiving bond with the infant (Wilkins *et al.* 2015). This bond is experienced as love.

Infants and children must also be encouraged to express their views and the parent is responsible for providing the stimulation needed for their development and to help them achieve their potential within a stable environment with consistent guidance and boundaries. While there is no 'perfect' model of parenting, having an understanding of what 'good' parenting looks like is helpful in recognising parents who may need support and determining what support might be required by the family as a whole (Powell, 2011).

Pause for reflection

What might be the difference between supportive parenting and unsupportive parenting?

Are you aware of the professionals who might be involved in supporting parenting?

Fatherhood

In recent years there has been increased attention given to fatherhood and the role of fathers in ensuring the health, safety and well being of their children (Reeves, 2008). The needs of young fathers in the UK have received less attention, but there is now growing recognition that fathers – particularly young fathers, resident or non-resident – may require support in order to parent effectively.

Within the United Kingdom the Fatherhood Institute is influential in ensuring that fathers are represented within policy and practice, and the Fatherhood Institute website (www.fatherhoodinstitute.org) provides legal advice about parental responsibility for unmarried fathers. The amendments to the original legislation as contained within the Children Act 1989 about the position of fathers and parental responsibility has created greater inclusivity for fathers, which should be reflected in the practice of those working with children and their families (Powell, 2011).

Terminology: safeguarding and child protection

The terms 'safeguarding' and 'child protection' are not synonymous: safeguarding pertains to wider activities that support the well being of children; child protection is *part of* safeguarding.

Safeguarding

Safeguarding is defined within statutory guidance (HM Government, 2015a) as:

- protecting children from maltreatment;
- preventing impairment of children's health or development;
- ensuring that children grow up in circumstances consistent with the provision of safe and effective care; and
- taking action to enable all children to have the best outcomes.

This definition reflects the move from an outcome-based approach to policy and practice within the UK. Contemporary policy advocates the provision of help and advice to parents, the promotion of healthy choices for children and gives more emphasis on well being (HM Government, 2015; Powell, 2011). The Children Act 2004 takes attainment of five outcomes as being core to its definition of well being. These are said to reflect what children and young people said they wanted from their childhood, which is to:

- be healthy
- stay safe
- enjoy and achieve
- make a positive contribution
- achieve economic well being.

While there has been debate about the outcomes and the terminology the outcomes remain and it is important to recognise that they are all linked. A child who is not healthy or safe might not enjoy and achieve (Powell, 2011).

Child protection

Child protection is part of safeguarding and promoting welfare.

What does it mean?

Child protection refers to the activity that is undertaken to protect specific children who are suffering, or are likely to suffer, significant harm as a result of abuse or neglect. It involves measures and structures designed to prevent and respond to abuse and neglect.

- Child abuse involves acts of commission and omission, which result in harm to the child.
- In line with statutory guidance, Local Children Safeguarding Boards (or their equivalent) produce local policies and procedures for inter-agency working to 'safeguard children'. Additionally, all organisations providing services for children will have their own local or 'in house' policies and procedures.
- It is also important that further or higher education institutions have guidance for students explaining what they should do if they identify concerns in practice.

Pause for reflection

Are you aware of how to locate and use these documents in your own organisation, locality or practice area?

Vulnerability and risks to children's well being

It could be argued that infants and young children are vulnerable in light of their age and dependency on others to ensure their safety. However, an infant's or child's vulnerability increases with increased risk to their health, safety and well being when factors impact on their parents' ability to meet their needs. These include parental mental health difficulties, substance misuse and domestic abuse and or violence. As mentioned earlier, these phenomena often co-exist and have been conceptualised as the toxic trio (Brandon *et al.* 2009, 2010, 2012). Children's vulnerability is also increased when their parents have never worked, or are long-term unemployed, when compared with the children of professional or managerial classes (Action for Children, 2012; Powell, 2011).

Although the extent to which children are vulnerable is difficult to measure (Action for Children, 2012), increasing attention is being given to the needs of vulnerable children with emphasis on a model of integrated services to meet these needs (Department of Health (DH) 2009). Current policy agendas highlight that if the inequalities in children's health, well being and achievement are to be reduced, practitioners need to be able to identify children with high risk and low protective factors and ensure that these families are referred to appropriate services for support (DH, 2009).

Poverty is one of the biggest risk factors related to poorer outcomes for children.

Pause for reflection

Are you able to identify the risk factors that are likely to impact on health, learning and achievement in early childhood?

Are you aware of the generic indicators that can be used to identify children who are at risk of poor educational and social outcomes?

Do you know how your practice area works with others to address health inequalities in your locality?

Parental capacity

Parental capacity relates to the ability of a parent to meet their child's needs. The NSPCC (2014) identifies that 'good enough parenting' comprises four elements:

- meeting children's health and developmental needs
- putting children's needs first
- providing routine and consistent care
- acknowledging problems and engaging with support services.

On the other hand, risky parenting is associated (Kellett and Apps, 2009) with:

- neglecting basic needs; putting adults' needs first
- chaos and lack of routine, and
- an unwillingness to engage with support services.

Keep the child in mind

Parenting capacity is one of the three core elements that need to be assessed when there are concerns that a child is vulnerable to maltreatment. The other two elements being the child's developmental needs, and the wider family and environmental factors. The three elements are, however, inter-related and cannot be considered in isolation (HM Government, 2015a).

Child maltreatment

Child maltreatment is the concept that relates to the abuse and neglect of a child. Abuse is a form of maltreatment. It is therefore important to note that child maltreatment is a challenging concept to define, mainly because what is, or is not, seen to be harmful to children can vary over time and within society according to contemporary knowledge, and the beliefs and values of both individuals and society as a whole (Corby *et al.* 2012). Definitions of maltreatment and what constitutes abuse and neglect are discussed in Chapter 2.

Pause for reflection

It might be useful to look at child maltreatment as being on a spectrum of 'poor to good parenting' (Powell, 2011).

What benchmarks would you use to help you decide whether or not a parent's behaviour is indicative of abuse?

What are the categories of abuse identified within UK policy?

It is also important to note that child maltreatment most commonly occurs within family settings, with the perpetrators being the parents. However, it can also occur in institutions, including educational and healthcare settings, and communities. The perpetrator is rarely a stranger and while 'stranger danger' is given attention, stranger abuse is relatively uncommon (Powell, 2011).

Significant harm

Significant harm is the benchmark used to determine whether or not compulsory, statutory intervention is required to protect the child from harm, i.e. the need to invoke child protection proceedings. The concept of 'significant harm' was introduced with the Children Act 1989 (England and Wales) as the key to child protection work. It recognises the need to consider a range of factors, including:

- the nature of harm;
- the impact on the health and development of the child;
- any special needs the child may have (including disability or a medical condition);
- parental capacity to meet the needs of the child; and
- the context of the family and environment.

It is important to note that there are no absolute criteria to judge significant harm. It depends on the extent, nature and severity of the abuse and/or neglect, as well as the seriousness and/or likely long-term impairment of physical or mental health or physical, intellectual, emotional, social or behavioural development.

Reflecting on the daily-lived experiences of the child can help practitioners determine whether or not a child is suffering significant harm. However, it is always important that concerns are shared. In schools, this will be with the designated safeguarding officer and in other organisations with the safeguarding lead. If there are any concerns that significant harm has occurred then a referral must be made to Children's Social Care under section 47 of the Children Act 1989 and local policies must be followed (HM Government, 2015a). Referral processes are discussed in Chapter 3.

The impact of child maltreatment

Recognising and responding to concerns about vulnerable children is crucial if outcomes for vulnerable children are to be improved. Furthermore, child maltreatment will have both short-term and long-term ramifications if interventions are not put in place to stop the harm. As Powell (2011) notes, these include:

- death
- neurological damage
- disability (physical and learning)
- physical injuries
- mental health problems (including depression and self-harm)
- poor self-esteem
- attachment disorders (for a useful resource on attachment theory see Wilkins *et al.* (2015))
- emotional and behavioural problems; and educational difficulties.

There is increasing evidence to confirm that child maltreatment is linked to poor health and social outcomes in adulthood. While some individuals do develop resilience to the effects of abuse and neglect, not all do and it is argued that the morbidity and mortality that results from what is essentially a preventable phenomenon is unacceptable.

The incidence and prevalence of child maltreatment

The incidence of child abuse is measured by the number of cases that are recorded by the authorities over the course of one year. Research studies provide an indication of the prevalence of child abuse within the population – which is the proportion of a population who were abused during childhood. So, for example, where a small sample of the population is asked about their life experiences, the proportion of respondents who were abused is then extrapolated up to give an idea of what proportion of a wider population has experienced abuse (NSPCC, 2015).

However, findings from research studies often reveal much higher numbers of children who have been abused than official statistics do. Some child abuse does not come to the attention of the authorities as many children do not disclose their abuse to anyone at the time because they are scared of the consequences of telling or are unsure *who* to tell or *how* to tell someone. In a research context people will often disclose abuse because they are able to do so anonymously.

Most research is done with adults, who may find it easier to talk about something that is no longer happening. After keeping the abuse secret for so long, it is a relief for some to be able to talk about it. For others, it is only after many years that they come to realise what happened to them as children was actually abuse. However, some may never disclose and as the NSPCC (2015) notes, there is no way of knowing how many people never tell anyone.

Studies do suggest that one in ten of all children suffer from some form of maltreatment during childhood but not all are captured in official statistics (Cawson *et al.* 2000; Radford *et al.* 2011; Harker *et al.* 2013; Department for Education, 2013). Cawson *et al.* (2000) undertook a study on behalf of the NSPCC and found that out of a sample of 2,869 young adults 18 to 24 years of age:

- 7 per cent reported serious physical abuse in childhood
- 1 per cent reported serious sexual abuse
- 11 per cent reported serious neglect
- 6 per cent reported serious emotional abuse.

In total, the study found that 16 per cent of the sample considered they had been seriously abused or neglected in childhood, with some respondents reporting multiple types of maltreatment. This is representative of one in six children in England. Radford *et al.* (2011), again on behalf of the NSPCC, interviewed young adults aged 18 to 24 years, and children aged 11 to 17 years. They found that one in four adults reported having been seriously maltreated in childhood. One in five of the children reported serious levels of maltreatment (Corby *et al.* 2012).

Corby *et al.* (2012) conclude that it is highly likely, if not proven, that child abuse and neglect is more widespread than official statistics can demonstrate.

There is still much hidden harm and therefore it is important that all practitioners whose work brings them into contact with children and their families are equipped with the skills and underpinning knowledge to recognise and respond to concerns. It is important that a vulnerable child can be recognised as well as the indicators of abuse and neglect.

The risk of abuse is greatest in infancy, although it is also evident that some groups of children and young people are at increased risk of abuse due to pre-existing vulnerabilities – for example, children with a disability, looked-after children, children seen as different and those whose needs have been missed or marginalised (Brandon *et al.* 2009).

Safeguarding children and public health: implications for all sectors

Successful safeguarding not only improves outcomes for vulnerable children but also improves the well being of the population as a whole (Department of Health, 2009; Powell, 2011).

Safeguarding is a major public-health issue but this does not mean that the responsibility for this lies within the field of public health. As mentioned above, everyone who comes into contact with children and families has a role to play (HM Government, 2015a). Fergussion (2009) discusses how safeguarding is part of the continuum of care provided by a range of practitioners working within children and families. It is those who come into contact with children and families within universal services (e.g. education and health) who are best placed to identify issues of concern about the safety and well being of a child. Fergussion (2009) emphasises how a public health model implemented by all allows a move from a disease model (which focuses on recognising the 'signs and symptoms' of abuse and referring on) to a model that engenders prevention and early intervention. While it is crucial that actual abuse is recognised, it is also important that practitioners across the children's workforce are able to recognise vulnerability and engage in early help agendas in order to prevent or reduce the risk of a vulnerable child being harmed as a result of abuse or neglect. Parton (2015) also supports the notion that a broad public-health framework is a useful approach but it does need to locate a children's rights perspective as the focus of safeguarding and child protection practice. In addition, there needs to be recognition that there are a wide range of significant factors that result in the maltreatment of children.

All practitioners therefore have a mandate for prevention, early intervention and proactive work with children and families, alongside their responsibilities to recognise and respond to concerns that a child may be suffering harm.

Providing early help is more effective in promoting the welfare of children that reacting later. Early help is about proving support as soon as a problem emerges at any point in the child's life.

Roles, responsibilities and skills

Effective communication and assessment skills as well as knowledge of childcare and development are important tools for best practice in the field of safeguarding children. Effective safeguarding is also dependent on the ability to practise in an authoritative way when concerns arise.

Documentation and record keeping must also be clear, factual and contemporary, demonstrating justification of decision making, including that which is related to information sharing with other practitioners and agencies. Poor record keeping is a common theme in findings from serious case reviews along with a lack of clarity about assessment, decision making, care planning and evaluation of interventions. Crucially, there is often a failure to reflect the views and wishes of the child. This is picked up in Chapter 6.

Practitioners must therefore be able to recognise concerns and make referrals as well as contribute, as appropriate, to strategy discussions, initial child-protection conferences, core groups, child protection review conferences, child-death review processes and serious case review processes as appropriate to their role.

HM Government (2015c) in the policy document *What to Do if You're Worried a Child is Being Abused* identifies four key steps that a *practitioner* should follow to help them identify and respond appropriately to possible abuse and/or neglect. These are:

● to be alert
● to question behaviours (of children and parents)
● to ask for help
● to refer.

The document highlights that it may not always be appropriate to go through all stages sequentially. If a child is in **immediate danger** or is at **risk of harm**, the first step would be to make a referral to children's social care and/or the police, but it is also important to identify the basic facts. It will then be the role of the social workers and the police to investigate cases and make a judgement on whether there should be a statutory intervention or a criminal investigation, or both.

It is important, though, that practitioners record in writing all concerns, and record all the discussions that have taken place about the concerns. This should include who the discussions took place with. Practitioners should also document the outcome of discussions and the decisions made, together with the reasons for those decisions.

Policy updates (2015)
Working Together to Safeguard Children (HM Government, 2015a)

This is the key statutory guidance for anyone working with children in England and it should be complied with. This guidance updates the previous version published in 2013 and has been amended to include:

● changes on how to refer allegations of abuse against those who work with children

- clarification of requirements on local authorities to notify serious incidents (where a child dies or is seriously harmed)
- a definition of serious harm for the purposes of serious case reviews.

Keeping Children Safe in Education (HM Government, 2015b)

This is the key statutory guidance for all schools, colleges and academies in England. It sets out what they must do to safeguard and promote the welfare of children and young people under the age of 18. This guidance replaces the previous version published in 2014. It has been amended to include:

- some changes on how to report concerns and allegations
- clarification about recruitment and vetting processes
- clarification around preventing radicalisation.

What to Do if You're Worried a Child is Being Abused (HM Government, 2015c)

This is a short document containing advice for practitioners. It has been produced to help anyone whose work brings them into contact with children and families to identify child abuse and neglect and to take appropriate action in response. This advice replaces the version published in 2006.

Information Sharing (HM Government, 2015d)

This has been updated since 2008 in order to provide advice for practitioners providing safeguarding services to children, young people, parents and carers. It aims to help people working with children or parents and carers to decide when and how to share personal information legally and professionally. It replaces the previous 2008 publication 'Information sharing: guidance for practitioners and managers'.

- It is important that the above documents are used in conjunction with each other.
- Information sharing with the relevant agencies and practitioners is crucial for effective safeguarding and child protection practice. If practitioners are not sure as to whether they should share information a good starting point is to consider: 'what will happen if I share the information and what will happen if I do not?' Always seek advice and refer to the above policy.
- Concerns about the maltreatment of a child must always be referred to children's social care and the practitioner should discuss their concerns with the designated safeguarding lead in the organisation and seek support from them with regard to making the referral.

Summary

This introductory chapter has provided an overview of the principles and contemporary perspectives that underpin practice. The main message is that safeguarding is about prevention and early help. Practitioners need to be able to recognise the vulnerable child and risk factors for maltreatment, as well as recognising the indicators of abuse and neglect.

It is important that practitioners not only recognise but also respond to concerns. The child should be the focus of all actions and responses and it is important to think child, think family and uphold children's rights. Subsequent chapters will address the nature of abuse and neglect, recognising concerns and responses, interventions and legislative and policy framework that guides practice.

Key texts

Harker, L. *et al.* (2013) *How Safe are Our Children?,* London: NSPCC

HM Government (2015a) *Working Together to Safeguard Children: A Guide to Inter-agency Working to Safeguard and Promote the Welfare of Children*, Department for Education

HM Government (2015b) *Keeping Children Safe in Education*, London: Department for Education

HM Government (2015c) *What to Do if You're Worried a Child is Being Abused*, London: Department for Education

Laming (2009) *The Protection of Children in England: A Progress Report.* London: House of Commons. Available online at: http://dera.ioe.ac.uk/8646/1/12_03_09_children.pdf

National Institute for Health and Care Excellence (2009) *When to Suspect Child Maltreatment*, London: NICE

NSPCC (2014) *Assessing Parenting Capacity: An NSPCC Factsheet*, London: NSPCC. Available online at: www.nspcc.org.uk/globalassets/documents/information-service/factsheetassessing-parenting-capacity.pdf

NSPCC (2015) *Statistics on Child Abuse: Incidence and Prevalence*, London: NSPCC. Available online at: www.nspcc.org.uk/services-and-resources/research-and-resources/statistics/incidence-prevalence/#tab-registers

Powell, C. (2011) *Safeguarding and Child Protection for Nurses, Midwives and Health Visitors: A Practical Guide*, Milton Keynes: Open University Press

Other useful sources of information

The Healthy Child Programme:

www.gov.uk/government/uploads/system/uploads/attachment_data/file/167998/Health_Child_Programme.pdf

www.unicef.org.uk/UNICEFs-Work/UN-Convention

www.fatherhoodinstitute.org

2 Defining vulnerability, abuse and neglect

Introduction

Definitions of abuse impact on policy, practice and research. This chapter explains and describes the main types of abuse and neglect, as they are covered within the child-protection policy guidance in the UK. It provides contemporary definitions as reflected in policy at the time of writing. It is important that practitioners understand the different kinds of abuse and the facts they are all equally important and constitute unacceptable treatment of children. The discussion focuses on early and middle childhood: children up to about eight years of age. But bear in mind that all these issues also apply to older children and young people up to the age at which they cease legally to be a 'child'.

As indicated in Chapter 1, there is increasing emphasis in policy agendas on the need to protect vulnerable children and improve outcomes for the most vulnerable. There is emphasis on the need to recognise risk factors as well as abuse and neglect. Children are still being 'missed' and abuse and neglect is not being picked up until it is significant. This chapter will first consider what is meant by a vulnerable child and vulnerability, before discussing the different types of abuse. Contemporary definitions will be given as these provide the conceptual framework for practice within which legislation and policy are located. Definitions also determine the incidence of abuse and neglect as well as providing the framework for recognising unacceptable behaviour towards children.

This chapter will cover the following: definitions of abuse and neglect, what constitutes a vulnerable child and vulnerability, emotional abuse, physical abuse, sexual abuse and exploitation and neglect. It will also discuss 'fabricated' and 'induced illness'.

Vulnerability

Conceptions of vulnerability are central to recognising risk factors to abuse (Bradford, 2004). A vulnerable child may be at increased risk of maltreatment. The concept of 'vulnerability' also informs how individuals and groups are managed and classified within society, including those with mental illness, learning disability, the elderly, within the criminal justice system, and children living with adversity and or those at risk of harm. Vulnerability is, however, difficult to measure (Action for Children, 2012). Nonetheless, it is important to highlight that findings from numerous inquiries and reports clearly articulate that vulnerable children are not always recognised early enough and there is much concern about 'poor' outcomes for vulnerable children (Laming, 2003; 2009; Munro, 2011; Coffey, 2014; Jay, 2014; Casey, 2015). There are particular concerns about 'missed opportunities' to identify neglect. The need to identify vulnerable children and the importance of reducing vulnerability are therefore key themes in contemporary policy for children in the UK.

Thus, it is clearly important that practitioners can identify vulnerabilities and risk factors to abuse and neglect. These vulnerabilities vary from child to child. Disabled children are particularly vulnerable to abuse, which may be because they have an impaired capacity to resist or avoid abuse. They may not recognise that they are being harmed and may not be able to distinguish between therapeutic and harmful interventions. They may have speech and language as well as communication needs and may not be able to articulate or tell others about what is happening to them. Children also develop and mature at different rates and so what appears to be worrying for a younger child may be 'normal' behaviour for an older child.

Parental behaviours may also impact on a child and so practitioners should be alert to parent–child interactions that are concerning, and other parental behaviours. Children are more vulnerable if they have parents who are misusing drugs or alcohol, or if there is a sudden change in a parent's mental-health well being, or they have a significant mental-health illness. Children exposed to domestic violence and abuse are also vulnerable and will experience harm as a result of the exposure.

By understanding the warning signs, practitioners can respond to problems as early as possible and make referrals to services to help ensure that the child and family will be provided with the right support and services.

Keep the child in mind

It is important to recognise that a 'warning sign' does not automatically mean a child may is being abused or neglected but it does indicate that the child is vulnerable (HM Government, 2015c). It is the exposure to the risk that increases the child's vulnerability.

What does it mean?

A useful definition of **vulnerability** is provided by Daniel *et al.* (1999) whereby vulnerability pertains to the innate characteristics of the child and those imposed by their family circle and the wider community which might threaten or challenge healthy development and therefore impact on the child's well being and welfare. All children are vulnerable to some extent and the younger they are the more dependent they are on older others to ensure their safety. The factors that render a child vulnerable to maltreatment can be separated into:

- **intrinsic** characteristics in the child that might make them more vulnerable – this might be their age, a disability or long-term health problem;
- **extrinsic** (external) vulnerabilities imposed by others and the environment around them in which they live.

(Webb, 2007)

There are also combinations of 'stressors' that may increase the vulnerability of the child, such as parental mental illness, substance misuse, and domestic violence. When these factors coexist together they are referred to as the 'toxic trio' and are viewed as indicators of increased risk of harm to children and young people (Brandon *et al.* 2012).

It is therefore important that the practitioner is able to recognise children who are vulnerable and be alert to the circumstances and contexts that might increase the likelihood of abuse and neglect.

Child abuse and neglect

Formal definitions of abuse and neglect are provided by HM Government (2015a, 2015b) in their policy guidelines and are therefore used as the definitions for this edition.

Abuse and neglect are forms of 'maltreatment of a child. Somebody may abuse or neglect a child by inflicting harm, or by failing to act to prevent harm. Children may be abused in a family or in an institutional or community setting by those known to them or, more rarely, by others (e.g. via the internet). They may be abused by an adult or adults, or another child or children' (HM Government, 2015a).

However, child welfare concerns may arise in many different contexts, and can vary greatly in terms of their nature and seriousness. For example, in the case of female genital mutilation, children may be taken out of the country to be abused. Additionally, an 'abused child will often experience more than one type of abuse, as well as other difficulties in their lives. Abuse and neglect can happen over a period of time, but can also be a one-off event. Child abuse and neglect can have major long-term impacts on all aspects of a child's health, development and well being' (HM Government, 2015b).

> ## What does it mean?
>
> In broad terms, **child abuse** covers:
>
> - doing something to a child that should not be done: anything that will injure them physically, distress them deeply and emotionally or seriously disrupt their development or well being;
> - failing to do something for a child that should be done, for the sake of their well being, safety or continued healthy development.

Within this broad framework there are different types of action, or inaction, which could be considered abusive and neglectful because of the consequences for children. This chapter discusses those issues from the perspective of what is considered to be maltreatment of children. In Chapter 4 you will find a further discussion about the signs and symptoms of abuse and neglect that practitioners may notice and that arouse concerns.

This section considers the four basic categories of abuse as they are identified in HM Government's 2015 *Working Together* guidelines.

Emotional abuse

Emotional abuse is the

> *'persistent emotional maltreatment of a child such as to cause severe and persistent adverse effects on the child's emotional development. It may involve conveying to a child that they are worthless or unloved, inadequate, or valued only insofar as they meet the needs of another person. It may include not giving the child opportunities to express their views, deliberately silencing them or "making fun" of what they say or how they communicate. It may feature age or developmentally inappropriate expectations being imposed on children. These may include interactions that are beyond a child's developmental capability, as well as overprotection and limitation of exploration and learning, or preventing the child participating in normal social interaction. It may involve seeing or hearing the ill-treatment of another. It may involve serious bullying (including cyber bullying), causing children frequently to feel frightened or in danger, or the exploitation or corruption of children. Some level of emotional abuse is involved in all types of maltreatment of a child, though it may occur alone'.*

(HM Government, 2015a)

Any kind of direct ill-treatment or neglect will affect a child's sense of security and trust. Such experiences shake their belief in themselves as worthwhile individuals who deserve care. Therefore, it is reasonable to say that emotional abuse plays a part in all types of abuse or neglect. However, for some children, a pattern of emotional abuse is the main or only form of abuse in their lives.

Emotional abuse is a persistent pattern of deliberate uncaring or emotionally cruel treatment of a child. A judgement of emotional abuse has to take account of patterns and a continuing experience for a child or children in a family, or in a setting, in which a child is regularly targeted. It can sometimes be hard to identify, especially when the burden seems normal to a child, but it is crucial not to underestimate the impact.

What does it mean?

Emotional abuse: a persistent pattern of cruelty by words or rejecting body language, such that children or young people feel disliked or unloved by carers from whom they have the right to expect such affirmation.

Persistent or severe emotional ill-treatment or rejection of a child has a negative effect on their all-round development and their behaviour. Children need to experience affection, security and encouragement. If these experiences are denied, children can doubt their ability to make relationships or their capacity to learn and deal with life. Children may be physically unharmed, but so badly affected by emotional abuse that they are in poor health or react by harming themselves. Children and young adolescents can be seriously depressed by this experience, so that psychological scars last well into adulthood.

Ways in which children and young people may be emotionally abused

Emotional abuse might take any of the following forms:

- Children are verbally abused, told they are 'stupid', 'useless', 'ugly' or 'should never have been born'.
- Some children and young people are burdened with the accusation from a parent that their birth 'ruined my life and stopped me being...'. The claims of lost opportunities that follow are often unrealistic and, in any case, children cannot be held responsible for their own conception.
- Sons or daughters are subjected to continuous criticism or faced with unrealistically high adult expectations, which no child or young person could ever meet. Perhaps their interests and achievements are ridiculed or compared unfavourably with someone else, for example a favoured sibling.
- Any apparent affection felt by the parent is made dependent on the child's behaviour or achievements. Children may never feel sure of their parents' love, nor easily predict what will make them withdraw signs of affection.

- Children may be overprotected, to an unrealistic extent, so they cannot gain any sense of confidence or appropriate self-reliance. The continual message is that they are incompetent to deal with ordinary daily life. Overprotection by parents, or other carers, can be hard to judge, especially where a child or young person's disability or health condition means that a high level of care is necessary.
- Communication with the child may be distorted so that adults use their maturity inappropriately to make a child or young person feel guilty for family situations that are not, and cannot be, the child's responsibility.
- One child in a family is sometimes pushed into the role of 'serious behaviour problem' as a way of explaining away entrenched family strife. The argument is that everything would be fine if it were not for this child or young person. The targeted child may be given little option but to behave in disruptive ways. Family support of any kind has then to separate the child's reaction from the unhealthy family dynamics.
- Children may also be emotionally damaged by experiences of domestic violence (see also page 245) or general family conflict. Children may feel torn between two disputing parents and the adults may deliberately use the children to vent their own feelings.
- Some children and young people face such a barrage of verbal threats and personal attack, even without physical abuse, that they describe their experience as a kind of emotional terrorising.

Some of the abusive treatment described above shows a pattern of blaming a child for situations over which they have no control, or where their behaviour is only one of many factors in their family's troubles. This process is called 'scapegoating': when one person, in this case a child, is made to feel personally responsible for the distress or deep dissatisfaction felt by others. Children can be especially vulnerable to this form of emotional abuse, because they have very limited resources to counter the accusations. Some children who are made the target for blame in their family also experience other forms of abuse and neglect.

What does it mean?

Scapegoating: a process by which an adult or child is made to feel personally responsible for the distress or deep dissatisfaction felt by others, and this judgement is not an accurate reflection of the true situation.

Some children experience an emotional rejection, akin to abuse, when their non-abusing parent retreats from them following a disclosure. Some children who speak up about serious physical or sexual abuse by one parent, or a step-parent, are further devastated when the other parent continues to doubt their word and chooses to believe the abuser over their son or daughter. Such an event may leave a child or young adolescent no choice but to go into care, unless other family members can provide an alternative home.

Families can go through difficult times and the majority of parents try their utmost not to take out their feelings of stress on their children. Some parents respond well to help from relatives, friends or trusted practitioners who are involved with the children and the family. These parents acknowledge the difficult situation that has developed and are prepared to work towards changing it. Other parents, and some carers, are resistant to acknowledging what is happening or to changing the situation. They persist in believing that the child deserves the emotional abuse, and that the fault and responsibility all lie with the child.

Children and adolescents can be emotionally and physically cruel to each other. Problems between children would usually be resolved through an effective bullying policy and practice in school, out-of-school settings and residential care (for more about bullying see page 220). However, practitioners should be concerned about children, or adolescents, who have a pressing need to be cruel to other people. To what extent are they recycling verbal or physical abuse and threats from daily experience in their own family?

Case study

Pike Lane Pre-school

Students on placement at Pike Lane have reported back to their tutor their distress on discovering how the children are treated in this pre-school. Three- and four-year-olds are subject to a very structured session in which they have no choice about activities. The children are expected to sit still for a long time. Children who fidget or who try to move across to the 'wrong' activity are told off at length and threatened with losing their short time out in the garden.

The students report that children who have toileting accidents are told they are 'dirty'. The end of session group time is run mainly as a way to highlight which children have failed to behave well during that day. The ground rules for the setting are all phrased as 'Don't…' or 'You must not…'. Adults regularly contravene the rules, such as by shouting. One student has written up an incident in which a child tentatively said to an adult, shouting across the room at him, 'But we're not supposed to shout. You said it's rude.' The practitioner strode across the room and, pointing a finger towards the child's face, yelled, 'That means you, not me!'

The students tried to raise their concerns with the pre-school manager and were told firmly that all the parents wanted this kind of approach to education and discipline, and so the pre-school was meeting the demands of partnership.

● What should concern you about this situation?
● What issues would you want to raise if you were directly involved?

You will find a commentary on page 47.

Making sense of the scenario

No adult, however caring, manages to be patient and considerate with children all the time. Parents are not perfect and sometimes they get cross, or their own concerns temporarily overwhelm them. Normally considerate practitioners may look back and feel that they did not give children the attention they needed. Adults may recognise they jumped to an unfair conclusion about a child's behaviour.

In the main, kind and reflective adults treat children with respect. Parents or practitioners will admit their mistakes and make the effort to put right their oversights. They will listen to another adult, fellow parent or colleague who points out that a child is being treated too severely, or that their expectations of the child are unrealistic. They will listen to the child, to the words they manage to express, or interpret the messages of their sad and disheartened body language. In contrast, an adult who is culpable of emotional abuse carries on with this treatment, regardless of the obvious distress of the child or young person. Some abusive adults look as if they actually enjoy the pain they cause.

Take another perspective

In this chapter, possible reasons appear for each of the different types of abuse, but the following points apply every time:

- There is no single pattern of cause and effect for abuse. So any hope of changing circumstances to benefit children has to be attuned to what probably created fertile ground for this abuse or neglect.
- Possible reasons or likely explanations are not, ever, excuses for ill-treatment of children and young people. Professionals try to make some sense of unacceptable adult behaviour only in order to gain a perspective on the possible dynamics.
- Some adults are breathtakingly cruel and will not be stopped without extraordinary measures, including imprisonment and other severe restrictions on their civil liberties.
- However, many adults whose behaviour brings them into the child protection system will be amenable to change, levered from an understanding of why and how.

Practitioners may be in a position to offer support to a child who needs to be reassured, even convinced, that the situation is not all their fault.

There are different factors that can cause adults to abuse children emotionally:

- Some adults may be reliving their own childhood experiences of cruel words and relentless criticism. It does not occur to them, without outside support, that there are better ways to treat children. Parents may really believe that they are unaffected by the treatment they received, and so they cannot possibly be harming their child(ren).

- Adults' own troubles may be projected onto children. In a life plagued by worries and doubts about their own competence, adults may boost their own self-esteem by verbally abusing more vulnerable individuals.
- Such *maladaptive* thinking and unacceptable behaviour are not restricted to the family. Self-centred adults working as practitioners may follow the same track: unloading their stress onto children in their nursery or school class. Such practice is excused by claims that their actions are justified by a child's behaviour, or that it does not matter because the children take no notice anyway. However, this is not acting in the best interests of the child and may impact negatively on the child's well being.
- Some emotional abuse in any environment seems to arise from an adult's dislike of a child. The abuse is excused on the grounds that the child is persistently naughty, awkward or insolent.
- In group settings, such as a school or leisure activity that takes place in a sports club, some adults argue that shaming a child also keeps the rest of the group in line. Such a tactic of motivation through fear is seriously inappropriate in any setting or service. Even at a low level this behaviour sets an unacceptable example of bullying by adults.
- Emotional cruelty from adults is connected with an abuse of their authority. The adult feels powerful by ridiculing a child or always finding something to criticise, however hard a young person strives to please.
- Some adults believe that children will not learn without being hit, or the threat of such punishment. In a similar way, other adults believe children learn only by being criticised and punished for their mistakes and that encouraging words will make them proud (in a negative way) and spoiled.

Physical abuse

What does it mean?

Physical abuse is defined as 'A form of abuse which may involve hitting, shaking, throwing, poisoning, burning or scalding, drowning, suffocating or otherwise causing physical harm to a child. Physical harm may also be caused when a parent or carer fabricates the symptoms of, or deliberately induces, illness in a child.' (HM Government, 2015a)

Abuse is the actual or likely physical injury to a child. Children may be physically abused through direct attack or by an adult's deliberate failure to protect them from injury or suffering; the two forms of abuse sometimes merge together. Physical abuse, with accompanying neglect, is a very dangerous form of maltreatment of children and young people. Serious injuries and damage to health can result; babies and children can die.

Abuse is also the non-accidental injury to children or young people, caused by direct attack or actions highly likely to put them at significant risk of physical harm.

Ways in which children might be physically abused

Children who are physically abused might be ill-treated in different ways. It is important to realise that attack and severe physical cruelty are inflicted even on babies. In fact, babies and very young children may be at increased risk from physical abuse, as a direct result of their reduced ability to fight back or escape.

- Children have been hit with hands, fists and implements. They have been shoved, thrown against walls and furniture or shaken hard, so that injury is almost inevitable.
- It is potentially dangerous to shake any child with violence, but babies are especially at risk from shaking. An older child or young person may manage to brace their head and shoulders, at least against limited shaking. However, babies do not have the muscle strength to protect themselves and their heads are relatively heavy. Babies easily sustain neck injury and brain damage.
- There is no doubt that it is dangerous to shake babies or young children. However, concerns have been raised for over a decade about the diagnosis of 'shaken baby syndrome' when there are no external injuries or other evidence of shaking. Medical opinion is divided on the ease with which internal injuries to the brain and retina can be attributed, without doubt, to violent shaking.
- Children have been bitten, burned or deliberately scalded, squeezed with violence or half-suffocated. Physical abuse has included deliberate poisoning of children with household substances and the inappropriate use of alcohol, drugs or prescription medicines.
- Abuse has also included physically rough handling and dragging of children. Ill-treatment, often in the name of discipline, has frightened children, for instance, who have been shut in confined, dark spaces.

It is the responsibility of adults to help protect children and this obligation extends to members of the family in which one adult poses a danger to the younger members. The Domestic Violence Crime and Victims Act 2004 (applicable across the UK) has made it possible to prosecute a parent or other adult family member who knew about the risk of violence and did not act so as to protect children. When a child has been killed, the parent or other family carer can be judged guilty of causing or allowing that foreseeable death. They failed to act directly to protect the child, or left the child with a person known to be violent. This provision also covers the situation when it is impossible to prove which of two or more adults, present at the time of a fatal attack, actually killed a child.

Make the connection with...

A responsibility to care

Physically abusive actions are not always directly inflicted through attack by an adult. In 2007, four women appeared in court in Plymouth (England) as the result of their behaviour towards a two- and a three-year-old. The mother of these young children, together with three of their adult female relatives, had bullied the boy and girl into fighting each other and had recorded the event on video.

During the trial, information became public that the children's father, who was not resident with the family, had borrowed the camera, seen the footage and contacted the police. Public statements by the women showed that they justified their actions as 'toughening up' the children and claimed to be doing no worse than many other people they knew. The women were convicted of causing the children to be ill-treated in a way that was likely to lead to unnecessary suffering or injury. The brother and sister were removed from the home for their own safety and custody was then given to their father's family.

The behaviour of these women was judged to be abusive because their actions could in no way be justified as supporting children's personal safety skills. It is abusive to ill-treat children as a means of entertainment. The women could be heard laughing in the video recording and the children could be seen distressed and trying to escape.

Pause for reflection

Who do you think is more likely to physically abuse children – females or males?

It is worth noting that children are more likely to be maltreated by females than males (See Corby *et al.* (2012: 108).

However, in situations of physical abuse, fathers including non-biological or social fathers are generally seen as the more likely perpetrators. Men are perceived to be more violent that women. However, women as well as men do physically abuse children (Corby *et al.* 2012).

Possible reasons underlying physical abuse

Children are physically abused by adults, or by young people, for a number of reasons. Support work with families and individuals has to take account of circumstances. But reasons are not, of course, justifications for abuse.

- Family stresses are sometimes taken out on the children. Financial and other worries may make parents less patient, or they may focus their anger on the person close at hand, the child.

- Young parents or carers who are unsupported may become overwhelmed with the responsibility of caring for babies or young children. Their frustration or panic may combine with a genuine ignorance of how their actions can injure children. For instance, an adult may believe it is less dangerous to shake a baby or child than to hit them.
- Physical discipline may get seriously out of hand as a parent's frustration or temper leads to fiercer attempts to control a child's perceived misbehaviour.
- Some adults, for a variety of reasons in their own background, relish inflicting cruelty on others, and children are easy targets. Powerless adults may enjoy wielding control over the young and vulnerable. They may exercise this power by other forms of abuse, in addition to physical. The consistent strand is that adults regard children, or vulnerable young people, as acceptable targets for adult frustrations or a twisted sense of entertainment.
- Within families, one child may be abused while another is left unharmed. The distorted thinking in the family may be that this child is the bad one or the unwanted child: the process of scapegoating described earlier.
- An abused baby may be harder to comfort or feed, or may cry a considerable amount. Parents under stress, or with little support, may find it very hard to put the baby safely in the cot and walk away to calm themselves.
- An abused child may show patterns of behaviour that are genuinely challenging, even to the most patient of adults. However, it can be hard to determine to what extent the child's behaviour led to the abuse (as a justification in the adults' eyes) or resulted *from* physical abuse.
- Physical abuse can follow actions that parents or other family carers strongly feel are for the child's own good. Girls are abused through the injuries that result from the cultural practice of female genital mutilation (see page 155).

Case study

Sajida

Sajida is seven years old and attends your after-school club, which is linked with her primary school. Sajida has Down's syndrome and her development is closer to that of a four-year-old. She has a helper, Alan, who stays with her during school time but does not attend the club. Your impression is that Sajida's mother still has difficulty in reconciling herself to having a disabled child and speaks with much more enthusiasm about her son, who is nearly five years old. You have never met the children's father.

Sajida seems to have a lot of accidents, both at school and at home. Within the last year, she has had a badly twisted ankle, a fractured arm and numerous bruises. On each occasion there has been a plausible explanation and Sajida's mother and Alan agree that the child is very clumsy. You have seen Sajida bump into tables and sometimes other children, but she has never sustained more than a mild bruise at the after-school club.

⇨

Today, Sajida arrived at the club with Alan, who said that the child had slipped in the school toilets and hit her head on the taps. Sajida has a large swelling and bruise over one eye and a reddened area on one arm, which, Alan says, is the result of his trying to catch the child to prevent her fall. Later that afternoon, you are sympathising with Sajida, saying, 'You have a lot of bangs, don't you? How did you slip?' Sajida looks puzzled and you say, 'Alan says you slipped over in the toilet.' Sajida shakes her head and says, 'No, didn't slip. Alan banged me.'

- What would concern you about this situation?
- What should you do about it?

You will find a commentary on page 47.

Fabricated or induced illness

Deliberate creation of illness in a child or young person by their carer is recognised as a form of physical abuse. The pattern was first identified in the late 1970s by Roy Meadow, and others. Adult carers, in most cases the mother, reported a series of imaginary symptoms for the child, and actually made the child ill (for instance, poisoning to cause fits) or interfered with medical investigations to make the claims appear true. This disturbed adult behaviour is called 'fabricated illness syndrome' or 'illness induction'.

What does it mean?

Illness induction or **fabricated illness**: physical harm when a parent or other carer feigns, or deliberately causes, symptoms of ill-health in a child or young person for whom they are responsible.

Roy Meadow and another medical professional, David Southall, were severely criticised during 2003–04 for the frequency with which they had diagnosed the syndrome in families who had experienced more than one unexplained infant death. Expert witness testimony was challenged and several convictions for child murder were eventually overturned on appeal. These miscarriages of justice highlighted the recommendation from the Butler-Sloss inquiry into the Cleveland sex-abuse cases (see page 55) that a judgement of abuse by families should not rest solely on medical opinion. A similar situation has arisen over appeals against prosecutions based on shaken baby syndrome, when there was evidence that the baby had been ill over a period of time.

There is reason to believe that illness induction syndrome exists and poses a threat to children. However, a serious problem arises with a rush to this diagnosis, because it becomes very difficult for parents to disprove the accusation. Induction of illness is not widespread and is different from parents who are highly anxious. It is important that nobody swiftly assumes illness induction, when a parent is persistently concerned about the ill-health of a child. Some concerned parents have been proved to be right in thinking their child to be ill, although medical professionals could not initially reach a diagnosis.

In the case of genuine illness induction, the most pressing action is to take steps to protect the child. There also needs to be appropriate psychiatric help for the adult, often a parent but sometimes an adult in a position of trust and authority, such as a medical professional. Parents and other carers who claim that healthy children are ill, or who deliberately harm children to create a medical emergency, seem to feed off the drama of the situation. They seek the reflected attention of having a dramatically ill child and being the self-sacrificing carer. The end result for children is unnecessary illness and medical intervention, plus confusion over their own health and well being. Some children have died as a result.

Concerns should be raised when:

- children or young people have unexplained and recurrent illnesses;
- there is a mismatch between the medical history and what the carer claims is the current problem or health history of the child or young person;
- extensive medical investigation has failed to explain the symptoms;
- there is an unexplained presence of drugs, chemicals, blood or other substances in the urine, stools or stomach fluids of the child;
- the symptoms do not occur if the child and carer are separated.

Neglect

Neglect is about unmet needs. It is:

'the persistent failure to meet a child's basic physical and/or psychological needs, likely to result in the serious impairment of the child's health or development. Neglect may occur during pregnancy as a result of maternal substance abuse. Once a child is born, neglect may involve a parent or carer failing to:

- *provide adequate food, clothing and shelter (including exclusion from home or abandonment);*
- *protect a child from physical and emotional harm or danger;*
- *ensure adequate supervision (including the use of inadequate care-givers); or*
- *ensure access to appropriate medical care or treatment.*

It may also include neglect of, or unresponsiveness to, a child's basic emotional needs.'

HM Government, 2015b

> ### What does it mean?
>
> **Abuse through neglect** is a continuing pattern in the treatment of a child or dependent young person. Persistent and severe neglect includes different kinds of failure to care properly for a child.

Reviews of child protection practice during the 1990s identified that neglect could be difficult to assess, especially when a family was not known to social care services. In that situation, services such as nursery or school were doubly important, since those practitioners could be the first ones to realise that a child's basic needs were not being met by family carers. Serious case reviews stressed the significant risks to children when their dire state failed to be recognised, even when a social worker had been assigned to the family. Following a number of tragedies, the firm recommendation is restated that professionals must insist on seeing a child and not depend on continued reassurances, or excuses, from a parent or other carer.

What does it mean?

Neglect: failure of a carer, responsible for a child or young person, to ensure their safety, health and general well being.

Non-organic failure to thrive: when neglect of a child's basic needs leads to persistent health and development problems, not explained by other causes.

Children suffering neglect of their basic physical needs have died, or been in a desperate state when they were found. However, neglect at less extreme levels can slow down all areas of development, including physical growth. This condition, which is caused by neglect and not an identified genetic or medical cause, has been called 'faltering growth' and, more recently, 'failure to thrive'. In Scotland, the child protection system includes 'non-organic failure to thrive' as a fifth category, separate from neglect.

Ways in which children might be neglected

Neglectful treatment can arise in the following ways, when adults responsible for the care of children fail to meet their basic physical needs for health and survival:

- Children might be given inadequate food, so that they are malnourished or actually starving. Neglected children have been found going through dustbins for food, sometimes in homes where their parents had enough to eat. Very young children are at even greater risk, since they are less likely to be able to scavenge.
- Very young children, and some older children with disabilities, need considerable support with feeding. Neglectful adult carers may unrealistically expect children to feed themselves. They may rush to feed a baby or child in such a careless way that the food will almost inevitably come back up again.
- Until the twenty-first century, neglect of children's nutritional needs was focused on insufficient food and malnutrition. However, it is now recognised that parents, and other key carers, are responsible for any aspect

of diet-related health. It can become a child protection issue if children are allowed to eat such excessive amounts of food, possibly also a seriously unbalanced diet, so that they become clinically obese (see also page 88).

- Children are not given warm enough clothes for the time of year, so are cold and ill throughout the winter months. Children may be left in unheated bedrooms with insufficient bedclothes for the temperature.
- Children have died of hypothermia and related neglect. Babies and young toddlers are especially vulnerable, since they are unable to climb out of their cot and try to find more layers. Some babies have died, lying in their own urine, while their parents lay in warmth in the next room.
- Sometimes parents or other carers have grossly neglected a child's basic physical needs so that they are dirty, remain for ages in unchanged nappies or have infections that would have improved with basic medical attention.
- Older children still need parents to pay attention to their physical needs – not only when disability or ill-health makes it difficult for children to take care of themselves. However, neglect of older children can arise because parents fail to set safe boundaries, have no idea of their children's whereabouts or are unable to control the behaviour of a son or daughter.

It is important not to underestimate the risks of severe neglect to babies, young children and older children or young people whose disabilities mean that they cannot take responsibility for their own basic care needs. Inquiries into child abuse have raised awareness that families who are neglectful of their children have sometimes drifted for a long time, perhaps years, even with social work support, because nobody had made a comprehensive assessment that the family had gone beyond the bounds of 'acceptable parenting'. The input of practitioners who see the child regularly can be crucial in this kind of situation. You notice what is happening with children, observe and record their health and general well being.

A concern that parents are doing what appears to be their best under difficult circumstances has to be balanced by an objective view of what is happening to the children. It is important that safeguarding guidelines explicitly recognise that support work focused on adults, for instance because of drug or alcohol addiction, must never be allowed to mask the importance of assessing children's well being when these adults are parents.

Pause for reflection

The case of Daniel Pelka

Read the Serious Case Review regarding Daniel Pelka: born 15th July 2007, died March 2012. At the time of his death 'Daniel was found to be malnourished and to have bruises on his body'. He had suffered abuse and neglect over a long period of time. He had been seen scavenging for food at school.

$\Rightarrow$

⇨

This report (Lock, 2013) highlights the significance of the need for practitioners to be aware of and to be sensitive to the needs of children in their work and highlights the importance of having knowledge about the potential indicators of abuse and neglect and knowing what to do.

The report can be accessed online (see References).

Home alone and young people caring for children – the interface with neglect

Young children, or older children with disabilities, are not able to take care of themselves without adult support. So parents, or other carers, who leave them alone will be judged neglectful, because of the high risk that children could come to harm. Across the UK there is no legislation that determines the age at which a child can be left alone at home. However, adults can be prosecuted for wilful neglect under the Children and Young Persons Act 1933 (and equivalent laws across the UK) if they have left a child unsupervised in a way that is likely to cause unnecessary suffering or injury to health. However, practitioners need to recall that child protection concerns can be raised, and serious action taken, regardless of whether a criminal prosecution is feasible.

Concerns about family decisions of this nature would consider the age and capability of a child or young person, how long they were left and whether this occurred during the day or night-time. Older children could well be judged safe to be left during the daylight hours or adolescents able to manage without an evening sitter. Part of growing up is that children are steadily taught the practical life skills that enable them to take care of themselves. However, concerns multiply if children, even adolescents, are left for long periods of time. Examples would include those cases that have hit the headlines since the 1990s when a parent has left children alone, or with adolescent siblings, while the adult takes a holiday.

Across the UK it is not possible for the under-16s legally to take responsibility for children. Parents make their own decision to pay a 14- or 15-year-old for evening or daytime sitting and some young people of this age are competent and trustworthy. However, parents remain legally responsible for the welfare of their own child. They can therefore be judged neglectful for entrusting a baby or young child to a young adolescent who proved to be unreliable or who reacted with panic to a crisis. Young sitters can themselves also be held accountable for abusive or neglectful actions that they can be expected to have understood.

Note: A 'young carer' is defined as a person under 18 years who provides or intends to provide care for another person (of any age, except generally where that care is provided for payment, pursuant to a contract or as voluntary work) (HM Government, 2015a).

Case study

Danny

Danny is the youngest child of five in the Sanders family. Danny attends the nursery class where you work and his three brothers are in the primary school. Danny is frequently dressed in clothes that are torn, dirty and smelly. His shoes and socks appear to be too small for him and affect how he walks. You have spoken with teachers of the other Sanders boys, who say that these children are usually in clean clothes and quite expensive trainers. When you mentioned Danny's shoes to his mother, Mrs Sanders told you firmly that she does not have money to burn and Danny should be grateful that he has any clothes that his brothers have not already ruined.

You continue to be concerned about Danny. Something he says to you makes you suspicious that he is shut in an enclosed space. But, when asked, Mrs Sanders says that Danny was shut in the cellar by one of his brothers as a joke and then the boy forgot. A singed area of hair and what looks like a burn on Danny's scalp are explained as, 'I got the hairdryer a bit close to him last night. Kid wouldn't sit still!'

One afternoon you overhear Mrs Sanders talking to another mother, who is expecting her second child and says she is hoping for a girl this time. Mrs Sanders says that Danny should have been a girl. 'I wanted a daughter. Do you think I wanted all these boys! But Danny fixed that for me. It ruined my insides having him and he was such a sickly little runt. They had to change all his blood when he was born, so it's not like he's really mine, anyway.'

- What would concern you about this situation?
- What pieces of the 'jigsaw' do you and your colleagues have already?
- What do you not know and perhaps need to explore?
- What would you do?

You will find a commentary on page 47.

Neglect by practitioners

Individuals or teams can also be neglectful of children: through direct unacceptable practice, reluctance to challenge colleagues, or acceptance of what they are told is centre policy.

- Children's physical needs **must** be met. Cost cutting in poor provision can undermine a healthy diet for children. Disregard for the importance of feeding routines and mealtimes can mean that children are not enabled to eat well. Refusal to deal with wet or soiled underwear may mean that children's clothing remains unchanged (see page 211).
- Neglectful practitioners who work alone or unsupervised may target one or more children through the same twisted logic of scapegoating used by abusive parents: arguing that the child is badly behaved and does not deserve care. The withdrawal of basics like food may be justified as a punishment. This is unacceptable.

- Children may be left in unsafe conditions by practitioners who are more interested in talking with colleagues, or who have been allowed to develop unacceptable habits, such as talking on their mobile phone during working hours.

Possible underlying reasons for neglect

Different factors can combine in leading to neglect and the accompanying risk to children and vulnerable young people (please recall the points on page 25). By definition, neglect occurs in families that are functioning poorly, but there are different reasons for the difficulties. Some adults appear to be fully aware of what they are doing and the consequent risks to the child. In this situation, neglect is often combined with emotional abuse (and perhaps physical as well), because the adult does not care and may even be pleased by the child's dire plight. In other families, neglect has arisen mainly through ignorance or the pressure of circumstances.

Lack of knowledge – omission

Some parents may not know what to do because their own childhood has given no useful experience of how adults care for children. They may themselves have been abused or neglected as children and have no positive model to help them. Parents with severe learning disabilities may not understand what a baby or young child needs and the consequences of poor care. Adolescent parents, especially those without family support, may have little idea of what the care of babies or children involves. They may feel overwhelmed by the responsibilities and the change brought about in their life. Young mothers may also be stunned that a baby whom they hoped would satisfy their own emotional needs is a very needy individual.

Parents of any age can be ignorant of the consequences of their actions – for instance, over diet. There have been tragic events in which babies have died of malnutrition. In one case that hit the headlines, very young parents fed their baby with an instant breakfast cereal, assuming it was the same as the more expensive packet baby food. In another instance, older parents had insisted on feeding their baby on a strict diet of only fruit, which again failed to provide enough nourishment.

These are all possibilities but, of course, there is no absolute link between these circumstances and child neglect or abuse. Some adults who have experienced disrupted childhoods can be good parents to their own children. They have looked for positive models outside their own experience or been guided by a supportive partner whose childhood was much happier. With appropriate support, parents with learning disabilities or very young parents can often cope.

Pressures – a constellated disadvantage

Some families would not be neglectful under more favourable circumstances, but adverse events have overwhelmed the ability of one or both parents to cope and the well being of the children suffers.

- Parents may be experiencing extreme financial hardship, debts and all the worries associated with this. It is important to realise that some families with serious money worries care well for their children, while some parents with no financial problems deliberately neglect one or more of their children.
- Physical or mental illness in the family may have incapacitated the main carer of the children. Psychological disturbance in the main carer may also lead this adult deliberately to neglect one child in a family, who is seen as a problem, unwanted or the 'wrong' sex.
- Alternatively, the parent's energy may be diverted to caring for a very sick or elderly family member. The children are then being overlooked, effectively forgotten or expected unrealistically to take care of themselves.
- Parents who have continuing problems of alcoholism, substance abuse and other addictions, such as gambling, are likely to lose sight of the welfare of their children. Time, attention and family money may be diverted away from the children's needs and towards the addiction.

Other factors

In some families, deeply held religious or philosophical views may lead to what is judged to be neglect from outside the family. Parents may refuse conventional medicines, even when their preferred alternative methods have failed to help a very sick child. Parents may also refuse life-giving interventions such as blood transfusions. These situations are very difficult, since an outside authority has to judge the limits to any parent's right to decide. When the consequences for a child are likely to be fatal, parental preference will usually be overruled legally.

Sexual abuse

Sexual abuse:

> 'involves forcing or enticing a child or young person to take part in sexual activities, not necessarily involving a high level of violence, whether or not the child is aware of what is happening. The activities may involve physical contact, including assault by penetration (for example, rape or oral sex) or non-penetrative acts such as masturbation, kissing, rubbing and touching outside of clothing. They may also include non-contact activities, such as involving children in looking at, or in the production of, sexual images, watching sexual activities, encouraging children to behave in sexually inappropriate ways, or grooming a child in preparation for abuse (including via the internet). Sexual abuse is not solely perpetrated by adult males. Women can also commit acts of sexual abuse, as can other children'

(HM Government, 2015a)

What does it mean?

Child sexual abuse: the exploitation of a child or young person, who has not reached an age or maturity to be able to give informed consent to involvement in any kind of sexual activity.

The majority of identified sexual abusers are male. But there has been increasing awareness that sexual abuse by women happens and has been underestimated. Michele Elliott (1993) was one of the first safeguarding professionals to raise this issue. She pointed out that part of the problem has been that many people, even within child protection services, resist believing that women would act in this way. Additionally, a strand of feminist tunnel vision has continued to assert that it is men are violent, sexually as well as in other ways, and not women. In 2009, the arrest and subsequent prosecution of an early years' practitioner, Vanessa George, brought home the dangers of complacency about who might sexually abuse children. George and four other women were fully complicit with Colin Blanchard in abusing children and uploading images of that abuse.

Pause for reflection

Read the serious case review report of the case of Vanessa George (Plymouth SCB, 2010). Serious issues for concern, such as George's use of her mobile phone camera in the nursery, are reflected in subsequent revised guidance, such as the welfare requirements in the revised Early Years Foundation Stage (for England).

Consider and discuss with your colleagues or fellow students the other important issues for effective safeguarding that emerge from this case.

Most sexual abusers are known to the children whom they abuse, because they are a relative, a family friend or a trusted person with access to children through their work or voluntary activities. Abduction and sexual assault by total strangers is very rare by comparison. Indeed, it's because such incidents are so infrequent that they receive significant media coverage.

Adults who sexually abuse children wish to satisfy their own sexual desires and impulses. (The situation with young sexual abusers – children or adolescents – follows a different pattern; see page 223.) Abusers often claim that the younger, or less mature, individual was a willing partner. However, abusers twist the idea of informed consent. Genuine consent means an agreement within an equal relationship – and abusing relationships are unequal. Abusers are in a greater position of power because they are older, larger or stronger and may have a position of authority over the child. Anyone who abuses a child usually builds a web of coercion to try to prevent discovery and reduce the likelihood that a child or young adolescent will be believed. But, sexual abusers are especially keen to force apparent co-operation and to impose secrecy: they know they are breaking an important social taboo.

A child's compliance and silence about the sexual abuse may be coerced through various means by the adult, and sometimes the adolescent who abuses peers or younger children:

- Abusers may directly threaten to hurt the child or young person or someone they care about (a person or a loved pet).
- Abusers may claim that nobody will believe the child if they tell, or that other people will blame and despise the child if the sexual activity is revealed.
- This threat can be especially effective if the abusing adult holds a position of authority over the child (through family or profession) or is a respected member of the local community.
- Some abusers attempt to bribe children with presents or treats and then induce a sense of guilt because the child accepted the gifts or outings.
- Some abusers work to convince children that what they are doing is normal or acceptable, as an activity within the family or between people who supposedly care for each other.

Ways in which children may be sexually abused

The key point is that sexual abuse operates to exploit the vulnerability of children (or young people), by coercing or forcing them into activity that is outside the boundaries for appropriate contact and interaction with minors.

- Sexual abuse of children sometimes involves full sexual intercourse, or abusers work their way towards this goal. Children and dependent young people have been coerced into tolerating oral or anal sex.
- But abusive use of children in a sexual way also includes intimate fondling and masturbation, either using a child in this way or requiring that they perform such acts on the abuser.
- It is also regarded as abusive for adults to engage in sexual activity in front of children. Sex between consenting individuals is a private, adult activity and trying to involve children as watchers is regarded as an abusive form of sexual exhibitionism.
- It is also regarded as abusive to coerce children into looking at pornographic photographs or films or to make them take part in such filming.

Available statistics indicate that more girls than boys have experienced some form of sexual abuse. However, both sexes are definitely at risk and it seems very probable that boys, especially from late childhood and into early adolescence, may under-report sexually abusive experiences. Some children are sexually abused only once, or for a very short period of time, but for some children and young people the experience carries on for years.

Child sexual exploitation

The National Working Group Network for Tackling Child Sex Exploitation (NWG, 2008) has defined the sexual exploitation of children and young people under 18 years as involving:

> *'exploitative situations, contexts and relationships where young people (or a third person or persons) receive "something" (e.g. food, accommodation, drugs, alcohol, cigarettes, affection, gifts, money) as a result of them performing, and/or another or others performing on them, sexual activities. Child sexual exploitation can occur through the use of technology without the child's immediate recognition; for example being persuaded to post sexual images on the Internet/ mobile phones without immediate payment or gain. In all cases, those exploiting the child/young person have power over them by virtue of their age, gender, intellect, physical strength and/or economic or other resources. Violence, coercion and intimidation are common, involvement in exploitative relationships being characterised in the main by the child or young person's limited availability of choice resulting from their social/economic and/or emotional vulnerability.'*

What does it mean?

Child sexual exploitation (CSE) is a form of child sexual abuse (CSA) but has nuances that separate it from the overarching concept of CSA. Victims of CSE are usually older, but children as young as 11 years have been known to have been sexually exploited.

The difference with CSE is that is involves an exchange and the victim often receives some form of reward from the perpetrator. The definition of CSE above highlights the exchange and power imbalance. The NWG (2008) definition is explicit about the power the perpetrator has over the young person they are exploiting, either through forceful acts or through persuasive techniques that might make a young person believe they are making a choice. It is also important that definitions for practitioners use language that reiterates the importance of looking beyond apparent consent, especially as young people may also describe exploitative relationships as consensual or withdraw claims as a result of coercion (Green *et al.*, 2014).

There are two coexisting factors that often increase the risk of CSE or indicate that it is occurring: 'The Dangerous Duo' (Webb and Holmes, 2015). These factors are gang involvement and missing children/young people.

Practitioners working with children aged 0–8 years need to be aware of CSE and be alert to concerns that may relate to siblings and older family relatives.

Other contemporary concerns include the sexual grooming of children via the internet and how mobile technology also poses a risk to young people (Chase and Statham, 2005; Barnardo's, 2011; Radford *et al.* 2011; CEOP, 2013). There are particular online key threats to children including the proliferation of indecent images of children, online exploitation, transnational child sexual abuse and contact child sexual abuse initiated online (CEOP, 2013). A significant proportion of children of all ages are exposed to pornography themselves both on and offline, which can lead to an unhealthy attitude to sex and relationships (Chase and Statham, 2005; Horvath *et al.* 2013).

Practice point: key message

Practitioners need to be vigilant to the concerns highlighted above. Traditionally, perpetrators of child sexual exploitation have been depicted as strangers, who appear threatening and dangerous. However, this perception is inaccurate (Lalor and McElvaney, 2010) and has probably led to missed opportunities for recognition of child sexual exploitation.

Case study

Sam

During the morning break, in the playground of the school where you work, you watched a vigorous physical game between the eight-year-olds that gradually began to concern you. The game involved a lot of shrieking and chasing in which the boys and girls were equally active. But one small group of boys, which appeared to be led by Sam, seemed to push the game beyond the limits that some of the girls wanted. A couple of girls were pushed against the fence and kissed, although they were shouting, 'Stop it!' You cannot be sure, but it looked also as if Sam was trying to put his hand up one girl's skirt. Sam is a boy who has concerned you because of the sexually explicit jokes that he makes sometimes.

- What would concern you about this situation?
- What should you do in response?
- What would your next steps be?

You will find a commentary on page 48.

Possible underlying reasons

Sexual abuse is possibly the hardest of the types of ill-treatment for practitioners, or anyone else, to consider in terms of possible underlying explanations. (Look back at page 25 at the points made for considering 'why' as well as 'what' and recall the important point that reasons are not ever excuses.) Adults, or young people, who sexually abuse others remain accountable for their actions, even when they have themselves suffered abusive treatment in the past, or it is still ongoing. They are not responsible for what was done to them; they have to accept the impact of what they have done to others.

Perpetrators of CSA and CSE

The term 'paedophile' is often used to describe unacceptable sexual behaviour towards children.

A paedophile is, by definition, an adult who is specifically sexually attracted to children and young adolescents, often pre-puberty. The roots of this term come from two Greek words: '*paedo*' meaning boy or child and '*phile*' meaning a strong or excessive liking. Paedophiles lose sexual interest in children as they grow out of childhood into adulthood. Children are their preferred objects for sexual activity and fantasy. Paedophiles may be heterosexual or homosexual. A disruptive myth still persists that gay men can be regarded as potential paedophiles. This assumption is false and can lead to discriminatory behaviour towards gay men. At the same time, children are likely to be put at increased risk if adults are reluctant to believe that 'happily married' men could ever be sexual abusers. A 'paedophile' is, though, a sexual offender and it is the term 'sexual offender' that is used to describe known perpetrators of CSA and CSE.

Perpetrators of CSA spend a great deal of time gaining a position of trust with children, in a paid job or through voluntary activity. Some target particular children and spend time getting to know the child and gaining the trust of their family, before attempting to create a relationship with the child. This process is called 'grooming' and some perpetrators target several children or young people at any one time. Such perpetrators feel sexually excited by steadily increasing their contact with a child, and their plans fuel their sexual fantasies. Some perpetrators become known to older children as the person who runs 'open house', where anyone (young) is welcome with no questions asked. Under these circumstances perpetrators may have contact with many children, and some are not abused.

The process of grooming works if the perpetrator is reasonably socially skilled. Some people are very adept at making contact and, in a twisted way, could be described as 'good with children'. They are very alert to children who are emotionally needy and without effective support from family or safe friends, either temporarily or over the long term. However, some perpetrators are socially unskilled and their attempts to make contact are so clumsy that even isolated children avoid them. Such abusers tend to make the headlines because they have abducted or attempted to abduct a child. The other type of sexual offender who hits the headlines is a subgroup and is predatory in a violent way. Such people are very dangerous indeed but appear, from available evidence, to be the less common pattern for perpetrators of CSA.

What does it mean?

Sexual abuser: an adult or young person who uses children or vulnerable peers to satisfy their own sexual needs.

Perpetrator: an adult who is specifically attracted sexually only to children or young adolescents.

Grooming: the process by which any kind of sexual abuser creates a relationship with a child or young person, making possible a pattern of sexual abuse.

Child pornography: the visual or written record of the sexual abuse of a child, or fantasies about this abusive behaviour.

Images of abuse: the visual record of sexual abuse. This term tends to be used now alongside, or instead of, 'child pornography'.

Other contexts of sexual abuse

Some adult sexual abusers are also in a sexual relationship with another adult, or have been in the past. These abusers seem to target children and young adolescents because they are available or easier to intimidate. What seems to happen is that such abusers turn to children or underage young people when they feel under stress or rejected in their adult relationship. They find children – their own, stepchildren or children of friends – less threatening and justify their abuse on the grounds that they are not harming the child, or that the child sought and welcomed their form of affection.

In isolated families, or whole communities, that close themselves away from outside contact, an abusive pattern has sometimes developed. A tradition is established that men have a right of sexual access to girls or very young women. Again, in examples that have come to public attention, the sexual abuse has been perpetrated by males. Most often, the women have been intimidated through pressure that this behaviour is acceptable, even required by the imposed cultural or faith tradition.

Some sexual abusers have themselves been abused as children. As a child or young person, they developed a distorted understanding of how to form affectionate relationships. As an adult, they may be exercising a sense of power over children, because they feel incompetent in relationships with adults. However, not all children who have been sexually abused go on to abuse as an adult.

Organised groups

The majority of sexual abusers, whatever their exact nature, appear to act on their own. However, there have been cases of groups of adults engaging in systematic sexual abuse of children. These may be within the family or external to the family. Such cases within families have involved either several generations of the same family or a linked group of local families. The organised abuse of groups of family and friends have involved men, women, boys and girls, although there are still proportionately more men involved than women. Scandals have broken about organised sexual or physical abuse in a few residential group settings, where children or young people were coerced into secrecy. They have also been told, with tragic justification in some cases, that nobody will believe them if they tell, because they are 'bad' children with a track record of misbehaviour and absconding.

The internet, technology and abuse

Pornography involving children can be part of sexually abusive behaviour. Organised groups of abusers do not just pass children between adults in real-time contact. They increasingly use webcam technology to provide interactive access to other abusers who may live at a considerable distance. Visual and written pornography involving children is not new. But communication via the internet has offered an easy expansion of the opportunity to access and exchange images of abuse. In their email communications and in chatrooms, sometimes linked with such websites, perpetrators support each other in the stance that their behaviour is acceptable and just another sexual orientation.

The arrival of mobile phones equipped with a camera function has simplified the process of taking and disseminating images, and this process can be used for unacceptable images just as easily as for photos of friends and family. Use of this technology was a key feature of the sexual abuse by Vanessa George (Plymouth, England in 2010) and also by Paul Wilson, an early years practitioner in Birmingham, England in 2011.

International police operations have uncovered significant internet websites. The ring called the 'Wonderland Club' was exposed in 2001 and during 2002 a huge subscriber website was discovered that operated out of Texas in the United States. In 2007 another international operation, led by the Child Exploitation and Online Protection Centre, dismantled an online ring that extended to more than 35 countries. This paedophile network was by that time largely controlled by one man living in Suffolk (England).

Such cases have shown the extent to which paedophiles exchange abusive images within well-hidden websites. Some participants in such websites claim not to be sexual abusers, because they only download the images. But, of course, children have to be abused in order to create the pornography. It is a profound shock for children and young people who have been sexually abused to discover their traumatic experiences have become public through the internet. This knowledge brings new levels of distress and a sense of powerlessness to children and young people who have already been damaged.

Trafficking and exploitation

Some children and young adolescents have been effectively prostituted by their own families, who have welcomed relatives or a network of friends to abuse their daughters and sometimes sons as well. Older children and adolescents of both sexes can become sexually exploited by non-family adults who approach them in the local neighbourhood. Some children and young people are brought illicitly to the UK, for sexual exploitation but also for work as household servants. Some children arrive accompanied by an adult who claims to be a friend of the family, if not a relative.

What does it mean?

Trafficking: movement of people, usually across national borders, for the purpose of exploitation, whether sexual or as forced labour.

Find out more

HM Government (2015a) *Working Together to Safeguard Children: A Guide to Inter-agency Working to Safeguard and Promote the Welfare of Children*, London: Department for Education. Available at www.gov.uk/government/uploads/system/uploads/attachment_data/file/419595/Working_Together_to_Safeguard_Children.pdf
These safeguarding issues are more likely to arise with children older than the 0–8-years focus of this book. The *Working Together* document has useful links to sources of information about safeguarding children who may have been trafficked and safeguarding children from sexual exploitation. These resources will support readers who work across an extended age range.

The harm of sexual abuse

Unless the sexual practices are very intrusive or violent, children are less likely to suffer direct physical injury than to be psychologically damaged by the experience. Sexual abuse matters because of the short- and long-term impact that the abuse has on children and young people:

- It is the responsibility of adults, especially those in a close relationship of trust, to help children to establish boundaries for appropriate physical contact and respect for others. Sexual abusers cross and disrupt the very boundaries that adults should help to create.
- Sexual abusers confuse and distort children's growing understanding of relationships, because they replace proper affection with sexual contact. The emotional upheaval is worsened by an atmosphere of coercion and secrecy. The experience disrupts children's legitimate wish for attention and care, because these needs are met with an inappropriate sexual reaction.

- Children's natural wish for physical contact and affection is manipulated through sexual abuse, and children can feel responsible. Yet it was entirely the adult's responsibility to offer appropriate intimacy to a child, not an abuse of trust.
- Children can experience, and be left with, painful feelings of guilt that somehow they brought the experience on themselves. They continue to believe they are to blame because they accepted gifts or treats from the abuser.
- When children's disclosures of sexual abuse lead to the break-up of their family, they may feel that this crisis is their fault. Some members of the family may be keen to blame the child or adolescent.
- Children may not be believed, or may be considered to be at least partly responsible, when the abuser is a respected member of the community and 'not the kind of person who would do this'. Children can be disbelieved about any kind of abuse or neglect. But claims of sexual abuse perpetrated by an adult with high status in the community seem especially likely to be rejected.
- Depending on the reactions that children experience when the abuse is disclosed, they may feel dirty, as if they are unpleasant and unworthy. The abuser may also have threatened children that they will be disliked and rejected if they break the secret.
- Children should be able to trust adults to protect them and not to violate them. The experience of sexual abuse can leave children feeling powerless and betrayed. The abuser can have shaken their trust in adults in general.
- Children's emotional and sexual development can be disrupted. They may have later doubts about their sexuality and how psychologically healthy relationships should operate. Adults who experienced sexual abuse in childhood may fear, with some justification, that their later adult partners will be disturbed or reject them if they knew what had happened.
- Children who are sexually abused by adults of the same sex may experience later confusion about their sexual identity and what would have been their chosen orientation without the imposition of abuse.

Other contemporary safeguarding concerns

It is also important that anyone who works with children has an awareness of child abuse linked to faith or belief. Belief in witchcraft, spirit possession and other forms of the supernatural can lead to children being blamed for bad luck, and subsequently abused. Fear of the supernatural is also known to be used to make children comply with being trafficked for domestic slavery or sexual exploitation. For further information see the national action plan to tackle child abuse linked to faith or belief (Department for Education, 2012).

Faith- and belief-based abuse is discussed further in Chapter 5.

Other contemporary safeguarding concerns relate to unaccompanied migrant children and with regard to this the NSPCC emphasises that separated children should be treated as children first and migrants second. Should concerns be raised about unaccompanied migrant children: 'all agencies and professionals dealing with separated children need to ensure that the statutory responsibilities under child welfare legislation are applied to all children in the UK, irrespective of their immigration status' (NSPCC, 2012).

Practitioners need to be alert to the needs of first-generation immigrants, asylum seekers and refugees and to make referrals to children's social care if they are aware of children in this context who need intervention to ensure that they are protected from harm.

Female genital mutilation is also a contemporary safeguarding concern and is discussed in Chapter 5.

Commentary on the scenarios
In each example, the commentary below offers possibilities and suggestions.

Pike Lane Pre-school (page 24)
The students need to be reassured that their concerns are valid; they have observed bad practice and they were right to challenge what they observed.

Their tutor needs to contact the pre-school manager and meet to discuss the concerns. If the students' account is correct, there are serious concerns about practice in this setting. The team has bad practice in terms of young learners, the adult approach to behaviour, and setting a good example to the children. Even if some parents are in favour of such an oppressive regime, this agreement does not excuse the team and the leader. This preschool is not a suitable work placement for students, as they are being given a negative model for early learning and partnership with families.

If the tutor meets with the same reaction as the students, then the matter will need to be taken further, both verbally and in writing. The most likely first step would be to contact the local advisory team for early years provision. It is possible to make a complaint, with descriptive support, to the regulatory body that inspects the group. However, first it would be appropriate to contact the local department responsible for this setting.

Sajida (page 29)
The after-school club team needs to talk now with Sajida's parents and the school, either through Sajida's key person at the club or the club's designated safeguarding lead.

It is important, of course, not to leap to conclusions. Perhaps Alan did 'bang' Sajida, but it was in the course of trying to catch her. However, the child seems to have more accidents at school and home than in the club. This difference between settings raises concerns that Sajida is either poorly supervised elsewhere, or is being directly hurt by somebody. Sajida has the ability to express herself in spoken words, but she may need help through signs and images to communicate the details of her accidents.

It is important that nobody comes to a premature conclusion that Alan or Sajida's family have hurt her. But equally, it is time to challenge the simple explanation that Sajida's clumsiness explains a series of accidents.

Danny (page 35)

The information about Danny raises the real possibility that he is neglected, and possibly physically abused, by his mother or older siblings. Teachers in the primary school are not concerned about his older siblings. But, in some families, one child is singled out for neglect or abuse. The way that Mrs Sanders talks about her son sounds very rejecting.

The nursery class team and the head need to keep descriptive records of Danny's condition each day and be clear with Mrs Sanders that their concerns are serious and could well be taken further. The nursery team needs to bring together what they have already observed and discuss with the designated teacher for child protection (in the school) what kind of regular contact they will plan, in order to make a more concerted effort to address the problems for Danny.

It will also be important to bring together, if this has not already happened in a thorough way, the knowledge of the Sanders family that is spread across the school staff team. For instance, is Danny's father at home or in contact with the family; might he be of any help? There appear to be five boys in the family but only four in the nursery and school. Have there been any concerns in the past about this other son; where is he placed in the birth order of siblings? Once all the information is made available to the school staff team, and if Danny's well being does not improve, it is probable the designated safeguarding lead will judge it is time to make a referral.

Sam (page 41)

The adults need to intervene in a game that has unacceptable elements of pressure and possibly touch. A first step would be to tell children that 'Stop it!' means precisely that and a game is no longer playful if anyone is hurt or distressed. It is also appropriate to explore the issue with the girls in question. You could ask, 'I was concerned about what was going on by the fence. What exactly happened?' The girls may need to be reassured that they were not responsible for the chasing game going too far. Depending on what emerges, there may be a need for a whole-group discussion about appropriate touch, listening to 'No' and play without pressure.

If Sam *was* putting his hand up a girl's skirt, that behaviour is unacceptable between children. It will be necessary for an appropriate person, possibly his class teacher, to have a serious conversation with him about what is and is not alright in play. If Sam was aware of being observed, and nothing is said, he is likely to assume that either his actions are acceptable or that adults do not have the confidence to challenge him.

Depending on the seriousness of what has emerged, there may also need to be a conversation with his parents. There should have been an earlier conversation, in which the practitioner raised with Sam's parents what had been said to him about the sexually explicit jokes and why these are offensive. If nothing was said about the matter, then it is overdue for the team to address the situation.

Summary

This chapter has considered the contemporary definitions of abuse and neglect and what constitutes the different types of abuse. It is important that practitioners have an understanding of contemporary definitions. Definitions do evolve but help to provide a framework for the recognition of abuse and neglect.

Up until the 1990s the main child protection concerns were with intrafamilial abuse, with the main forms being physical, sexual, emotional and neglect. Concerns then began to emerge about extrafamilial abuse including that of organised sexual abuse and 'child prostitution', shifting and extending the focus of practice. Child prostitution is now recognised as a form of CSE. The period from the mid 1990s to 2008 can also be seen as a time when policy shifted from a narrow child protection orientation towards a more family service and, in particular, child-focused orientation. However, if safeguarding is to be effective, legislation, policy and practice must have at their core a children's rights perspective. The next chapter will discuss the legislative and policy framework for safeguarding practice.

Key texts

The NSPCC website offers many short briefing papers that will enable you to explore each broad area covered in this chapter. Useful sources on the site include the Child Protection Research Briefings and the Research Findings, both of which are best accessed through this home page:

www.nspcc.org.uk/Inform/research/research_wda48228.html.

The research briefing on child sexual abuse (NSPCC, 2013b) also has useful references to follow up for further reading.

Real Love Rocks provides tools for young people, families and educators on healthy relationships: www.barnardosrealloverocks.org.uk

Barnardo's *Spot the Signs* provides a short overview of the key risks and indicators surrounding child sexual exploitation:

www.barnardos.org.uk/spot_the_signs_professionals.pdf

Families and Communities Against Child Sexual Exploitation, D'Arcy *et al.* (2015):

www.barnardos.org.uk/university_of_bedfordshire_FCASE_report.pdf

DCSF (2009) *Safeguarding Children and Young People from Sexual Exploitation: Guidelines for LSCBs from the Department for Children, Schools and Families* includes information on the roles and responsibilities of different professional organisations, prevention of CSE and managing individual cases.

www.gov.uk/government/uploads/system/uploads/attachment_data/ file/278849/Safeguarding_Children_and_Young_People_from_Sexual_ Exploitation.pdf

The Government provides further sources of information and supplementary guidance on particular safeguarding issues including the following Department for Education guidance:

- Safeguarding children who may have been trafficked.
- Safeguarding children and young people who may have been affected by gang activity.
- Safeguarding children from female genital mutilation.
- Forced marriage.
- Safeguarding children from abuse linked to faith or belief.
- Radicalisation – Prevent strategy.
- Radicalisation – Channel guidance.
- Use of reasonable force in schools.
- Safeguarding children and young people from sexual exploitation.
- Safeguarding children in whom illness is fabricated or induced.
- Preventing and tackling bullying.
- Safeguarding children and safer recruitment in education.
- Safeguarding disabled children: Practice guidance.

3 The legislative and policy framework

Introduction

The view is now well established that parents, or any other family members, cannot simply deal with children, or adolescents, as they please. Society, backed by legislation, leaves parents considerable flexibility in how they raise their sons and daughters, but reserves the right to intervene when their safety or continued well being is under threat. Services and settings are also accountable for their practice; professionals cannot argue that their knowledge or expertise places them beyond challenge. Of course, laws do not automatically change people's behaviour or attitudes. However, legislation makes a very public statement about what is acceptable or unacceptable within society.

The activities and practice of those working with children are very present orientated but historical perspectives provide insight on how legislation, policy and practice has evolved. This chapter will provide an overview of the legislative and policy framework and key events that have influenced how these frameworks have developed. It will provide a historical perspective and an overview of the key areas of legislation of which practitioners need to be aware.

Historical perspectives

The main framework for safeguarding and protecting children from harm in the UK is a relatively recent development. However, it would be wrong to assume that previous generations were uncaring about the ill-treatment of children. Some of the national children's charities were set up before the twentieth century, by individuals who were deeply moved by the plight of abandoned children. Captain Thomas Coram fundraised tirelessly to open his Foundlings Hospital in 1741 and the Coram Family organisation still operates in London today. Dr Thomas Barnardo set up his first orphanage for homeless boys in 1870 and Barnardo's continues to be an active national organisation. The National Society for the Prevention of Cruelty to Children (NSPCC) was established in 1884 by the Reverend Benjamin Waugh and like-minded people who were shocked by the fact that a law against cruelty to animals had been passed, with no equivalent legislation about children. Energetic lobbying by the NSPCC led to the first English Prevention of Cruelty to Children Act in 1889, which created the option of prosecution. The

NSPCC set up a national network of centres and inspectors, and for many decades they were more active in child protection than local authorities.

Children with repeated, hard-to-explain injuries remained a medical puzzle until 1961, when Henry Kempe, in a presentation to the American Academy of Paediatrics, described what he called 'the battered child syndrome'. This public discussion opened up a serious debate about the notion that adults, including parents, sometimes intentionally injured children. Tragically, it took the non-accidental death of a child to bring the reality of physical abuse effectively into the public arena when, in 1973, seven-year-old Maria Colwell was killed by her stepfather. Maria was known to be at risk by the local authority (Brighton, England). The public inquiry in 1974 criticised the lack of communication between the various agencies involved with the family. The child protection register, first known as an 'at risk register', was established in 1975 as a national requirement for local authorities to improve contact in such situations.

The Maria Colwell case was pivotal to the development of Safeguarding Practice as it is today.

Table 3.1 identifies significant events that have occurred and related policy and practice implications.

Child protection practice	Events
1974–1990 The first era of child protection practice: child abuse work	Definitions of abuse broadened; Interventions into families became more focused and intrusive but with concerns emerging in the 1980s about an over-intrusive and very punitive approach towards families suspected of abusing their children.
1990–2000 The second era: child protection	Wider concerns emerged with regard to extrafamilial abuse: organised abuse, child prostitution, and child abuse via the internet as well as institutional abuse. A changing emphasis for practice, towards one of early intervention and prevention of harm through recognising vulnerable children early. Messages from research and a need to be more child-focused.
2000 onwards The third era: safeguarding, of which child protection is part	An increased focus on childcare, child welfare and a supportive approach to vulnerable families as well as an increased focus on child protection. Increasing emphasis in policy on the need to protect vulnerable children from harm and improve outcomes through early intervention. The emergence of the 'early help' agendas and the need to 'think family' while keeping the child in mind.

Table 3.1 Historical events and influences on safeguarding and child protection 1990 onwards

The twentieth century and beyond

Over the second half of the twentieth century, a far greater awareness grew of the complexity of child abuse. Children and young people could be physically attacked but they were also put at serious risk by neglect of their basic needs, emotional maltreatment and sexual abuse within, or from outside, the family. Initially, the focus for abuse was on ill-treatment of children from their own family. But cases emerged, some dating back many years, where children had been abused by adults within the context of their professional role. Physically abusive and neglectful regimes had sometimes been justified as necessary discipline or tough training regimes. Any hopeful predictions about likely abusers were swept away as it became clear that there are no neat certainties. Abusers can be men and women, from any social class, ethnic group, cultural background and faith. The most likely abuser is an adult, but young people (under-18s) have also abused peers or younger children.

Find out more

www.barnardos.org.uk/who_we_are/history.htm
Barnardo's

www.coram.org.uk/section/about/our-heritage
Coram Family

www.nspcc.org.uk/what-we-do/about-the-nspcc/history-of-NSPCC/history-of-the-nspcc_wda72240.html
NSPCC

Laws and guidance

Within the UK, some laws passed by the Westminster Parliament apply to all four nations: England, Wales, Scotland and Northern Ireland. However, some legislation only applies to England and Wales and those two nations may differ in their application of the final details of practice. Scotland passes laws applicable only to that nation through the Scottish Parliament, and Northern Ireland has the same power within the Northern Ireland Assembly.

The laws described in this section are primary legislation (see 'What does it mean' on p. 54) and the requirements built into the laws must be obeyed. However, legal language is not expressed in ways that make it easy for people without a legal background to understand what laws mean for daily life. Sometimes the relevant government department issues further information through books of guidance. These documents do not have the same force as primary legislation. But when they are described as 'statutory', it is required that local authorities, or relevant organisations, follow the details of guidance or a code – or can provide a very good reason for variation.

For example, *Keeping Children Safe in Education* (HM Government, 2015b).

Guidance documents often describe what would be regarded as best practice wherever you work within the UK. However, you need to be aware that statutory guidance from elsewhere may refer to law that does not necessarily apply to your provision. Some good practice guidance is 'recommended', meaning that the associated government department strongly advises that the suggestions and examples are followed. The process of developing guidance often goes through a consultation phase. The draft guidance, or a report with practical recommendations, is available on the relevant website and anyone can make comments and suggestions.

The devolution process for Wales did not extend to the right to set its own laws. However, the Welsh Assembly exerts considerable influence over how legislation is implemented. Documents such as *Children and Young People: Rights to Action* (Welsh Assembly Government, 2002) set out a clear national plan that is stronger than the equivalent government documents for England on implementing children's rights.

What does it mean?

Primary legislation: laws that have been passed for a given country. The detail of law defines what is legally required or has been made illegal. The name of a law is given with the date when it was passed by Parliament or Assembly. Sometimes parts of a law do not become fully applicable until a given later date.

Statutory guidance: material issued by the relevant government department to explain in non-legal language what must be done or not done.

Good practice guidance: material to support professionals to put law and statutory guidance into daily practice. These publications may be 'recommended' by the relevant government department.

Consultation: the process by which draft guidance is made available on a government website. Anyone can make comments or suggestions.

Procedures, guidelines and advice

Statutory guidance, backed up through the process of inspection, sometimes requires that services have a clear code of practice or policy on an important issue. It is expected that local authorities will develop their own child protection guidelines, grounded firmly in the relevant law and statutory guidance, in order to support local practice. Some procedures apply across authorities, with the aim of creating consistent application of safeguarding practice. For example, the London Safeguarding Children Board Committee has published the *London Child Protection Procedures* (updated October 2015, see www.londoncp.co.uk).

The *All Wales Child Protection Procedures*, issued by the Social Services Improvement Agency (SSIA) in 2008 applies legal requirements within the context of every Welsh authority (www.childreninwales.org.uk/our-work/safeguarding/wales-child-protection-procedures-review-group/).

These substantial documents not only explain the details of good practice, linked with national requirements, but also give information about relevant services and organisations for the area or country. Reliable websites, such as those of Local Safeguarding Children Boards and the Social Services Improvement Agency (Wales), are also a valuable source of information and procedures for professionals facing a particular safeguarding issue.

The law and child protection

The shape of child protection across the UK was determined during the late 1980s and 1990s. The first new legislation was the Children Act 1989, which applied to England and Wales. The Cleveland Inquiry contributed serious concerns about a thorough process of assessment, avoiding sudden and unjustified removal of children from their family. Chaired by Dame Elizabeth Butler-Sloss, this report investigated claims of widespread sexual abuse during 1987 within families in Cleveland (England). However, plans for revising family law were already well advanced before the final report. A number of avoidable child deaths during the 1980s, caused by the actions or inaction of children's own families, had raised serious concerns that the existing legislation was not working effectively. Legislation followed in the rest of the UK: the Children (Scotland) Act 1995 and the Children (Northern Ireland) Order 1996. Subsequent legislation has changed some details of how the child protection system works, but much of this legal framework still applies.

All these laws cover child welfare and family support in the broadest sense. The sections covering child protection are part of more wide-ranging legislation that also encompasses services for children in need. The Children (Scotland) Act 1995 stands out as the legislation that most took account of the United Nations Convention on the Rights of the Child 1989. Each Act or Order also covered the registration and inspection of early years services that fell outside the state educational system. Each law shares the key principles that should underpin all practice with children and young people:

- The welfare of the child must be paramount in any work with a family; this is known as the 'paramountcy principle'.
- Work must be conducted in partnership. Professionals are expected to work together in a spirit of inter-agency co-operation and to work in a co-operative way with parents.
- Children are not the possessions of their parents. Parents have responsibilities for their children, not absolute rights.
- Children should preferably be raised within their own family, but their welfare requires limits to family privacy and decision making.

- Each law assumed that childhood, and the need to protect, extended up to an individual's 18th birthday – with the exception of Scotland, which placed the boundary at 17 years of age.

Each law also established two broad areas of concern:

- Children and young people are judged to be 'in need' when their development and health cannot be guaranteed without extra support for children and their families. All disabled children were defined as 'in need', although Scotland extended the definition to include all children in a family where any member, adult or child, was disabled.
- Serious concerns about a child's health and development raise the possibility that they are at risk of suffering 'significant harm'. A child's parents or other carers are failing to ensure that the child can thrive and be safe, compared with what could be expected for children of a similar age.

Keep the child in mind

Promoting the well being of children in need and safeguarding children who are at risk of significant harm should be seen as two sides of the same coin. The judgement that children are suffering, or are at risk of significant harm, triggers compulsory intervention in family life through the child protection process. However, a range of actions can be taken to protect children who are in need, as well as at risk of significant harm, including family support services. The legislation also established the types of abuse recognised in law: physical abuse, emotional abuse, sexual abuse and neglect. In Scotland, a fifth category, that of non-organic failure to thrive, was given separately from neglect.

New laws do not always repeal (or revoke) existing legislation – that is, remove a similar earlier law from the statute book. Legislation relevant to safeguarding, introduced since the Acts and Order described here, have not repealed the legislation of the late 1980s and mid-1990s. In fact, some details of safeguarding are still decided by the Children and Young Persons Act 1933. Other laws also affect safeguarding and family issues around that task; you will find examples throughout this book. In general, law affecting child protection is of two kinds:

- *Civil law* includes the public law that has determined the systems of child protection. It also includes private law that deals with family proceedings such as divorce and the ways in which separating adults can continue to be parents to their children in relation to issues such as contact.
- *Criminal law* relevant to child protection identifies what are offences against children and young people: crimes that inevitably bring police involvement.

UK law to safeguard children and young people includes a wide range of provisions to protect that do not require there to be a crime, nor for evidence to be presented that meets the standard of a criminal court case.

What does it mean?

Civil law: guides and determines disputes or problems between individuals that do not involve a criminal act.

Criminal law: determines which actions are criminal under a specific law and the likely consequences of being convicted in court for that criminal act.

Repeal or revoke: the legal step, built into some new laws, that specific sections now replace named sections in an existing law.

Developments since the 1990s

Law, guidance and the application to practice do not stand still. Since the 1990s, there have been significant reviews of how well the child protection system is working to safeguard children and young people effectively from harm.

These developments are discussed below with an overview of key events presented in Table 3.2.

Date	Key event
1989	Children Act (Implemented October 1991)
1991	New *Working Together* Guidelines
1995	Children (Scotland) Act
1999	Protection of Children Act
2000	Framework for the Assessment of Children in Need and their Families
	Death of Victoria Climbié
	Criminal Justice and Courts Service Act
	Leaving Care Act
	Care Standards Act
	Publication of *Lost in Care*, the report of the Waterhouse Inquiry into the abuse of children in a residential home in North Wales
	Publication of *Working Together Guidelines to Safeguard Children Involved in Prostitution*
	Murder of Sarah Payne

Date	Key event
2001	Review report into the death of Lauren Wright
	Review report into the death of Kennedy McFarlane
	Publication of Department of Health research *The Children Act Now*
	Review of child protection in Scotland
2002	Review into the death of Ainlee Labonte
	Murders of Jessica Chapman and Holly Wells
2003	Publication of the Victoria Climbié *Inquiry Report* (Laming)
	Publication of the Green Paper *'Every Child Matters'*
	First publication of *What to Do if You're Worried that a Child is Being Abused*
	Local Safeguarding Children Boards established (replacing Area Child Protection Committees)
	Every Child Matters Agendas launched
2004	Children Act
	Publication of the Bichard report
	Publication of the *Hidden Harm* report on the children of parents who misuse drugs
2007	Death of Peter Connelly
2009	Publication of *The Protection of Children in England: A Progress Report* (Laming)
2010	New *Working Together* Guidelines
2011	*The Munro Review of Child Protection*
2012	Death of Daniel Pelka
2014	Coffey, A. (2014*) Real Voices: Child Sexual Exploitation in Greater Manchester, An Independent Report.*
2015	New *Working Together* Guidelines
	New guidelines on *'What to do if You're Worried that a Child is Being Abused*
	Updated guidance on *Keeping Children Safe in Education*

Source (up to 2012): © Corby, B., Shemmings, D. and Wilkins, D. (2012) Child Abuse: An Evidence Base for Confident Practice, **Milton Keynes: Open University Press.** Reproduced with the kind permission of Open University Press. All rights reserved.

Table 3.2 Key events in safeguarding and child protection since 1990

Review and public inquiry

Government departments sometimes commission research reviews: overviews of safeguarding as a whole or reports on specific aspects of child protection. Public inquiries follow those cases when child protection has failed in some way. The different strands of overview sometimes merge in practice – for example, the 2002 review by Nina Biehal and Jim Wade of children who go missing. An overview of this kind often makes practical recommendations, which contribute to the development of practice guidance. For example The Department for Children, Schools and Families has published such guidance in 2009 (*Statutory Guidance on Children who Run Away and Go Missing from Home or Care*) and it has since been updated by the Department for Education in 2014.

Around the UK, a local inquiry has to follow the death or very serious injury of a child if child abuse is either confirmed or suspected. A report is made to the Child Protection Committee or Local Children Safeguarding Board (currently the Health and Social Services Board in Northern Ireland) for the area. Such a report does not necessarily become public, although sometimes the decision is made that publication is in the public interest. That step is sometimes taken when the death of a child was avoidable and professional practice had been inadequate to protect.

Changes to legislation and policy can occur in light of reviews and public inquiries, as discussed below.

Pause for reflection

Read the report about the death of Peter Connelly, known initially as Baby P, who died in Haringey, North London in 2007 (Haringey LSCB, 2009).

Like Victoria Climbié (page 66), Peter was a child known to social care services; his name was on the child protection register and a number of agencies were involved with the family. Yet his mother's vague explanations were accepted for a litany of injuries, key medical professionals were absent from important case meetings and no proper investigation was made of the adults living in a house where Peter and other children had already been judged to be at risk.

Also, if you have not done so already, read the report about the death of Daniel Pelka who died in Coventry in March 2012 (Lock, 2013). Daniel died of a head injury. At the time of his death Daniel was found to be malnourished and to have bruises on his body.

Daniel had been starved, assaulted, neglected and abused. His mother had relationships with three partners between moving to the UK in 2005 and the time of Daniel's death, all of which involved high consumption of alcohol and

⇨

⇨

domestic abuse. There was a history of incidents of serious domestic abuse and violence and a chaotic lifestyle with multiple house moves. Issues identified in the Serious Care Review findings include:

- The deception of agencies and services by the mother, which included coercing Daniel's older sister to lie about injuries sustained by Daniel, his eating habits and his mental development;
- The impact of witnessing violence on the children in the household;
- The impact of culture, race and language on service provision; and
- Daniel's isolation and 'invisibility'.

Recommendations included: a review of information sharing and notification systems in respect of domestic abuse; ensuring a robust system for recording injuries or welfare concerns by school staff; and guaranteeing that health professionals consider child abuse as a differential diagnosis, when assessing the welfare of children who present with unclear concerns.

- Consider and discuss with colleagues or fellow students the significance of the issues that emerge from these reports.
- What are the implications for practitioners?

The Department of Health (for England) is obliged to commission regular overviews of serious case reviews, following avoidable deaths or serious injuries to children. These overviews draw out the consistent themes from many case reviews, while keeping the details confidential, as in, for example, the 2010 report and the 2012 report by Brandon *et al.*

Significant public inquiries are organised when the events of a particular case raise serious questions about the adequacy of the existing system to protect. Such reports make recommendations, often leading to a change in guidance, and sometimes to new legislation. There have also been public inquiries following investigations into child abuse when professional opinion has been sharply divided; for instance, Lord Clyde's judicial inquiry following the claims about ritual sexual abuse in the Orkneys (1990). Public inquiries also usually follow the discovery of significant professional malpractice in provision for children or young people; for example, the abusive 'Pindown' system used in Staffordshire Children's Homes (1990).

The long-term abuse in residential children's homes in Clwyd, North Wales, exposed finally in the mid-1990s, led to the report *People Like Us*, by Sir William Utting in 1997. The government's response was to introduce the Quality Protects Programme for England – Quality First in Wales – to improve provision for looked-after children and young people. A review in 2004 by Marian Stuart and Catherine Baines identified that changes made since the Utting report had brought improvements in some aspects of practice. However, improvements were slow in some areas, such as children and young people in custody or in psychiatric hospitals.

Find out more

Brandon, M., Bailey, S. and Belderson, P. (2010) *Building on the Learning from Serious Case Reviews: A Two Year Analysis of Child Protection Database Notifications 2007–2009*, London: The Stationery Office.

Brandon, M., Sidebotham, P., Bailey, S., Belderson, P., Hawley, C., Ellis, C. and Megson, M. (2012) *New Learning from Serious Case Reviews*, London: Department for Education, DFE-RR226.

Focus on professional practice

A major consequence of reviews throughout the 1990s was to show that children's welfare may not only be endangered by their families, but also that professionals may have the potential to harm children through their actions or inaction. The concept of 'professional dangerousness' came into use to describe behaviour from members of relevant professions that failed to protect children effectively. This concept remains highly relevant in the twenty-first century, along with the commitment to reflective practice that it entails.

What does it mean?

Professional (or organisational) dangerousness: when inappropriate values, priorities or methods lead professionals to act in ways that fail to reduce the risk to children or young people.

It was found that significant practice issues could increase the risk for children, even though professionals were involved with their family:

- Unsafe professionals had inadequate supervision and sometimes impossible caseloads.
- An additional issue has arisen with pressure to get considerable amounts of data entered on computer files. The risk of what has been called 'technology-driven practice' is that hard-pressed professionals may slip into placing a higher priority on inputting data than on spending time with a child whose welfare is in doubt.
- Whole teams were sometimes perplexed about how to balance anti-discriminatory practice with child protection. Anxiety about avoiding what could be interpreted as racist decisions remains a live issue that complicates safe decision making in some cases.
- A proper focus on children had sometimes been lost in favour of addressing the problems of adults and accepting their perspective on family life.

- Some professionals held on to an unrealistic optimism about the family's ability to cope, even in the face of poor outcomes for the child.
- Some professionals had avoided contact with the family because of unacknowledged fears for their own personal safety. This situation, combined with poor support within the team, meant that nobody confronted how a child could possibly be safe in a household that professionals were afraid to visit.

A key theme in professional dangerousness for work with families is that the child has been lost as the priority in child protection. Even where parents are doing their best, given serious stress or very limited understanding of a child's needs, the final judgement has to be the well being of the child. No child can be left at risk of abuse or neglect on the grounds that, although their care is seriously inadequate, the parents could not be expected to manage any better. All involved professionals must place the child's safety and well being at the very centre of attention. Social workers, and other professionals directly involved with families, face a challenging task. They have to make genuine efforts to work with parents, who may well be supported to keep their child safe. Yet these professionals must also be alert to parents who are only co-operative on the surface – masking an inability, or refusal, to change behaviour or a home situation that endangers a child.

During the 1990s it became clear that the full possibilities of family support services were not always used. Each Children Act and Order was set up to enable support for children 'in need' as well as action to protect children at risk of significant harm. Reviews highlighted that the key point of the process was not exclusively whether to place a child's name on the register and that this action didn't in itself protect children without effective follow-up. Family support services could be crucial to ensure that a child who was currently 'in need' did not slide towards 'at risk' and a crisis situation. Reports emphasised the obligation to involve parents as much as possible, but that professionals must not overlook listening to children, taking their views properly into account.

Make the connection with ...

Procedures have to be implemented to be effective

Carefully drafted procedures, like any safeguarding policy, do not in themselves protect children. Two linked reports from Wales highlighted how abusive treatment was allowed to continue because the adults responsible for safeguarding made other considerations a higher priority than the welfare of children and young adolescents. ⇨

> ⇨
>
> Sir Ronald Waterhouse reported in *Lost in Care* (Waterhouse Inquiry, 2000), the North Wales Child Abuse Inquiry, on allegations of abuse of looked-after children and young people in the Gwynedd and Clwyd areas dating back to 1974. The Waterhouse inquiry documented allegations made by some children about abusive treatment during the time they stayed at Gwynfa, an NHS facility in Colwyn Bay for children and adolescents with mental health problems. Sir Alex Carlile led the subsequent inquiry into these allegations (Carlile Report, 2003). He highlighted the risks that arose from secrecy and a feeling among staff that it was unacceptable to express any concerns about practice within their team. The Gwynfa facility had clear guidance on child protection but failed to implement procedures, using excuses such as staff shortages.

Focus on the child in 'child protection'

The subtitle of the Carlile Report was *Too serious a thing*. The full quotation from Charles Lamb (a nineteenth-century writer) is given on the front page of the Report: 'A child's nature is too serious a thing to admit of its being regarded as a mere appendage of another being.' The reports from Wales highlight the great risk to children and young adolescents when protection of them becomes less important to adults than their own concerns and priorities. Adults can be culpable of neglectful inaction, even when they are not the active abusers.

Good practice in protection also has to respect the welfare and development of children as individuals in their own right. A criticism made in the public inquiry on the Cleveland sex abuse cases in the late 1980s was that the children themselves ran the risk of being lost in the flurry of diagnosis and professional counter-claim. A telling phrase from that report is still quoted: 'The child is a person, not an object of concern.' However, problems continued through the 1990s, as shown in later reports on professional misconduct in dealing with claims of widespread sexual abuse within a community (for example, in the Orkneys). There is a significant risk to children and young people when professionals are so convinced that abuse has occurred that they refuse to believe the children's protestations; indeed, the denial was sometimes taken as a sure sign that something *had* happened (the child was 'in denial'). Such public inquiries also highlighted that professionals must follow codes of conduct for how a child is interviewed and a high standard of documentation of that process.

Agencies must work together

An additional problem arose when a service simply did not view children and adolescents as part of their brief. There are now stronger messages for professionals within adult disability, mental health or addiction services: to look beyond their own adult client or patient. Such services should at least check whether an adult who faces a daily struggle to take care of themselves is also responsible, in theory, for a child or young person. The review by Marian Brandon *et al.* (2009) confirmed the risks to children and adolescents when professionals stuck rigidly to their own brief, either in terms of a narrow focus on a child or being oblivious to the possible risks to children within the same home as an adult with serious problems. The message is that this insular 'silo practice' has to be challenged by professional understanding that safeguarding children is everybody's business.

If all the different sources of knowledge are brought together, then the seriousness of the situation for a child or young person can be far more obvious.

- The most useful image is that of a jigsaw, for which different professionals or services each have only a few of the total number of pieces.
- Children are not well protected when roles and responsibilities between agencies are not clear.
- It is too easy for everyone to assume that somebody else 'knows about...' or 'is doing something about...'. Yet the real situation is that nobody has taken responsibility for this matter.
- Action to protect is undermined when there is a different professional approach to confidentiality and information sharing, perhaps worsened by feelings about professional territory.
- Those practitioners in different professions who are vital to the full safeguarding picture need to address potential communication problems that may result from placing a different meaning on terms such as 'vulnerable', for example.

More than one inquiry has stressed the need to use observations and assessments made by people who see the child(ren) regularly. If all the different reports and knowledge of children are brought together, then the seriousness of the situation for the children can be far more obvious than when considering one perspective. Some reviews stressed the great importance of consulting individuals and group settings where children and young people were seen on a regular basis, sometimes daily. To return to the image of the jigsaw, practitioners in nursery, school and out-of-school facilities, or the childminding service, can hold significant pieces.

Lessons learnt

The final reports of public inquiries, and reports of local reviews that have been made public, usually make recommendations. However, the broad impact of high-profile cases is that everyone becomes unsettled, not only those in that geographical or professional area. The experience of tragedy or the discovery of professional misconduct shakes general morale and confidence. A well-run public inquiry can identify key issues for best practice that need to be addressed. However, systems and policies are only as effective as the people who put them into practice day by day, week by week. Changes in the law or guidance do not in themselves transform practice to protect children. Adults have to change, or be enabled to change, their professional behaviour, priorities and outlook.

The high level of media involvement in tragedies involving children is now a complicating factor. Social workers, and other professionals, can find themselves criticised, even vilified, in public, well before it is clear what went wrong. One of the alleged consequences of everything that happened around the death of young Peter Connelly has been an increase, maybe short term, in over-cautious moves to take vulnerable children into care. Social workers can then find themselves heavily criticised for overreacting and failing to give families opportunity and support to change for the better.

Nick Alford and Roger Bullock were commissioned to undertake a research overview of child death and significant case reviews as part of the Child Protection Reform Programme (CPRP) in Scotland. Their report (Alford and Bullock, 2005) highlights several key points that are still relevant today:

- Child deaths resulting from abuse or neglect are relatively rare. It can be problematic, if significant changes are made to the safeguarding system, specifically to avoid the repetition of an unusual event. The point is not, of course, to ignore inexcusable failures to apply existing guidance to protect.
- The majority of children who are in need of protection experience levels of abuse that, although unacceptable, are not life threatening. Their safety can be ensured, with effective child-protection practice, while they continue to live with their family and promptly receive appropriate services.
- Patterns of cause and effect can appear more obvious with hindsight. Indeed, some children's injuries, trauma or death have been the result of serious failures of people and services. However, it is much harder in most cases to predict the likelihood of a very serious or tragic outcome while the situation is ongoing.
- The important focus for safeguarding is that a great deal is now known about factors that increase the level of risk to a child or young person. The aim of detailed assessment procedures is to assess that risk and not try to predict the future in detail. Effective safeguarding is a matter of 'most probably could', 'easily might' and rarely of 'definitely will'.

Take another perspective

You need to remind yourself that serious mistakes and tragedies are far more likely to become public knowledge than when children have been protected and are therefore safe. Headlines are not created from 'Social workers intervene and life is much better for young Matthew'. Partly, such events are not deemed to be newsworthy, but also the details remain confidential to the family and involved professionals. There have been serious failures of safeguarding that have led to deep distress, injury and even death for some

$\Rightarrow$

children. This section has focused on overviews that highlight good practice, as well as that which is less adequate, and public inquiries that arise because safeguarding has not worked to protect children or young people. The clear message of more recent inquiries is that problems are not ancient history. Systems still fail some children and young people through the actions or inactions of key people or their inadequate knowledge.

Changes in the child protection system since 2000

Two public inquiries have exerted a significant impact on the system for child protection, and changes continue to evolve.

The Laming Report 2003

The lack of effective change for protection was brought home forcibly by the suffering and death of eight-year-old Victoria Climbié in 2002. The avoidable death of this young girl was especially shocking because she was known to a wide range of North London services, professionals and community groups. The public inquiry led by Lord Laming identified 12 separate occasions when Victoria could have been safeguarded through direct action or information sharing between agencies.

The report makes such depressing reading because many practice issues, clearly identified over the 1990s, were shown to have undermined effective child protection in the early years of the new century. The Laming report (2003) documents a list of serious problems: poor inter-agency working and information sharing, under-resourced social work departments and inadequate support for front-line professionals, and continued confusion over anti-discriminatory practice. For more detail see: www.victoria-climbie-inquiry.org.uk

Key practice points need to be reconfirmed and the continuing focus on evidence-based practice has encouraged government funding for useful research reviews. Caroline Hart and Harriet Ward reported in 2011 on the consistent messages from a range of studies about effective responses to maltreatment of children. The review was in response to the death of Victoria Climbié, but also that of Peter Connelly. One issue raised was the pressing need for knowledge of child development for social workers. No professional will be effective in the safeguarding role unless they are able to recognise seriously delayed development or out-of-the-ordinary patterns of behaviour. Any professional can only make sense of what they observe against the backdrop of confident knowledge about the range of ordinary and safe development for children.

Pause for reflection

The full reports of research reviews can be long, but many of them have a summary version which is still rich in detail.

Look at the key points summarised by Carolyn Davies and Harriet Ward (2011) *Safeguarding Children Across Services: Messages from Research*. What points can you see that apply directly to your professional involvement in safeguarding? What can you and you colleagues or fellow students identify that you need to understand, although this may not be your direct professional role?

The Bichard report (2004)

Sir Michael Bichard reported in 2004 on the circumstances that led to the employment of Ian Huntley as a college (secondary school) caretaker. This position of trust enabled him, in 2002, to murder Holly Wells and Jessica Chapman, who attended the nearby primary school (in Soham, Cambridgeshire, England). Huntley was known to police and social services in Humberside as a result of a series of sexual relationships with young adolescents who were under the age of consent. These incidents had been viewed separately, rather than brought together as a pattern to reveal an individual who posed a risk. The police database in Humberside was inadequate for effective safeguarding. Also, ignorance in the team about the working of data protection law meant that vital information was not passed on to the Cambridgeshire police authorities. The final report led to changes in the law around vetting and barring individuals for work in close proximity to children and young people (see page 174).

Changes in England and Wales post 2003

The recommendations of the Laming report in 2003 led to the overarching framework called *Every Child Matters*. This approach established five key outcomes by which to judge the success of any policies for children and young people: being healthy, staying safe, enjoying and achieving, making a positive contribution, and economic well being. Legal changes were made through the Children Act 2004, and Section 11 introduced a duty on agencies involved with children and young people both to safeguard them and promote their welfare. A considerable amount of the best practice described within *Every Child Matters* documents remains current, although this term has disappeared from official discussion. The coalition government that came into power in 2010 has chosen to archive a significant number of documents from the previous Labour government, not only about safeguarding.

The Children Act 2004 was followed by a revised version in 2006 of *Working Together to Safeguard Children*, since updated with three subsequent publications. This 2006 version introduced into policy the concept of 'safeguarding children'. Safeguarding includes conventional child protection:

actions to protect children and young people once a risk or actual harm has been identified. The concept extends that approach to be more proactive: an obligation for all agencies and services to take effective measures to minimise risks and to anticipate what might threaten the welfare of children and young people.

Good practice is not exclusively about children known to be vulnerable, nor about putting all the energy into reacting to a crisis in protection. It is about recognising risk factors or vulnerabilities, prevention and early intervention as well as responding to signs of abuse and neglect.

Children are protected by all the aspects of best practice in taking good care of them and empowering older children and young people to share the responsibility of keeping themselves safe. Chapter 8 of this book focuses on those aspects of your work that definitely contribute to safeguarding but whose relevance you may have underestimated.

What does it mean?

Safeguarding: the process of creating a safe environment for the whole younger generation, as well as protecting those children and young people who are vulnerable or have already been harmed.

The main changes for England and Wales, brought about by the Children Act 2004, include that Area Child Protection Committees were replaced by Local Safeguarding Children Boards (LSCB). These are statutory, rather than just recommended, and are given a more formal responsibility to ensure local inter-agency working. The boards still bring together relevant agencies and services. The government now has powers to intervene if local social services are unsatisfactory – in a similar way to that which works already with schools. The Act creates the option of addressing the problems of unregulated private foster care – the situation in which Victoria Climbié lived. Local authorities now have a legal duty to promote the educational achievement of looked-after children and young people. The Act also introduced the appointment of a Children's Commissioner for England, although without the same remit and power of those commissioners already in post elsewhere in the UK.

The Laming Report 2009

This report was commissioned to examine what had been achieved since the 2003 Laming Report. Laming (2009) looked at the barriers to effective safeguarding work and what actions could be taken by the government to overcome these barriers. Laming made 58 recommendations. However, this report was then superseded by the more wide-ranging and in-depth Munro Report, of which the final report was published in May 2011 (Corby *et al.* 2012).

Eileen Munro undertook a significant review of the current system, with the intention of finding a way forward that did not rest on yet more pages of guidance and ever more complicated procedures. Her final report in 2011 makes a series of recommendations which aim to move professionals away from a culture of targets, of 'doing things right' by placing a high priority on following procedures. The avowed aim is to refocus the child protection system on 'doing the right thing': that is, checking and ensuring that children and young people have been made safe and helped. The Munro Report takes a systems theory approach: a focus on how different parts of any whole system work together and influence each other. The report notes that for many decades the official response to serious problems or tragedies within safeguarding has been to issue revised, ever longer guidance and more complex procedures. The aim now is to reduce paperwork, and the guidance documents published since then have been considerably slimmed down.

Other relevant legislation
(Please note that this is not a definitive list.)

The Human Rights Act 1998 came into force on 2 October 2000. It incorporates the rights and freedoms guaranteed under the European Convention on Human Rights (ECHR) into domestic law. All authorities in the UK are required to act compatibly with ECHR.

The Sexual Offences Act 2003 covers all sexual offences, including those perpetrated against children. The list of offences is long and considers a multiplicity of events. For example, making indecent images of children, grooming a child, abusing a position of trust, inciting a child under 13 to engage in sexual activity.

The Care Act 2014 reformed the law relating to care and support for adults and the law relating to support for carers (this includes children who are carers) to make provision about safeguarding adults from abuse or neglect, to make provision about care standards, to establish and make provision about Health Education England, to establish and make provision about the Health Research Authority, and for connected purposes.

The Children and Families Act 2014 considers a wide range of issues that affect children, including: adoption and contact, family justice, children with special educational or medical needs, childcare and the wider welfare of children, particularly those children living away from home (including looked after).

The Acts from 1987 onwards can be accessed via: www.opsi.gov.uk

Changes in Scotland
The Child Protection Reform Programme (CPRP) was a significant audit and review of the system in Scotland. The programme was led by a report commissioned by the Scottish Executive entitled *'It's everyone's job to make sure I'm alright' Literature review* (2002). This detailed overview combined information from research studies, public inquiries in Scotland and elsewhere

in the UK and information about child protection in some countries outside the UK.

The CPRP covered a range of safeguarding issues, including the implications of the Laming and Bichard reports, a review of how local Child Protection Committees operate in Scotland and the operation of child-death and significant-case reviews. The final shape of child protection in Scotland is described in *National Guidance for Child Protection in Scotland* (The Scottish Government, 2010, updated in 2014).

This updated guidance in Scotland emphasises 'partnership working', and to support this partnership and 'to keep up the momentum on child protection' the Scottish Government has introduced additional policy guidance, which includes the *National Risk Framework for Assessment of Children and Young People*, the *National Framework for Child Protection Learning and Development,* the *National Parenting Strategy*, the revised *Pink Book* and guidance for supporting those working with children affected by parental substance misuse, *Getting Our Priorities Right*. Additionally, the Scottish Parliament has passed the Children and Young People (Scotland) Act 2014 with the aim to further improve outcomes for children and young people.

Changes in Northern Ireland

An audit in 2004 by the Department of Health, Social Services and Public Safety considered the child protection system in Northern Ireland against the 108 recommendations in the Laming report. The Social Service Inspectorate for the province then reviewed all aspects of safeguarding in Northern Ireland. The final report (DHSSPS, 2006) acknowledged good practice and positive developments in the province but also made a series of firm recommendations.

The SSI report 'Our children and young people – our shared responsibility – inspection of child protection services in Northern Ireland and the Standards for Child Protection' was followed in 2008 by Standards for Child Protection. The main changes have been:

- A Safeguarding Board for Northern Ireland has brought together the services involved in child protection and work to improve practice across the province.
- Five Local Safeguarding Panels have been created to replace Area Child Protection Committees. The aim is to ensure that child protection remains a top priority and with clear lines of accountability.
- Clear criteria have been established for local Case Management Reviews (when a child has died or suffered life-threatening injuries) and steps to improve the quality of inter-agency working.
- A single assessment framework has been developed. *Understanding the Needs of Children in Northern Ireland* (DHSSPS, 2011) is known as the UNOCINI Guidance.

- A database has combined the details of children on all the local child-protection registers, so that national statistics are now available for Northern Ireland.

The process and steps of safeguarding

The process of responding to concerns about children and young people is determined by law and related guidance. There are agreed steps in the sequence to protect vulnerable children or to act decisively for children who have been harmed. Once concerns have been raised about a child, these steps are not negotiable depending on local or personal preferences. The procedures are laid down by the national guidance, and local authorities have to follow time limits on steps in the process; it is not allowed to drag on indefinitely. Practitioners need to understand the big picture of how protection works in the UK in order to place their own role in context (which is covered later in the book).

It is important that practitioners have an understanding of the relevant aspects of the Children Act 1989 and the Children Act 2004.

A number of very important principles are embodied in the Children Act 1989:

- the *welfare* of the child is the *paramount* consideration S.1(1)
- wherever possible, children should be brought up and cared for within their own families.

Referrals to children's social care

If practitioners are making a referral to children's social services they will be making the referral under section 17 or section 47 of the Children Act 1989. They must be clear as to the nature of the referral.

Section 17 pertains to a child in need. Children who are defined as being 'in need', under s17 (10) of the Children Act 1989, are those whose vulnerability is such that:

- they are unlikely to reach or maintain a satisfactory level of health or development

or

- their health or development will be significantly impaired, without the provision of services
- plus those who are disabled.

The critical factors to be taken into account in deciding whether a child is in need under the Children Act 1989 are:

- what will happen to a child's health or development without services being provided
- the likely effect the services will have on the child's standard of health and development.

Section 17 concerns the duties that childcare professionals have to contribute to assessments of 'children in need', or vulnerable children whose families may need guidance and support to reach their potential. These assessments are now carried out by all professionals using the guidance and knowledge base provided by 'The Common Assessment Framework.'

Section 47 concerns the duty of local authorities to assess and investigate situations where there are suspicions that a child has suffered significant harm (or could in the future) from lack of care or a deliberate act by her/his carers. These assessments are carried out in accordance with the Assessment Framework, as these children are also in need, but there are additional concerns regarding risk of harm. The child's well being and protection from harm may require 'safe-guarding' and urgent or more formal intervention by professionals.

If there are concerns that a child has suffered significant harm or could in the future, then practitioners should make a referral under section 47.

The concept of 'harm' and 'significant harm'

Significant harm pertains to the harm caused by the maltreatment.

Harm is defined in the Children Act 1989 section 31(9) as amended by the Adoption and Children Act 2002:

- '**harm**' means ill-treatment or the impairment of health or development, including, for example, impairment suffered from seeing or hearing the ill-treatment of another;
- '**development**' means physical, intellectual, emotional, social or behavioural development;
- '**health**' means physical or mental health; and
- '**ill-treatment**' includes sexual abuse and forms of ill-treatment which are not physical

Significant harm:

- The Children Act 1989 uses the concept of significant harm to justify compulsory intervention in family life.
- The local authority is under a duty to make enquiries where it has reasonable cause to suspect a child is suffering significant harm.
- Under section 31(10) of the Act, 'where the question of whether harm suffered by a child is significant turns on the child's health and development, his health or development shall be compared with that which could reasonably be expected of a similar child. It is though always important to consider and note the child's reactions, and his or her perceptions, according to the child's age and understanding'.

There are no absolute criteria for identifying significant harm.

The severity of ill-treatment depends on:

- the degree and extent of physical harm
- the duration and frequency of abuse and neglect
- the extent of premeditation
- the degree of threat and coercion, sadism and/or unusual elements.

Who is involved in safeguarding?

A considerable range of professionals and services shares the responsibility to protect children and young people. The situation is summed up well by the title of the review, *It's Everyone's Job to Make Sure I'm Alright* (Scottish Executive, 2002). Their roles are different but equally important. In brief, the range includes:

- social workers, who take the lead in assessment and investigation, but who will not be directly involved in much of the safeguarding practice that ensures the well being of children and young people who are not at risk;
- the police service, who will be involved in some steps for emergency protection and when there is the possibility that actions could be criminal;
- related services such as the courts, probation service and youth offending teams, the prison service and young offenders institutions;
- services for looked-after children and young people: residential homes, foster care and secure accommodation;
- health services of all kinds: hospitals, clinics, health visitors and the wide range of specialist medical professionals;
- education services for children and young people of school and college age, including related services such as careers advice;
- early years services of all kinds: full day and sessional groups, drop-ins and crèches, and the childminding service;
- out-of-school services for children and young people of school age;
- local services such as housing that have contact with families;
- the wide range of play, sport and leisure services;
- faith groups and communities that have contact with families and sometimes also offer religious instruction to children;
- organisations such as the armed services, which have a responsibility for families through the nature of the job, but also accept under-18s into the service.

The community as a whole has a responsibility to look out for children and young people. Anyone may contact social services with a concern; it is not exclusively professionals who can make that phone call. Community groups and organisations have a definite responsibility, when they have regular contact with families, children and young people. Many informal services depend on an atmosphere of trust that anyone involved will not take advantage of younger or vulnerable members of that community.

Children's hearings in Scotland

In this part of the UK a unique system deals with juvenile and family matters, including some aspects of child protection. Concerns about a child are dealt with by local social-work departments through a similar process described in this section, including the use of case conferences. However, a referral to the Children's Reporter must be made whenever a local authority has information which suggests that compulsory measures, including emergency legal action, may need to be taken as the result of abuse or neglect, or arising from a child's or young person's own behaviour. Anyone, not only professionals, can contact the Children's Reporter with such concerns.

The Reporter will work in partnership with social workers to decide whether the case should be dealt with by the Children's Hearing, comprising volunteer lay people drawn from the local Children's Panel. The Children's Hearing can deal with emergency orders, but the Procurator Fiscal is the person who decides if a child protection case should go on to court within the criminal system.

Children and young people have not only a right to attend their own Children's Hearing, but also an obligation to do so, with few exceptions. A 'safeguarder' can be appointed to support individual children and young people to enable them to express their views and to speak on their behalf.

The Children's Hearings (Scotland) Act 2011 is leading to some changes in how the system works, including the development of a national body: Children's Hearings Scotland (CHS). The aim is to strengthen some aspects, including advocacy support for children and young people.

Summary

This chapter has provided an overview of legislative and policy developments that frame and guide practice. Since the 1970s there have been significant key events that have influenced legislation, policy and practice. Safeguarding is more than child protection and it is everyone's responsibility.

- Safeguarding children applies to individuals from pre-birth to 18 years of age.
- Children's rights and a child centred approach are essential to the delivery of safe, effective care and the achievement of best outcomes.
- Safeguarding requires a multi-agency approach.

Key texts

Young Person's Guide to the Munro Review on Child Protection (2011): a summary written in straightforward language, definitely worth reading first of all and available at: www.education.gov.uk/publications/standard/publicationDetail/Page1/DFE-00063-2011

The Munro Review of Child Protection: Final Report (2011) www.gov.uk/government/publications/munro-review-of-child-protection-final-report-a-child-centred-system

A Child-centred System: the Government's Response to the Munro Review of Child Protection (2011) www.gov.uk/government/publications/a-child-centred-system-the-governments-response-to-the-munro-review-of-child-protection

4 Child protection in action: recognising and responding to concerns

Introduction

Part of the whole process of child protection will be the involvement of your own setting, service or home-based practice as a childminder or foster carer. This chapter focuses on ways in which child protection concerns can arise and offers guidance on good practice in how to respond in accordance with legislative and policy frameworks.

Practice will differ depending on your type of provision and your role if you work in a group setting. However, everyone contributes to protecting children and keeping them safe from harm.

This chapter will therefore cover the signs and symptoms of possible abuse or neglect and how practitioners should respond to those concerns. It will also consider patterns of disclosure and how practitioners should manage disclosure. Roles and responsibilities for safeguarding by those practitioners working with the 0–8 years age group will be addressed.

The first part of the chapter is concerned with signs of vulnerability before discussing possible signs of abuse or neglect. It is essential that practitioners are able to recognise concerns in order to respond to them. The chapter then goes on to discuss the steps to take when concerns are identified as well as addressing referral processes.

Vulnerability

Within contemporary literature, including findings from numerous inquiries and reports, it is clearly articulated that vulnerable children are not always recognised early enough and there is much concern about 'poor' outcomes for vulnerable children (Laming, 2003; 2009; Munro, 2011; Coffey, 2014; Jay, 2014; Casey, 2015). As noted earlier in the book there are particular concerns about 'missed opportunities' to identify abuse and neglect. Furthermore the importance of being able to identify vulnerable children early and the need to reduce vulnerability is now a significant feature of welfare policy for children (HM Government, 2015; Parton, 2015). Perceptions of vulnerability also influence how services are received by children who are vulnerable. More importantly, vulnerability is often missed until the harm experienced by the child has become significant.

It is also worth noting that there are different perspectives on who are seen as vulnerable. Young children are depicted as victims and therefore vulnerable within the context of child protection, while the ideas of vulnerability in older children are sometimes perceived as being synonymous with challenging and difficult behaviour (Hanson and Holmes, 2013). Yet the reason for their deviance might be due to their vulnerability and increased risk of abuse. While there is no clear definition of what constitutes a vulnerable child, and vulnerability is difficult to measure (Action for Children, 2012), there are contexts that increase the vulnerability of a child and increase the risk of a child being abused.

As discussed in Chapter 2, generally children are vulnerable because of the intrinsic and extrinsic factors that impinge on their development (Daniel *et al.* 1999). There may be pre-existing vulnerabilities that increase the risk of abuse.

From both a rights and a legal perspective, children aged 0–18 years have a right to protection from harm whatever the context of their vulnerability. It is therefore important that where possible vulnerabilities are picked up and early intervention put in place to support the child and families in order to prevent further harm or significant harm occurring.

● If practitioners, and indeed the wider community, are alert to vulnerability and able to recognise underlying needs of vulnerable children the problem can be made visible and responses may be more effective;
● Practitioners, parents and families must be empowered to identify early indicators of abuse and neglect and to report concerns for the safety of the child.

Factors that increase a child's vulnerability to abuse and neglect include:

● Age – babies are more vulnerable than older children, particularly if they are born prematurely or disabled.
● Parental substance misuse.
● Parental mental illness and or learning disability.
● Domestic abuse and domestic violence within the family.
● Deprivation/family isolation/poor parenting/financial worries.
● Uncertain immigration status.
● Female genital mutilation.
● Young parents – not all young parents will abuse or neglect their children but the likelihood is increased if they themselves have had 'poor' childhood experiences, lack problem-solving skills and are without family support.

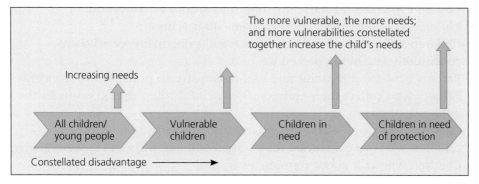

Figure 4.1 The spectrum of vulnerability (Webb and Holmes, 2015)

There is a spectrum of vulnerability (see Figure 4.1). When assessing a child's needs, at whichever point they are on the spectrum, consider:

● What does this child need?
● What does this child need me to think about?
● What does this child need me to do?

Signs of possible abuse or neglect

This section covers separately the different types of abuse and neglect, with examples of observations that would concern you. You need to continue to bear in mind that a similar worrying pattern might link with experiences such as bullying by other children. A child might really want your help, but the problem is not a safeguarding issue. Also, bear in mind that some children's ill-treatment includes more than one type of abuse.

It is also not your role to diagnose a particular form of abuse but to identify and respond to concerns.

Some of the following signs might be indicators of abuse or neglect:

● Children whose behaviour changes – they may become aggressive, challenging, disruptive, withdrawn or clingy. They might have difficulty sleeping or start wetting the bed;
● Children with clothes that are ill-fitting and/or dirty;
● Children with consistently poor hygiene;
● Children who make strong efforts to avoid specific family members or friends, without an obvious reason;
● Children who don't want to change clothes in front of others or participate in physical activities;
● Children who are having problems at school – for example, a sudden lack of concentration and learning, or they appear to be tired and hungry;
● Children who talk about being left 'home alone', with inappropriate carers or with strangers;
● Children who reach developmental milestones late (such as learning to speak or walk), with no medical reason;

- Children who are regularly missing from school or education;
- Children who are reluctant to go home after school;
- Children with poor school attendance and punctuality, or who are consistently late being picked up;
- Parents who are dismissive and non-responsive to practitioners' concerns;
- Parents who collect their children from school when drunk, or under the influence of drugs;
- Children who drink alcohol regularly from an early age;
- Children who are concerned for younger siblings without explaining why;
- Children who talk about running away; and
- Children who shy away from being touched or flinch at sudden movements.

HM Government (2015c)

The possibility of emotional abuse

Any of the following patterns of behaviour in children should concern you. They may indicate emotional abuse by an adult, but are not, of course, proof that this kind of experience is the source of the problem:

- When your observations show that a young child is developmentally delayed, especially if your efforts to help a child have not led to much progress. There are many different reasons for developmental delay, but persistent emotional abuse can stunt children's motivation to learn.
- When children indicate, through words and body language, that they think they are worthless, stupid or unattractive.
- When children persistently blame themselves, or seem to expect you to blame them or punish them. Be aware of children who are very distressed by their mistakes. However, some children are by temperament, as well as experience, hard on themselves, or set themselves tough standards, so you cannot afford to jump to easy conclusions.
- When children harm themselves with persistent hair pulling, picking at their skin, or head banging, or have compulsive rituals such as very regular and lengthy hand washing.
- When children find it difficult to make friends and the reason seems to be that they do not see themselves as worthy of being liked.
- When children mistrust adults and appear to expect them to be unpredictable and unpleasant.
- Alternatively, you should be alert to children who are prone to cling in an undiscriminating way to any adult who is kind to them.

The above possibilities need to be placed in context as some of these developments arise because a child is being relentlessly harassed by one or more siblings. However, all practitioners in contact with children should know that it is not within the normal range of behaviour for children to harm themselves, nor to have compulsive habits that cause them injury. It is not usual for children to say they wish they were dead or make similar desperate statements.

Deliberate self-harm during childhood (and adolescence) is provoked by serious distress, although not always by abusive treatment – emotional or otherwise. It is possible that deliberate self-hurting by younger children could be misinterpreted by adults as accidental injury, or a child not being able to foresee the consequences of actions. There is no typical profile of someone who self-harms: a wide range of children and young people, and adults too, of both sexes deal with their emotional turmoil by cutting, otherwise hurting themselves or putting themselves deliberately in danger.

Case study

Sally

You are the manager of a large nursery and a parent asks to speak with you in private. Sally, her child, is three years old and spends her time in a group run by Richard (who is the child's key person) and Jessica. The parent says, 'I know it's awkward to ask you, but I'm worried that Richard is leaving this job. We've always been a bit concerned about Jessica. She's very sharp with the children. Our daughter says some amazing things when she's playing with dolls, and it's not the kind of stuff that we say to her. Richard seemed to keep a balance, but now he's going. Could you get our daughter moved into another group? I really don't want Jessica to become Sally's new key person.'

- What would concern you about this situation?
- What else would you need to explore?
- What should probably be your next steps?

You will find a commentary on page 132.

Physical observations	Behavioural observations
• Failure to thrive or grow • Sudden speech disorders • Delayed development; either physical or emotional 	• Compulsive nervous actions, e.g. hair twisting or rocking • Unwillingness or inability to play • Excessive fear or making mistakes • Self-harm or mutilation • Reluctance to have parents contacted • Excessive deference towards others, especially adults • An excessive need for approval, attention and affection • An inability to copy with praise

Figure 4.2 Features of emotional abuse

The possibility of physical abuse

The most likely warning signs of the physical abuse of children are injuries, perplexing illnesses, or a continuing pattern of accidents to a child for which the responsible adult(s) give no believable explanation. It is important to remember that young children collect many bumps and bruises in the normal course of play. Physically lively children, with a limited understanding or concern about risks, can have a childhood full of minor but understandable injuries. So a consideration of possible physical abuse has to include both the visible injury to the child and the explanation of how this injury was caused.

Accidental or non-accidental injury?

It will not be your job to make an assessment of whether a child's or young person's injuries are definitely accidental or non-accidental. However, your attention should be caught by aspects such as the age and mobility of a child. For instance, a baby or a profoundly disabled older child will not manage the kind of lively play and getting into 'mischief' that can be usual for an active three- or four-year-old. One good reason for keeping proper records (see page 197) is that documentation will show whether a child has many accidents, each of which has a credible explanation but when looked at as a whole, the sequence forms a significant catalogue of events.

There are no certainties about visible injuries, but in general:

- Accidents that occur during normal play or boisterous activities tend to lead to several bruises to the bony parts of children's bodies, such as elbows and knees, which stick out and are likely to be hit in a fall.
- Children usually trip forwards so are likely to hit themselves on the forehead, face or other parts of the front of the body. They may also injure their hands, once children have learned to put them out to break their fall.
- However, some children have been directly hit in the face by abusive adults, or pushed with such force that they fell forwards. So injuries to sites that are often the focus of genuine accidents cannot be overlooked.
- Injuries on the bottom and back of the legs are regarded as more suspicious sites, because that is often where abused children are hit by an adult hand or with implements. However, if children accidentally slip on the stairs or lose control of equipment like roller blades or ice skates, they can land very heavily on their bottom.
- Bruising to less-accessible parts of the body, such as upper arms or thighs, is more likely the result of deliberate pinching, biting or hitting. But you may not know who did it; it could be from bullying by another child.
- The genital or anal area is a less likely site for accidental injury. However, children have lost their footing on climbing apparatus, or when riding a bike, and landed heavily on their crotch area. This experience is painful for both girls and boys.

- Very young children, especially babies, do not usually bruise inside their mouths. It is, in fact, very hard to imagine how they could gain that kind of injury in what should be the normal pattern of a baby's day.
- Symmetrical bruising is unlikely to be accidental, since children tend to hurt themselves naturally in one place. It is difficult, although not impossible, to gain two black eyes at the same time by accident. Patterns can arouse suspicions, for instance, three to four small bruises on each side of a child's face could be finger marks. Outline rather than solid bruises may be the mark of a belt or hand. (See page 207 about benign skin markings that may look like bruising.)
- Young children sometimes bite each other. But an oval or crescent shape larger than three centimetres is more likely to have been made by an adult or older child with permanent teeth.
- Burns or scalds with clear outlines are regarded as more suspicious by medical practitioners; so, too, are burns of uniform depth over a larger area or splash marks above the main burn area. Children who can step into their own bath do not sit down voluntarily in very hot water. So they cannot accidentally scald their bottom without also harming their feet. The adult should have tested the water temperature for babies or young children.
- Babies are more vulnerable.
- Physical abuse in babies is more serious and the results can be catastrophic
- Bruising in a non-mobile baby should be followed up.

Take another perspective

Some sites for an injury will raise more concerns than others. But it is unwise to assume that some locations are sure indicators of non-accidental injury. Working in a group of colleagues or fellow students, copy the front and back body outline in Figure 4.3.

Now mark up the sites of injuries that you definitely know to have been accidental because you were there and observed events. Your knowledge may arise because you, or a sibling or friend, injured yourself in that way during your own childhood. Or you may be marking up genuine accidents for a child that you observed, but could not prevent, as an adult.

Maintain confidentiality about the details of any accident involving a child other than yourself.

Now look together at the patterns that have emerged. This exercise works best if your group, or combination of a number of smaller groups, brings contributions from at least a dozen or more people. If you have several groups, then mark up one large outline on flipchart paper. ⇨

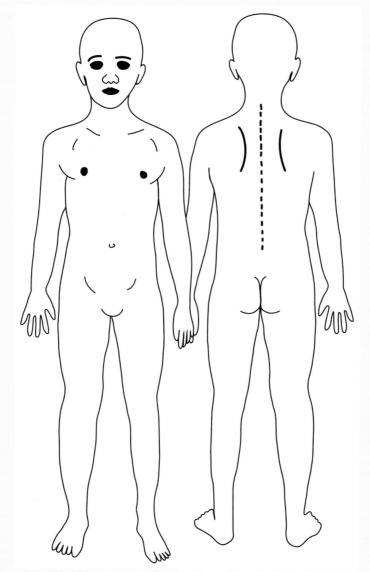

Figure 4.3 A body outline

- Where on the outline do you have most crosses?
- What parts of the body outline have few, if any, crosses?

It is very likely that many sites of accidental injury will be the more predictable places. However, you will probably have reliable anecdotes that illustrate how a child or young adolescent managed to sustain accidental injury in sites that usually raise concern about non-accidental injury.

Explanations of an injury

It makes sense to ask those children who have the language to answer about a visible mark or an apparent discomfort on part of their body. Your question does not have to be intrusive. It may include comments such as, 'That's an impressive bruise, Jonathon. How did you manage that?' or 'Yasmin, you look as if your leg hurts. What's up?' The response in words or actions may reassure you or add to your concerns.

- Children are often rather proud of minor injuries from falls or understandable domestic accidents. They are only too keen to show you and tell their tale. Indeed, one narrative often leads to rolling up of trousers and sleeves as other children contribute their own drama and sometimes now invisible marks.
- It is a different situation if children are evasive (rather than appearing genuinely perplexed about the origin of, say, a long scrape mark), look very uneasy or refuse absolutely to discuss the injury.
- Initial unlikely explanations still cannot be seen as proof of abuse. Some children give a strange reason for their injury. But further conversation reveals they produced this story because they were doing something they should not. The children are worried about getting into trouble themselves. They do not foresee that their version of events could bring suspicion on their parent or other carer.

There are features in a conversation with a parent that could put your mind at ease or alternatively add to your existing concern. The same considerations hold if you are a senior practitioner in conversation with a member of staff who was responsible for the group when an accident happened. Injury as the result of a genuine accident is likely to have most or some of the following features (Webb, 2007):

- The parent (or other carer) did not delay in seeking help, with appropriate first aid or by seeking further medical intervention. Some people are prone to panic, but what happened after the panic subsided? If a team member seems incompetent or froze in a crisis, then this problem must be addressed.
- After a full conversation, the explanation of the child's injury makes sense: given the nature of the injury, the child's age, what you know of the child (some children are reckless) and their overall development.
- But, again, do not just be persuaded by your knowledge that these individual children are lively and fearless. Given their age, does it sound as if they were being properly supervised?
- The description of the incident given by all the individuals involved, including children who are old enough to talk about what happened, is very similar. You hear a consistent narrative about what happened.
- The history of the injury fits the picture presented.

Note: You would suspect non-accidental injury if the pattern varied significantly from the above, also if the explanation kept changing. But be aware that, since child abuse now has a high profile in the media, parents may seem uneasy even though nothing wrong has happened. Perhaps they are genuinely worried that matters may get out of hand and they will be accused of maltreatment.

A worrying pattern still cannot be taken as proof of abuse or neglect without further exploration. Careful consideration may reveal health problems. For example, some children have problems of physical co-ordination or may be found to have failing eyesight. A few children have brittle bone disease (*Osteogenesis Imperfecta*), which means that very minor accidents can create fractures and breaks. Remember that the child protection system across the UK is also set up to respond to these situations: the child and family are in need of appropriate support and help.

Children can also present with injuries that do fit the 'picture' and are in places where children are able to injure themselves. The issue might still be concerning if there was a lack of supervision when the accident occurred.

If a child presents to you with an injury ask yourself:

- Could the child have done that to themselves? Accidents do occur in children as they go through various stages of development and children are naturally inquisitive.
- What happened?
- Does the injury fit the account?
- Has this child got more injuries or recurrent injuries beyond normal occurrence?
- Has the child been given opportunity to disclose?
- Has a multi-agency meeting allowed information sharing?

Recognising physical abuse:

- An explanation that is inconsistent with an injury.
- Several different explanations provided for an injury.
- Unexplained delay in seeking treatment.
- The parents or carers are uninterested or undisturbed by an accident or injury.
- Parents are absent without good reason when their child is presented for treatment.
- Repeated presentation of minor injuries or illnesses (which may represent a 'cry for help' and if ignored could have a more serious outcome or lead to a more serious injury).
- Family use of different doctors and hospital Emergency or Urgent Care Departments.
- Reluctance to give information or mention previous injuries.

Physical observations	Behavioural observations
• Black eyes without gross bruising of forehead • Bruises on trunk, cheeks, inner thighs (soft tissue areas of the body) • Bruises on upper arm consistent with gripping • Finger tip bruising; marks on fingers • Cigarette burns • Human bite marks • Burns caused by lengthy exposure to heat • Scalds with upward splash marks or tide marks • Fractures – particularly spiral fractures • Swelling and lack of normal use of limbs • Untreated injuries • Any serious injury with no explanation, conflicting explanations or inconsistent accounts	• Unusual fearfulness • Unnaturally compliant • Frozen watchfulness • Refusal to discuss injuries – fear of medical help • Withdrawal from physical contact • Aggression towards others • Wearing clothes that cover arms and legs in all weathers • Reluctance to have parents contacted • Running away or showing fear of going home • Flinching when approached • Reluctance to undress for sport • Depression or moods that are out of character

Figure 4.4 Features of physical abuse

The child's behaviour is also important to note. Children may tell you that someone is hurting them. However, sometimes they are as concerned to hide their ill-treatment as the adults who inflict it. So you should be alert to a child who is very reluctant to undress for games or for a routine medical check and to uncover their limbs in hotter weather. The exception is when there is an alternative explanation for their unease. Some families feel strongly about modest dress, for reasons of faith or cultural traditions. Children may continue to wear long sleeves and cover their legs when their peers are wearing shorts and a T-shirt. Other children are very self-conscious about their bodies because other children have been rude about their size, shape or skin problems like eczema.

There may be behavioural signs that all is not well with a child or young person, and the underlying reason may be experience of physical abuse. Children who are persistently aggressive towards other children will need clear adult guidance in order to change this pattern of behaviour. However, supportive adults need to notice children who have developed strong habits of cruelty and physical attack. You have to question how they have learned this pattern of behaviour and whether there is a possibility that they are imitating what has been done to them.

Make the connection with ...

Normal range behaviour

Young children need to learn how to be careful with animals and understand that pets can be hurt. It is appropriate to be concerned about older children who are cruel to animals and unresponsive to clear boundaries set by practitioners.

Children may have been physically abused and are working out their anger and pain on a more vulnerable creature than themselves. It may also be that children imitate the cruelty that they have observed from other family members. Joint work between the RSPCA and NSPCC has identified that cruelty to animals within a family highlights the possibility of other risks. The RSPCA have a protocol for reporting concerns about children following a family home visit in connection with allegations of animal cruelty. Some social care services have strong links with the local RSPCA and share concerns in return.

Find out more

NSPCC (2005) *Understanding the Links: Child Abuse, Animal Abuse and Domestic Violence*
www.nspcc.org.uk/globalassets/documents/research-reports/understanding-links-child-abuse-animal-abuse-domestic-violence.pdf

The possibility of neglect

Neglect is about unmet need and it will have an impact on physical and emotional health and well being. Unfortunately, neglect is often not picked up until the child is suffering significant harm. Children who are neglected will show a pattern of the results of inadequate care from the adults who should have their best interests at heart.

- Children look malnourished and underweight and health records show that they fail to put on weight. A malnourished child can be tired and lethargic. Severe malnourishment in babies and very young children can cause damage, including to their brain, which can never be completely reversed, even with very high quality later care.
- If you feed children in your setting, you may find that a child arrives desperate for food and eats a large amount when it is available. Their state of hunger may be noticeably greater after the weekend.
- It is not usual for children to hide food because they are afraid that they, or their siblings, will be hungry later. It is relatively usual for children to hide food that they do not want to eat and when they feel nagged at mealtimes by adults.
- Children may be seriously overweight and this condition may have affected their ease of movement and their ability to join in physically active games and may be causing observable emotional distress.
- Children may be regularly dressed inappropriately for the weather: for instance, thin summer clothes and sandals on a cold winter day. They may show signs of being cold on a regular basis: chapped hands, chilblains or unnaturally reddened skin (noticeable against a light skin colour).

- Children and their clothes may not be kept clean – and it takes time for a child to develop an unpleasant body odour. Soiled clothes, such as underwear, may be put back on a child rather than removed for washing.
- Parents may be unreliable in bringing the child to the setting on a regular basis or in picking the child up at the end of the day or session. The parents themselves may be in an unsafe state to care for children: drunk or showing the effects of drugs.
- Children may have untreated medical conditions or infections that are left to worsen rather than improved with basic home care or medical treatment. Parents, or other key carers, are responsible for taking up ordinary healthcare services, such as dental checks and ensuring that young children's teeth do not decay in their mouths.

Sometimes all the children within a family are neglected, but it can happen that one child is singled out and is visibly treated worse than other siblings – the process of scapegoating, described on page 23.

Case study

Fazila

You are playing tea parties with four-year-old Fazila, who appears to enjoy making tea and laying out the table. Fazila lines up the dolls in readiness for joining you both for tea. But she puts one doll at some distance from the others. You ask if this doll is coming to the tea party and Fazila replies, 'She's a smelly-poo. Nobody likes her.'

You have been working with Fazila's mother to try to improve the child's care, but her clothes are still changed infrequently and Fazila often has an unwashed smell about her.

- What would concern you about this situation?
- What should probably be your next step?

You will find a commentary on page 132.

Physical observations	Behavioural observations
• Being constantly hungry • Stealing food from others • Being unkempt, dirty or smelly • Loss of weight or constantly underweight • Overweight or obese • Dressed inappropriately for conditions • Untreated medical conditions or injuries	• Being tired all the time • Frequently missing school • Lateness for school • Failing to keep hospital appointments • Having few friends • Left alone regularly • Compulsive stealing

Figure 4.5 Features of neglect

Concerns about weight

In recent years there has been growing concern about childhood obesity and debates about whether or not it is a child protection issue. It is, however, a safeguarding issue within the wider context of safeguarding as obesity can impact on a child's overall health. This is in both the short- and long-term and therefore increases their vulnerability.

Children who are neglected sometimes fall into the group described as showing faltering growth or a failure to thrive. Records of a child's physical and general development can be crucial in making sense of whether a child is being neglected. Careful monitoring may need to establish a child's pattern of ill-health and their weight gain, or lack of growth. When care for a child is shared, either inside or outside the family, neglected children may be in considerably better health and energy after spending time away from a particular family carer.

An integrated approach across all agencies is required. The experience and records of all the professionals involved with the child and the family have to be taken into consideration. Some babies and children have digestion or allergy problems that affect their ability to keep food down or to digest it properly. Other children have eating problems and parents' understandable concern over mealtimes has inadvertently worsened difficulties. Such families may appreciate advice from a practitioner, but they are not neglecting their children.

As mentioned above, being significantly overweight brings serious health problems, starting in childhood, and can also create emotional distress for children and young people. It is an adult responsibility to offer a nutritious range of food and drink and not allow a child to develop the poor eating habits that arise with a seriously unbalanced diet, high intake of sweets and snacks or fizzy drinks. However, it is unlikely that obesity alone would trigger a child protection investigation and assessment.

A public statement in April 2012 by the Royal College of Paediatrics and Child Health (RCPCH) expressed concern about the high numbers of overweight, and clinically obese, children in the UK and the causes of this phenomenon. They identify that nearly a third of children aged 2–15 years are overweight or obese. RCPCH (2012) argue that the prevention and treatment of obesity depends on all levels of society and government taking action. This includes not only health professionals but also teachers, parents and children themselves. They argue that that there needs to be a cultural shift in improved nutrition and improved exercise.

In July 2015, the National Institute for Health and Care Excellence published a Quality Standard that was concerned with childhood obesity. The Quality Standard 'covers a range of approaches at a population level to prevent children and young people aged under 18 years from becoming overweight or obese. It includes interventions for lifestyle weight management. These statements are particularly relevant to local authorities, NHS organisations, schools and providers of lifestyle weight management programmes' (NICE, 2015).

The RCPCH endorsed these standards during June and July 2015 (Royal College of Paediatrics and Child Health, 2015).

Regarding more general issues regarding growth and nutrition also see:

www.rcpch.ac.uk/child-health/standards-care/nutrition-and-growth/nutrition-and-growth

There is some debate with regards to whether or not obesity is a safeguarding issue. What is clear, though, is that practitioners would be right to monitor the situation and first of all to work in partnership with parents (and their health visitor, school nurse or GP) to bring the weight of a child or young person back within healthy parameters. The best way forward is to establish healthy habits for eating, with sufficient physical exercise, and then let the natural upwards growth pattern even out the excessive weight.

Take another perspective

The interface between child protection and obesity

Would you consider the actions of a parent to be acceptable if they directly caused the following:

- social isolation
- weight-based teasing and bullying – peer abuse
- type two diabetes
- cardiovascular disease
- a quadrupled chance of having hypertension in adulthood
- asthma
- mental health problems
- skeletal and muscular problems.

The issue here is that the above are preventable and could potentially impact on a child's physical, emotional and social well being. If a child's obesity is the direct result of the actions of the parents and the child is suffering, or likely to suffer, significant harm then it could be contextualised as a child protection issue, as the threshold for child protection procedures has been reached.

Pause for reflection

Tackling obesity is a public health issue and should in the first instance be tacked as such. Interventions to address obesity are part of the Healthy Child Programme (Department of Health, 2009). Rudolph (2009) provides useful guidance and a framework to support the tackling of obesity through the Healthy Child Programme.

Where child protection would become an issue, with concerns about neglect, is if parents refused to accept and engage in help, and the level of obesity posed an immediate threat to their children's health. If you are unsure, always discuss your concerns with a colleague, manager or safeguarding adviser before deciding the next steps.

Care by siblings

Within some social and cultural groups it is very usual that children help with domestic tasks and with the care of younger siblings, so it would be important to avoid criticism of a family pattern only because it does not fit your own cultural experience. However, practitioners still need to be alert to situations in which inappropriate or heavy responsibilities are placed on a child, and to the well being of young siblings if an older brother or sister takes on much of their care. There would also be cause for concern if responsibilities meant that older siblings missed school or were unable to complete homework on a regular basis. (See also 'Young carers' on page 249.)

The possibility of child sexual abuse

Remember that within normal development, children can be very physical in their contact with one another and often like to be close to adults whom they trust and like. Children often show curiosity about their own and others' bodies and are sometimes quite uninhibited in their behaviour. Any concerns must be put within an understanding of the normal range of children's development and their likely grasp of socially accepted behaviour.

A child's behaviour

Any of the following observations should catch your attention:

- Highly sexual behaviour from young children, rather than affectionate physical contact, is of concern. It is not within normal development for children to persist in trying to make physically intimate contact with other children or with adults, especially once another child or adult has said 'No'.
- Children who are being sexually abused may express their worries and experiences in their pretend play or with dolls and small figures. Their explanations of drawings and paintings or created stories may show unusual knowledge (for their age) about sexual activity.
- You must consider how far this child's play is out of the ordinary. For instance, allow for the fact that younger children are interested in bottoms and 'willies'. Young children are often interested in these body parts in relation to going to the toilet, which is a direct part of their daily experience. The detailed sexual function of those same body parts should not be part of their knowledge.
- Young children often fiddle with their private parts, but you should be concerned if a child masturbates a considerable amount. Even if careful checking does not raise child protection concerns, a child who self-comforts a great deal needs significant emotional support.

- Some children with learning disabilities behave like much younger children, and may be less aware of the boundaries between public and private behaviour. Practitioners and parents need to focus on supporting children as they learn, but should not easily dismiss worrying behaviour patterns as an inevitable consequence of a disability. You need to ask 'Would we be worried if this child were not disabled?'
- What children say may cause you concern if it shows a sexual knowledge or curiosity unlikely for their age. Again, it is important to have a broad framework in which to make sense of any concern. Some parents are honest in answering children's questions about the new baby. So a four or five-year-old may be relatively well informed about 'where babies come from'.

Children may use language or show behaviour that raises concerns in different ways, which could also indicate other kinds of abuse or neglect. Possibilities might be that children regress in their development, start to have nightmares or experience many daytime fears. Reactions to sexually abusive treatment are varied: some children turn their distress inwards, perhaps with self-harm. But others express their turmoil through aggressive behaviour or abusing others in their turn (see page 223 about young sexual abusers). Children do not like everyone equally and sometimes they are uncomfortable with someone for reasons that have nothing to do with abuse. However, it is important to follow up if a child really does not want to be taken home by a family member or friend, or seems deeply uneasy about a practitioner or a frequent visitor to your setting.

Practitioners who work in schools and out-of-school services will know that the playground language of some children can be robust. Even when families are careful about their own language and conversation in front of their children, those same boys and girls may imitate peers who have heard sex-related and offensive lyrics of some forms of music. Practitioners need to track the origin of dubious phrases that children say or sing. The words may need attention in terms of 'We don't sing that song here, because ... ', but there may be no further concerns about a child's direct experiences.

Physical conditions

These physical symptoms should concern you and they need prompt attention. Most of them do not imply clear evidence of abuse, although all could be linked with this kind of ill-treatment of children or young people:

- Pain, itching or redness in the genital or anal area needs medical attention, but the condition could be the result of thrush or threadworms. Both these conditions cause very uncomfortable itching and can lead to broken skin if the child has scratched vigorously. Persistent constipation can cause redness and anal fissures, or bleeding from the strain.
- Bruising or bleeding in the genital or anal area again needs a medical check, as does any child's clear discomfort in walking or sitting. But you have to keep an open mind, as does the doctor who examines the child,

because children do sometimes slip or fall and land heavily on their crotch area.

● A vaginal discharge or apparent infection in a girl should be checked. Again, be aware that children sometimes stick small objects into their bodily orifices and an otherwise harmless object creates an infection if left.

● A doctor would conclude sexual abuse if a medical examination showed evidence of a sexually transmitted disease in a child. STDs are caught from very close, intimate contact with an infected person, not from toilet seats.

Case study

Olwyn

You are the specialist support assistant for Olwyn, who has learning and communication disabilities. Olwyn is 10 years old and her developmental level is estimated to be more like a six- or seven-year-old's. Olwyn has managed with support in mainstream school, but her pattern of behaviour has now raised concerns.

Olwyn appeared to have learned some of the boundaries between private and public behaviour, but has recently started to masturbate when she is in the classroom. You have raised this issue with her father, who is the main family contact for the school. He said that the behaviour had also become an issue at home. You were glad Olwyn's father seemed able to talk about this sensitive problem, but are now uncomfortable that he wants to recap the situation each time you meet.

Today you found Olwyn without her underwear in the boys' toilets and a couple of sheepish-looking boys just leaving. You have previously spoken with Olwyn's class teacher, who took the view that the child was showing immature behaviour as part of her disability. In that conversation, the teacher dismissed your unease about Olwyn's father, saying you are just embarrassed.

You feel today's events raise a new and different pattern and that it should be taken seriously, but you are disinclined to speak with the class teacher again. Additionally, you have become uneasy about how Olwyn behaves towards the new driver on her transport to school for some days of the week. You find it hard to identify what is awry, but are concerned to hear that he also runs a specialist sports club that Olwyn attends. You do not want to overreact, but equally you do not feel her behaviour should be explained away as part of the disability.

● What are the main issues that concern you about this situation?
● What should probably be your next steps?

You will find a commentary on page 132.

Physical observations	Behavioural observations
• Pain, itching, bruising or bleeding in the genital or anal areas • Sexually transmitted disease • Recurrent urinary tract infections • Stomach pains or discomfort when the child is sitting down or walking	• Sudden or unexplained change in behaviour • An apparent fear of someone • Running away from home • Nightmares or bed-wetting • Self-harm, self-mutilation or attempt at suicide • Abuse of drugs or other substances • Eating problems such as anorexia or bulimia • Sexualised behaviour or knowledge in young children • Sexual drawings or language • Possession of unexplained money • Taking a parental role at home • Functioning beyond their age • Not being allowed friends (particularly in adolescence) • Alluding to secrets • Telling other people about the abuse

Figure 4.6 Features of sexual abuse

Patterns of disclosure

Sometimes children and young people themselves communicate that they are worried: about what they fear may soon happen, what they are currently experiencing or what happened in the past that they now feel able to talk about in confidence. This kind of communication from a child or young person is called a 'disclosure' and is not always made through words.

What does it mean?

Disclosure: verbal or non-verbal communication by a child or young person about ill-treatment: potential, current or in the past. Children will, however, usually disclose abuse if they feel that they can or 'feel comfortable 'doing so.

Ways of 'telling'

The communication that practitioners recognise as a disclosure can vary, and sometimes it is only later, on reflection, that you realise a remark should not have been left without your comment. So do not be reluctant to revisit a conversation with a child. You might use an open-ended phrase such as: 'I've been thinking over what you said yesterday ...' or 'Can we go back to what you told me this morning? What did you mean by ... ?'

Talking with you directly

Children may seize the chance to confide their fear or distress in response to your friendly question, perhaps about how they got a visible new bruise or cut, or that they have been looking 'sad' for much of this week. A child may take the opportunity for a long conversation in which many details emerge. However, disclosures are not always 'big' events.

It can be possible to miss or overlook the significance, when children make a brief, almost throwaway remark. They may approach a disclosure through an apparently unrelated comment, by asking you a question or for your opinion. Slightly older children, much like adults, sometimes begin with expressions such as: 'What would you think if somebody ... ?' or 'My friend is worried about ... '. Of course, the disclosure may actually be on behalf of a friend.

'Telling' through actions

Children may look fearful or very reluctant to follow a routine. Young children are unlikely to behave in this way deliberately; their distress is simply manifesting itself through their actions. Older children may let their feelings show in a rather more conscious way, hoping that a trusted adult will pick up on the non-verbal message. Children, like adults, sometimes deal with extreme distress by burying the experience in their mind. The emotional pain may emerge in less obvious ways such as panic attacks or nightmares.

Children who have been damaged by abusive experiences may have reactions that are out of all proportion to what seem to be ordinary events. Something in a normal routine (such as a story at bedtime), an aspect of conversation or a television drama might trigger memories, sometimes strong enough to be described as flashbacks. Younger children, and sometimes those who are older, may show the impact of abusive experiences through play, including the themes they weave into their imaginative play. Practitioners may realise that the theme of a game or long sequence of pretend play is not entirely imaginary.

Case study

Cameron

Cameron is six years old and was born when his mother, Becky, was nearly 17 years old. Becky has tried to continue her own life and, although there have been no concrete worries about Cameron, neither his nursery nor his primary school feel that they have been able to get Becky to focus on being a parent to her son. This summer she went on holiday to Greece with a new boyfriend and left Cameron for three weeks with some friends of hers. Cameron was very distressed while Becky was gone and has been loath to let her out of his sight ever since. Becky finds this very irritating and continues to say that she explained everything to her son and that it was not a suitable holiday for a child and asks 'So what was I supposed to do?'

Cameron does not seem to like his mother's new boyfriend but Becky says that her son is only jealous and does not like sharing her. The teachers have noticed that Cameron is quieter than he used to be. Recently he said to the one male teacher in the school, 'I hold my willy, don't I? Nobody else should hold my willy.' Cameron was unwilling to say any more but he was later overheard saying to one of the other boys, 'Does your Daddy hold your willy?' Sometimes the new boyfriend comes with Becky to pick up Cameron from school and

$\Rightarrow$

Cameron refuses to take his hand. This afternoon it is just the boyfriend, without Becky, and Cameron has flatly refused to leave.

● What would concern you about this general situation for Cameron?
● How should you deal with the immediate problem today?

You will find a commentary on page 133.

Barriers to disclosure – what stops children telling

Children sometimes do not tell about abuse or neglect, or they delay for some time before making a disclosure. Children may keep quiet about their situation for several different reasons:

● Children may fear that telling will only make matters worse. Adults or young people who abuse sometimes make direct physical threats that ensure children's silence. The abuser may threaten to hurt the child if they tell, or make realistic threats towards someone else for whom the childcares.
● Abusers also make emotional threats, which can be just as effective as physical ones. They may say that if the child tells, then the family will be broken up, or the abuser will lose his or her job. Sexual abusers may claim that nobody will believe the child or that others will think the child is 'bad' or 'disgusting'.
● The aim of these emotional threats is usually to make the child feel inappropriately responsible for the negative consequences of telling; effectively the abuser is saying 'It will all be your fault!'
● Children who have long experiences of abuse or neglect may simply assume that their experience is ordinary. They believe that it happens in all families or that that it happens to 'bad' children like themselves who deserve ill-treatment.
● Slightly older children may postpone telling because they keep hoping the situation will get better, especially if they are fond of the abuser. An adult who is a relative or family friend may further abuse the trust of a child or young person by continually promising to stop.
● Finally, there is the possibility that children have told, or made a tentative disclosure, and the adult they trusted did not pay attention, or actually dismissed what they heard.

Children will usually only disclose if they trust the person to whom they disclose and they feel safe to do so.

Responding to disclosure

When children tell about ill-treatment, whether abuse by adults or bullying from their peers, they generally want:

● the abuse (or bullying) to end as soon as possible, ideally right away;
● to feel safe from now on and to be able to access help as and when they wish.

They do not want:

- their telling to make matters worse, because they are not believed or protected after telling;
- to have their life, or that of their family, turned upside down and then to feel guilty about having told;
- to find that circumstances spiral way out of their control, with additional adults, some of whom they do not know, presuming to know what is best.

Hearing the voice of the child: listening matters

There is no set pattern of response to be followed by all practitioners. Any fixed form of words undermines an authentic reaction from a trusted adult. The most important skill you can offer is to listen to what the child is telling you, and be attentive to how they behave. Good listening is a core strand in any work with children, so practitioners should draw on existing skills when a child starts to confide.

- **Listen** and **hear** the words children are using and the way they share this confidence. Watch children so that you can also 'hear' what they tell you through their facial expressions and whole body language.
- Be guided by children; the conversation finishes when they wish. If you are responsive, they are very likely to talk in confidence another day. On the other hand, if you press them now, they will almost certainly become evasive, silent and possibly distressed.
- Children may choose a time when they can speak with you without being overheard, but sometimes you need to create a confidential space. If other children come to get your attention, you can courteously ask them to wait by saying, 'I'll be with you shortly. Andrea wants to have a word with me' or 'Can you just let Delroy and me talk in private for a while?'
- Slightly older children may pick a time when their trusted adult's attention is partly elsewhere. Foster carers and residential workers report that some children prefer to talk during a shared domestic activity or when adult and child are driving somewhere. It seems that some children do not want full eye contact, so it is an advantage that the adult is still washing up or watching the road ahead.

Making sense of communication can be especially difficult when children have severe learning or physical disabilities. Practitioners need to be confident in using sign and image systems, although with great care, to ensure that they do not over-interpret what the child communicates. A joint project by Triangle and the NSPCC addressed the gap in many signing and image systems for children to communicate about personal safety or experiences of abuse. They developed a booklet to help in this area entitled *How It Is*. You may find this a useful resource, which can be accessed online at: www.triangle.org.uk/howitis

Case study

Kitty

Kitty is four years old. There is strong suspicion that she was sexually abused by her grandfather when he cared for her on a regular basis. The evidence was not certain, but Kitty's mother was worried enough to agree that her father-in-law would no longer come to their home and that Kitty would never be left alone with him at any family gathering. Kitty has said very little in the nursery but, when she draws, sometimes she does a figure on the paper then scribbles all over it. Today she whispers to you, 'No more Grandad.'

- What sense might you make of this observation?
- What should probably be your next step?

You will find a commentary on page 134.

Use open-ended questions

Concerned practitioners need to resist feeling, 'But I must find out everything'; children are people and not cases. It is your responsibility to **hear** what they want to tell you, in the way that children want to tell it. You are not responsible for gathering significant amounts of information from the outset. If something worrying has really occurred, then there will be a time later for exploration in more detail, led by a social worker in a child protection investigation.

Sensitive conversations with children will be supportive, and effective, so long as you avoid cross-questioning or leading questions.

- A long sequence of questions unbalances any conversation – not only a sensitive exchange. The pattern puts pressure on children to confide more details than they may wish, or at a faster pace. There is the risk that children agree with a persistent adult questioner just to end the conversation.
- Leading questions tend to be guided by guesses or unsupported suspicions ('Did Daddy do this to you?') and will distort the disclosure made in the conversation. Children may start to say what the adult seems to want to hear.
- From the police perspective there are concerns that leading questions may be judged later to have contaminated evidence in the minority of cases that reach court. So be cautious about how you gather information from the child. Moreover, it is important to note that that cross-questioning is experienced as oppressive by children.

You can avoid cross-questioning by appropriate and kindly use of language:

- Depending on what the child tells you, you might ask an encouraging question that is part repetition of what a child has just said. If a child says, 'My big cousin is nasty to me,' you could follow with, 'Nasty in what way?'

- A child might whisper, 'Somebody hurt me' and you ask quietly, 'You say somebody hurt you?' (in a questioning tone of voice). You often do not have to ask the more specific question, 'Who hurt you, Daria?' This kind of gentle questioning is called 'reflective listening'.
- Depending on the flow of the conversation, other open-ended questions might be, 'You say you were frightened?' or 'What has happened to make you cry?' You can also simply encourage a child by your open and attentive expression and simple questions like 'Yes?' or 'Anything else you want to tell me?'

Dealing with feelings

It is important to avoid telling children how they are feeling: such a response is too directive and also disrespectful. Be attentive to their words and actions, rather than try to guess their emotional state.

- Listen to what children say about how they are feeling: 'I'm cross with him,' 'She makes me cry and she doesn't care' or 'He says I'm a bad girl, that nobody will like me anymore.' Show empathy and support for the child, with comments such as 'You're feeling cross now,' or 'I will always like you, Mario. Please tell me what has happened.'
- It is not for you to criticise the person who has hurt the child. In some cases, the abuser is a loved relative and the turmoil of mixed emotions is part of the problem. You can still reassure the child with more general support such as 'Tania, nobody should make you this upset' rather than laying blame with 'Your uncle is a bad person.'

Listening and your own feelings

As you listen, you may feel anger, shock or distress. But you cannot assume that the child necessarily shares your emotions. Children may feel all of these and more, but you can only find out by listening and by gently watching their expression and body language. It is also important that a child does not feel overwhelmed by your reaction. It will have been hard for them to tell; children do not need the additional burden of feeling that now they have caused you to feel shock or distress. You do not have to pretend to have no emotional reaction at all; that would be unrealistic and confusing to the child. But strong emotions that trouble you need to be expressed to a fellow professional later.

Children who disclose troublesome secrets need reassurance from the adult, but you should not give commitments that you cannot honour. You cannot promise a child that you will keep disclosures about abuse a secret; you have a responsibility to take such concerns further. But you must be able to reassure them that their experience will not become general knowledge in the setting or local neighbourhood.

Record keeping and documentation

As the person in whom the child confided, you are responsible for making notes on the conversation as soon as possible, and certainly with no more delay than later in the same day. If you work in a team, then the Designated Safeguarding Officer/Safeguarding Lead/Safeguarding Adviser should help you, especially if this is the first time you have faced the task (see also page 104). You will need to think through what you saw as well as heard. You need to be factual and not interpret what you saw and heard.

- Your impressions and opinions can be valuable because you know this child. But support them with your reasons: for instance, 'I believe Sandy is very upset. When he said to me "My big cousin is nasty to me," Sandy was twisting his hair around one finger – the way he does when he is really distressed.'
- Your responsibility is to take seriously what the child said to you. But you are not trying to assess the exact truth of what you have heard; it is therefore important that unsupported assumptions do not go into your written account. There is a difference between taking further the concern of 'Delia told me that her evening sitter shows her "naughty pictures"' and the unsupported conclusion that 'Delia's sitter is definitely abusing her.'

Keep the child in mind

Children very rarely lie about abuse. They are far more likely to have difficulty in telling you, especially if the person harming them is part of their family or a respected authority figure. But it is possible that a child may give an account of only part of what is happening from a complex and troubling situation. So the assumption that the child has told you the whole truth in one conversation could be a harmful conclusion to draw.

It would be bad practice to assume that children who disclosed abuse, especially unlikely claims (from the adult's perspective), are probably lying. However, it is also poor practice to take the naïve view that children never lie about abuse. There have been cases when children have been bullied by one parent into making false accusations against the other parent, as part of vicious custody disputes. It also has to be accepted that older children (and adolescents) have sometimes made false allegations against teachers, foster and residential carers. Some children have not really understood the consequences of such claims. Others appear to have been so distressed or angry as a result of their own disrupted experiences that they are keen to spread that emotional damage.

When parents or other adults say something

Worries that may have child protection implications can arise because of what an adult tells you. There are several possibilities:

- Parents may speak with you about their own child. The concerns may relate to that parent as an individual, to a partner or other family member, or to other people involved with the family.

- Alternatively, parents may express concerns about another child in your setting, or that parent's deep worries about the other child's family life.
- Parents may voice direct concerns that something is amiss. Alternatively, what they say in passing could act as a warning for you, because it links with other incidents or information unknown to this parent.
- Parents or other adults who visit your setting may communicate concerns or wish to clear up issues about the actions of a practitioner or volunteer.
- Concerns might be raised by one of your colleagues, a volunteer or another professional who regularly visits your setting.

Case study

Longmead Primary School

Staff and parents are keen for the children to learn to swim and groups are walked to the nearby leisure centre. Several children say that they do not like the swimming coach, that he is 'horrid' and 'shouts all the time'. There is an incident in which two parents, who are helping with the group, get into an argument with the coach about his insistence that tired children continue to swim widths without stopping. Their concerns are raised in a meeting but the head takes the view that, although the coach can appear sharp and rather impatient, he is successful in getting children to swim. Plans are raised that the eldest children form a swimming team for a gala and that the coach will give them extra tuition. Parents start to say that their children do not want to have extra lessons from this swimming coach.

- What do you judge are the main issues in this situation?
- What do you think should happen now?

You will find a commentary on page 134.

Taking a positive approach when an adult tells you something of concern has many features in common with good communication with children:

- Listen with care to what you are being told. Give this adult your full attention and ensure that you understand what is being said to you.
- Ask open-ended questions. You might repeat part of what the adult has said, but with a question implied by your tone or a few words of encouragement. For instance: 'So, you've seen Marsha's mum hit the child a lot recently' or 'You're really anxious about the baby. Please tell me more about what worries you.'
- You do not have to work out the truth of what you are hearing. You should take seriously what you are told, even if what the parent says seems unlikely. Do not dismiss it, even if you feel this parent is a gossip, or dislikes the accused person.

An adult may want you to keep what they say a secret, or ask that you promise to keep their name out of any further enquiries. You cannot make either of these commitments. Remind a parent of your setting's policy and obligation to pass on any concerns about children. But you may also be able to reassure the parent that your next step will be to talk with the Designated Safeguarding Officer/Safeguarding Lead/Safeguarding Adviser for your setting or service. You will not phone social services without any further consideration.

A parent (or a member of staff) who raises many child protection worries that prove to be unfounded needs to be challenged in a private conversation. There may be a number of possible explanations. For instance, this adult may believe an unrealistically high estimate about the prevalence of child abuse. Alternatively, a parent or colleague may be seeking attention through raising concerns. Frustrations with such a person should not be handled by automatically disbelieving them.

Responding to concerns

This section of the book focuses on the steps that should be taken to deal with concerns.

Social workers always lead an investigation when there are child protection concerns. This will be under section 47 of the Children Act 1989.

Other professionals will not take on this role, no matter how experienced they are in their job. Yet the child protection system cannot work well without the full involvement of practitioners who work on a regular basis with children and their families. You could therefore be directly involved in different ways:

- As discussed above, concerns might be raised first within your setting, or by you as an individual practitioner.
- On the other hand, you might be contacted by a social worker or other professional, because concerns have been raised elsewhere.
- You, or a member of your team, will be required to contribute to child protection processes. Your knowledge of the child and the initial and/or any on-going concerns raised will be an important part of the assessment, investigation and full discussion at a case conference.
- One element of a child protection plan should be what will be best undertaken during your time with a baby or child. Your contribution will arise from your professional skills and your close relationship with key children and families.
- Nurseries and childminders can be the crucial front line for vulnerable children, because you ensure the important basics such as whether an individual child has arrived at the setting; you do not simply accept an absence, you find out why.

Certainly, if a child has a child protection plan, then a social worker should inform and involve you and your setting. Without this professional communication, a significant piece will be missing from the protection jigsaw.

Before a referral: making sense of concerns

Sometimes it is a 'gut' feeling that initially provokes a concern. It is important that this 'gut' feeling is explored to determine why you had the 'gut feeling that something is wrong'.

Nobody should dismiss the possibility of child abuse with claims that 'I don't work with that kind of family' or 'No practitioner would ever behave like that.' On the other hand, individuals, or a team, must not become so focused on the likelihood of abuse that they assume all problems or accidents are caused by deliberate ill-treatment.

Every practitioner needs a sound basis of knowledge about development across the age range. Some problems are fairly usual within an age group, like tantrums from young children who have limited ability to deal with frustration or to express it in words. These situations merit adult attention and support for the child, but are not usually a sign of something untoward that should worry adults. No professional can make sense of behaviour or patterns of development that might give rise to concern if they do not have a firm grasp of the range and variety within ordinary child development.

Practitioners may worry about being wrong in their concerns. It is responsible to allow for uncertainty, but it would be against the children's interests if those doubts led practitioners to do nothing. The child protection system described in Chapter 1 shows that there is a sequence of steps between expressing a concern and serious action to protect a child, including intervention in the family. Nor is it safe to assume that 'surely someone else will speak up'. Perhaps nobody else has noticed, or perhaps

Take another perspective

Child protection materials sometimes describe worrying signs in brief, but good practice is not led by simple checklists. Careful observation and discussion will raise a number of 'ifs and buts', because practitioners are usually looking for patterns rather than single incidents. Bland statements about 'obvious' symptoms of abuse can also be disruptive of genuinely good practice, because worrying signs are not a matter of simple cause and effect.

Bed wetting is often on an abuse checklist and some children who wet the bed are reacting to the distress of being abused. But not all children who wet the bed have definitely experienced abuse and the child's age is obviously a key issue in making sense of this.

Children who have been reliably dry at night sometimes start to have wet sheets because they are very worried and the stress leads them to regress in this skill. The bed wetting is a sign of children's distress and the need for emotional support. However, the cause may be that they are feeling upset at their parents' separation, being bullied at school or experiencing panic because of the impending maths test.

this childminder or key person is the only one to whom the child has confided their abusive experience.

This uncertainty should not be seen as a problem for practitioners because:

- It is not your responsibility to determine exactly what kind of ill-treatment is threatening a child's health or a young person's emotional well being.
- It is your responsibility to be knowledgeable about patterns of development within the normal range and familiar with children as individuals. You are then in a strong position to be alert to what is out of the ordinary for this age or for this baby or child.

What to do

As mentioned in Chapter 1, in March 2015 the government published updated advice for practitioners, *What to Do if You're Worried A Child is Being Abused*. It is non-statutory and its aim is to help practitioners identify child abuse and neglect and take appropriate action in response. It is written to complement *Working Together to Safeguard Children* (HM Government, 2015a), which is statutory guidance.

The policy document is for anyone whose work brings them into contact with children and families, including those who work in early years, social care, health, education (including schools), the police and adult services. It is relevant to those working in the statutory, voluntary or the independent sector, and applies in relation to all children and young people irrespective of whether they are living at home with their families and carers or away from home.

The guiding principles are:

1. 'No matter where you work, you are likely to encounter children during the course of your normal working activities. You are in a unique position to be able to observe signs of abuse or neglect, or changes in behaviour which may indicate a child may be being abused or neglected.
2. You should make sure that you are **alert** to the signs of abuse and neglect, that you **question the behaviour** of children and parents/carers and don't necessarily take what you are told at face value. You should make sure you know where to turn to if you need to **ask for help**, and that you **refer** to children's social care or to the police, if you suspect that a child is at risk of harm or in immediate danger.
3. You should make sure that you understand and work within the local multi-agency safeguarding arrangements that are in place in your area. In doing so, you should be guided by the following key principles:
   - children have a right to be safe and should be protected from all forms of abuse and neglect;
   - safeguarding children is everyone's responsibility;
   - it is better to help children as early as possible, before issues escalate and become more damaging; and
   - children and families are best supported and protected when there is a co-ordinated response from all relevant agencies.

4. You should not let other considerations, like the fear of damaging relationships with adults, get in the way of protecting children from abuse and neglect. If you think that referral to children's social care is necessary, you should view it as the beginning of a process of inquiry, not as an accusation.'

(HM Government, 2015c)

Professional roles and responsibilities

The role of the designated professional lead

National safeguarding policy determines that there should be a 'designated professional lead' (or for health provider organisations, **a named professional**) for safeguarding. Their role is to support other professionals in their agencies and to recognise the needs of children, including rescue from possible abuse or neglect. Designated professional roles should always be explicitly defined in job descriptions. Professionals should be given sufficient time, funding, supervision and support to fulfil their child welfare and safeguarding responsibilities effectively (HM Government, 2015a).

This person should:

- be a more experienced member of the team, with the authority to meet the responsibilities of leading on safeguarding and child protection. This practitioner does not have to be the head or senior manager of the setting but if not the head, then they must communicate regularly with their head or manager.
- It should be clear who steps into the designated safeguarding lead role when that practitioner is absent for any reason.
- The designated safeguarding lead is central in effective safeguarding for a setting but they do not start a child protection investigation; that remains the responsibility of a social worker.
- The designated safeguarding lead's role is to ensure that policy and procedures for safeguarding children are up to date and that practice in the setting is consistent with policy. This obligation is shared with the team; practitioners do not simply hand over concerns to the designated safeguarding lead.
- Conversation with the designated safeguarding lead does not replace careful discussion between colleagues when practitioners work together with the same group of children. However, it should be easy for any practitioner to consult with the designated safeguarding lead.
- The designated safeguarding lead should be told promptly when a child has made a disclosure that suggests the possibility of abuse or neglect (see page 99). The only reason not to talk with the designated safeguarding lead would be if the disclosure implicated that practitioner in some way. Then any concerns should be taken to the head of centre or other person in a management role.

- The designated safeguarding lead will be responsible for ensuring that information about children for whom there have been concerns is shared with the next provision when children leave. Copies of written records about child protection will also need to be passed on in a careful, professional manner.
- The designated safeguarding lead will be responsible, in partnership with the head of a setting, for the continued professional development of all staff with regard to safeguarding.
- The designated safeguarding lead should keep the team up to date with developments in safeguarding practice and resolve any misunderstandings.
- They may run information sessions, but could also organise staff training to be led by an external trainer. The designated safeguarding lead should facilitate information sharing from team members who have recently attended safeguarding courses.

The designated safeguarding lead should be able to offer well-informed support that respects other practitioners' ongoing relationships with children or parents but does not take over the task. Every team member needs to have sufficient understanding of child protection to be able to talk and listen to a child who has chosen to confide in them. Any setting must ensure that all staff can be trusted to understand their role, including what is meant by both confidentiality and the obligation to pass on information in a professional way.

In schools

Governing bodies and proprietors should ensure that the school or college designates an appropriate senior member of staff to take lead responsibility for child protection. This person should have the status and authority within the school to carry out the duties of the post including committing resources and, where appropriate, supporting and directing other staff.

The broad areas of responsibility for the designated safeguarding lead include managing referrals:

- 'Refer all cases of suspected abuse to the local-authority children's social care and:
  - the designated officer(s) for child protection concerns (all cases which concern a staff member),
  - disclosure and Barring Service (cases where a person is dismissed or left due to risk/harm to a child); and/or
  - police (cases where a crime may have been committed).
- Liaise with the headteacher or principal to inform him or her of issues, especially on-going enquiries under section 47 of the Children Act 1989 and police investigations.
- Act as a source of support, advice and expertise to staff on matters of safety and safeguarding and when deciding whether to make a referral by liaising with relevant agencies'.

(HM Government, 2015b)

However, please note that the person who identified the concern should be involved in the referral as it is their observations that should be recorded factually by them. These facts about what they observed should then be referred, in person, by or with the support of the safeguarding lead.

Anyone has the right to make a referral to children's social services if they have a child protection concern.

For further information see *Keeping Children Safe in Education* (HM Government, 2015b).

The local authority designated officer

Where there are concerns about a practitioner, local authorities have a designated 'officer, or team of officers (either as part of multi-agency arrangements or otherwise), to be involved in the management and oversight of allegations against people that work with children. Any such officer, or team of officers, should be sufficiently qualified and experienced to be able to fulfil this role effectively – for example, qualified social workers. Any new appointments to such a role, other than current or former designated officers moving between local authorities, should be qualified social workers. Arrangements should be put in place to ensure that any allegations about those who work with children are passed to the designated officer, or team of officers, without delay' (HM Government, 2015a).

Case study

Ciaran

Consider the following scenario and the two options at the choice point.
- What do you judge are the likely consequences of each option?
- Overall, which option do you think would be in the best interests of the child?

You will find a commentary on page 134.

You are a specialist teaching assistant (STA) and also undertake lunchtime duties in the playground. Ciaran is now aged eight and since you have known him has been a quiet child, but recently he has chatted much more to you.

One lunchtime last week he started to discuss one of the regular 'soaps' on television that has a current storyline of serious rows in the fictional family. Soon you got the impression that Ciaran was talking about his own family. He has continued to chat with you on most days and you have been very careful not to lead the conversation in any way. Over the last week you have become sure that Ciaran's mother and father have serious rows, that Ciaran and his younger sister have been hurt at least once, that they are distressed and frightened, yet under pressure to say nothing to outsiders.

Yesterday you made notes of what had emerged so far and discussed the matter with the Designated Safeguarding Lead in your school. This teacher agreed that you should continue to listen to Ciaran and says she will inform

⇨

the head about the situation. Today, the Designated Safeguarding Lead passes on the head's instruction that any further conversations with Ciaran about his home situation must be undertaken only with her.

Choice point: you have two main options here and both have consequences:

1. You feel that the head's instruction has to be followed: as an STA you are not in a position to argue. During the next lunchtime, as Ciaran starts to talk about his family, you say that he needs to have that conversation with the head.

2. You question, with the Designated Safeguarding Lead, whether the head's instruction is appropriate for Ciaran. You want to support and protect Ciaran effectively and ask the Designated Safeguarding Lead to talk now about other possibilities.

Talking with fellow professionals

Good practice within every setting or service is that it should be possible to raise concerns at any level. Practitioners need to be able to say their worry is at a low level and not have someone else insist on making a referral 'just in case'. However, it is important that the 'low level' concern is documented and the outcome of decisions is documented. If the family have been sign-posted to support services, or if there has been a referral made to other 'universal services' such as a health visitor, school nurse, GP or education welfare officer, this should also be documented clearly. It is also important to document who is aware of the outcome.

Note: It is best practice to keep the child and parents informed of decisions and who is involved. The only reason that parents might not be informed would be if there were concerns that the child's welfare would be in jeopardy or there are risks to the practitioner. In this situation, it would more likely to be a section 47 referral. It is important to document and inform other professionals in writing that the parents *do not* know of the referral. Talking with parents is discussed below.

Equally, practitioners need to feel confident that their knowledge of child development, and of this individual in particular, is respected when they express serious concerns. Practitioners need to be able to think over what they have observed, but it is often useful to talk it over with a fellow professional.

- In a group setting, you should clarify your concerns with another colleague and/or the safeguarding lead. The only reason for not talking with these colleagues would be if you had serious concerns relating to their behaviour.
- Some duty social workers will listen on the telephone and give advice about a non-specific concern. However, local teams vary and some insist on details for a referral before they will continue a conversation with a fellow professional.

- Every local area will have departments responsible for the different types of settings. If you do not know the details, find out by going on your local authority's website. You may find a good contact for advice within the specific team covering your service.
- There will be someone with local responsibility for the childminding service and there should be a support worker linked with any childminding network. Foster carers should have their own link worker.
- The national organisations for childminding are willing to listen and give professional support (during office hours). Check their websites for the current contact details: the Professional Association for Childcare and Early Years (PACEY) (www.pacey.org.uk), the SCMA (Scotland) (www.childminding.org) and the NICMA (Northern Ireland) (www.nicma.org)
- Nannies are the most isolated practitioners if child protection concerns arise. The childminding organisations encompass home-based childcare in general and will listen to nannies who call in need of a sounding board.
- The NSPCC (www.nspcc.org.uk) has a 24-hour, seven-days-a-week helpline open to anyone – call the Child Protection Helpline on 0808 800 5000.

Clarifying concerns

Practitioners will think through some issues without the need for support, but sometimes a sounding board is necessary. The following points will help as you listen to a fellow professional and, phrased differently, are also relevant when you mentally talk yourself through your observations and possible concerns.

- Listen to what the other person is telling you, without prejudging the issue one way or another.
- Ask open-ended questions that do not direct or assume. You might ask, 'What else did he say to you?' or 'What sense do you make of this?'
- Intuitions are important, but vague yet persistent concerns need to be grounded in what a practitioner has actually observed. You might comment, 'So, you feel Justin humiliates his son. Can you give me an example of something that's happened recently?'
- Another approach can be to invite: 'You say your worries about Karen came to a head this morning. Can you talk me through what happened?' Sometimes it helps to be encouraged to re-run 'this morning', like a visual and sound recording in your memory. It is important that the person listening only encourages and does not shape the memory with direct questions.
- Encourage the other practitioner to make notes on their observations, if this work has not yet been completed.

Talking with parents

One option would be to talk with the child's parent or other key family carer when that is appropriate. For instance, some children are looked after by their grandparents or by foster carers. Practitioners are often uneasy about the prospect, but this conversation is not always awkward. Sometimes a direct question brings a straightforward and credible explanation. Alternatively, parents may be pleased you have spoken, because they share your concerns. The appropriate follow-up action may go no further than your own setting, because no child protection concern arises. Perhaps the key issues are about the child's development or an understandable reaction to distress in the family, such as bereavement.

Even if the outcome is not to make a referral to Children's Social Care it is still important to document factually the initial concerns and the outcome.

Without doubt, conversations with other practitioners or parents will be easier alongside good practice based on partnership working with other practitioners and the family. Practitioners should have made the effort to build a friendly working relationship with families. Such a relationship gives parents a different context in which to make sense of your question about Sandra's bruises on her thigh or Mike's puzzling remark about 'seeing a strange man's willy'. Regular conversation will have created a two-way relationship: you have shown you believe parents have a right to be informed and offered explanations. A good working relationship with parents may also mean that Mike's mother tells you, without you having to ask, that yesterday she and her son had an unpleasant encounter with a flasher in the park, or Sandra's father tells you that his daughter fell out of the tree house at the weekend.

Anything that you say to parents needs to be in your own words and so come across as a genuine communication. There is no format that is always right or that will avoid any unpleasantness. However, there are better, as well as unwise, ways of expressing your concern or question. Your aim is for clear and honest communication: avoid unnecessary apology as well as any tone of confrontation.

Decide what you want to tell or ask a parent (or other relevant carer):

- What exactly is puzzling you about what the child said or did?
- What and where are the bruises, cuts or other marks?
- What patterns of behaviour from the child or young person have concerned you?
- What is happening or not happening?

Which of your feelings are relevant and could be voiced?

Some examples are:

- 'I'm uneasy about the games Jared tries to play with two other children.'
- 'I'm confused about what Tara said. What sense does it make to you?'

- 'I'm concerned that Nathan is so very quiet when your au pair picks him up. It's like he a different child on the days that you or your husband come.'

It is unlikely to be appropriate to add apologies such as 'I'm sorry but … ' or riders like 'Please don't think I'm interfering but … '. The communication will be more straightforward if you express the facts and any relevant feelings simply. See also the commentary on page 201.

You could take time during the day to consider, with a colleague or the designated safeguarding lead in a group setting, what you will say to a particular parent at the end of session or the day. You could practise the words you intend to use, either in your head or out loud with your colleague. Keep your message simple; for instance: 'Wai has several big bruises on her upper arms. Do you know how they came about?' or 'Davie said an odd thing to me today. He said, "The ghosties will get me if I tell about Uncle Ned." He seemed very upset. What sense do you make of it?'

In some families, you may see someone other than parents on a regular basis. Maybe a childminder picks children up from your morning session or it is understood that one father picks up his son and his son's best friend. You will then need to contact the parent directly, to arrange to meet.

You should never avoid talking with parents because:

- You are too busy. It is crucial that you make the time and, if necessary in a group setting, a senior practitioner must rearrange their time to enable you to have an uninterrupted conversation with the parent.
- You are concerned that the parent will get angry or start swearing. Having someone shout at you or disagree in a loud voice is not a pleasant experience, but you need to face this possibility for the child's sake. However, you do need to consider your own safety and it may be appropriate to have another colleague with you when discuss concerns raised with a parents. At no point, though, should you make an allegation of abuse or start any form of investigation yourself.
- You cannot believe that anything dubious could possibly happen in this family, so you are going to ignore the whole incident. There are no certainties for patterns of abuse or neglect, so you must take further appropriate action.
- You are worried about the consequences if your concerns are groundless: that you will spoil a friendly relationship with the parent that has been hard to establish. Social work practice has been criticised when undue priority has been given to maintaining good relations with the parent. All the UK child-protection legislation stresses that the welfare of the child must be the most important consideration and should therefore take priority over adult feelings.

Some practitioners have gained the impression that even minor concerns should be referred immediately to social care services. Sometimes this message has been given through child protection courses, with the rationale that talking with parents raises the possibility that abusers will cover up the evidence. However, the law and official guidance are clear: it is good practice to talk with parents, unless there are very sound reasons not to do so. Bear in mind that practitioners would be seriously taken aback if parents' first reaction to their own concerns were to contact social care services rather than first have a conversation with their child's key person or childminder.

Reasons not to talk with parents

The premise for safeguarding work is that one is open and honest with parents. However, there may be times when it is not appropriate to ask the parents or inform them of your concerns and what you are going to do about them.

A sound reason for not talking with parents and going straight to a referral is if the current situation, or past events with this family, genuinely support a belief that the child is at immediate and significant risk. High levels of concern might arise from the nature of what a child has disclosed, such as a serious level of physical threat.

Local guidelines sometimes specify that practitioners should go straight to referral if they have a sound basis for concerns about sexually abusive treatment, that a child is involved in organised abuse by several people or there is good reason to fear that a carer is deliberately making the child ill (for more on illness induction see page 30).

Alternatively, you could have good reason for thinking that this parent will have an extreme and violent reaction to what you say. In such a case the safety of you, your colleagues and the children is paramount. Your judgement, which you can justify to other professionals, is that the child's immediate safety requires that you contact social care services to set other procedures in motion.

The police have an important role in child protection (see page 121), but it would be unusual for you to telephone the local police force about your concerns. The exception would be if a parent, or other carer, became aggressive or threatened to become violent. You would then be concerned for your safety or that of the children, and it would be appropriate to call for the emergency help of the police.

Make the connection with ...

Safety at home

It is a serious matter if practitioners are already so worried about their own safety that they hesitate to raise concerns with a parent or other family carer. This fact increases the level of concern significantly. It also raises the crucial question of how children can be judged as safe from harm if they are living with adults (or older siblings) who frighten practitioners working in a nursery, school or club or as a childminder.

Outcomes of talking with parents

You may talk with parents and they give a plausible explanation of what had concerned you. Good practice would still be to make a note of the conversation in the child's record. This is easier if you and the parents have a continuing relationship of openness and share written records appropriately.

Alternatively, you may talk with parents and your concerns are not put to rest. Perhaps what they say only adds to your concerns. Maybe the parents are relieved you have opened the subject and make a disclosure about themselves or someone else involved with the family. Even if parents press you to keep the matter within the setting or your own practice as a childminder, you cannot agree to this request. Tell parents what you will be doing next and when you will speak with them again.

Making a referral

Your concerns may not be resolved or this incident may be part of a sequence that is not improving at all. In that case, your decision, or that of the designated safeguarding lead in a group setting, may be to make a referral to social care services.

You should already know the telephone number and, if appropriate, the name of the person to contact. This person would most likely be the duty social worker, or possibly the local NSPCC, if they are prominent in child protection in your area. Out of normal working hours, there should still be emergency social work cover at the end of the telephone. If you have not been provided with relevant numbers by your local authority, then track the information through their website, or that of the Health and Social Services Board in Northern Ireland.

You need to have all the information about a child and family ready so that you can give details in a straightforward way. Your setting or service should have a pro forma: a prepared layout in which you can fill in the details of a referral. Use this form to ensure that you have all the information in front of you while you make the telephone referral. You should then send the completed form with a covering letter in confirmation of the referral. If your setting does not have a pro forma, then the designated safeguarding lead should contact the relevant department for your service to obtain the recommended local form.

You will need to articulate your concerns clearly and factually.

The social worker will want to know:

- Your details, including your name and contact details for your setting or service, and your involvement with the child and family.
- Personal details of the child and family, including names and home address and who is in the immediate family. At this point, they may also want to know relevant details such as the family language(s) and whether the child is disabled.
- The nature of your concern, expressed in a concise way, and any sequence of events.

- Whether this referral is about an incident that requires immediate or emergency attention. You might be seriously concerned about the well-being of this child, or other siblings, given what has just happened.
- Whether you have spoken with the parent(s) about your concerns and what that conversation added to your views.
- Also whether you have informed parents that you are about to make this referral. You would usually tell parents, unless the circumstances were such that you judged this action would increase the level of risk.
- Details of other services or professionals who (you know) are already involved with the child or family, such as their GP or the child's school, if you are a childminder or from the child's after-school club.

Case study

Monica, Sergio, Rory, Yvette and Marsha

For each scenario, please consider the following questions:
- Does this situation concern you? If so, in what way? Be specific by thinking about the concerns that you might have if you were the practitioner.
- Should you talk with the parent in this situation? What will you say?
- Practise some real phrases, or explore the situation in a role play with a colleague or fellow student.
- What further information might you or others want to explore with care?

Monica

You are an experienced childminder and have cared for Monica since she was a young toddler. Monica is now nearly six years old and you are about to take responsibility for her younger brother, a baby nearly five months of age. The parents are strict vegetarians and you have been happy to ensure that Monica's food in your home meets the family's requests. Monica has been healthy and full of energy until the last couple of months. Her family now explain that they have shifted to a new kind of vegan diet and want you to do the same for Monica, as well as following their food guidelines sheet as you help to wean the baby.

You are concerned when you see the family's food list, because the diet is very restricted even for vegans, and seems to depend on excessive levels of vitamin pills. You are very uneasy that Monica, and even more so the baby, will have nutritional deficiencies in some ways, yet could overdose on some vitamins and minerals. You had planned to talk with the parents about Monica's health, because she has become very listless, normal scrapes take a long time to heal and she has had a sequence of colds. A conversation this evening has not gone well. Monica's mother became very irritated and demanded that you respect the family diet or else she would find another childminder. You do not feel that partnership with parents should mean that you follow requests that could endanger the health of Monica or her baby brother.

$\Rightarrow$

Sergio

Four-year-old Sergio has been persistent in trying to grope the female practitioners in your children's centre. When you started at the centre two weeks ago, you were warned never to turn your back on the boy, but this was explained as 'macho Italian stuff – it's the family'. Within a week you have noticed how practitioners stand with their back to the fence out in the garden and you noticed that your room colleague avoids sitting close to Sergio. Today, he tried to push his hand up your T-shirt and persevered despite your firm, 'No, Sergio, that is a private area of my body.' You had to hold his wrist and move his hand away. Sergio then grinned at you.

Rory

Rory is two years old and seems to have a lot of accidents at home. His mother, who runs her business from the house, has offered a reasonable explanation for each incident so far. You know Rory as a bold child whose curiosity and self-confidence can lead him into risky situations, even in the day nursery. This morning Rory has a very large bruise on his forehead and you ask his mother what happened. She replies, 'I think he pulled out the kitchen steps to get to the biscuits. He must have fallen off. It was a while before I realised.' You ask, 'Oh, weren't you in the kitchen with him, then?' She looks a bit embarrassed and then says firmly, 'I had an assignment to finish. I can't turn down work and you won't have them later than 6.30. And his father won't watch him.'

Yvette

Yvette is seven years old and attends your after-school club. Her mother dresses Yvette in what you feel are inappropriate clothes for a girl of her age. She wears mainly crop tops, tight short skirts and her shoes often have little heels. Yvette wears nail polish and has three earrings in each ear. You have become increasingly uneasy on hearing Yvette's comments about someone called Martin. Yvette has said things like, 'I'm his little princess' and 'Martin is going to get me a CD player if I'm good.' Yvette seems to become even more flirtatious with your male colleague than previously. He has just said to you that Yvette wanted to sit on his lap this afternoon. He made an excuse to get her off, because she seemed to be wriggling back very firmly against his crotch.

Marsha

The local child protection team is making initial inquiries about Marsha's family because of concerns that their mother is hitting Marsha and the young baby in the family. Marsha is usually very quiet in the playgroup but today you hear her shouting in the home corner. When you go closer, you can see her violently shaking the baby doll and calling out 'Be quiet! Be quiet! I'll give you such a one!' Another child in the home corner is looking at Marsha with disapproval and says, 'You shouldn't shake the baby. You'll make him cry.'

You can return to these scenarios when you have read other sections of this chapter. You will find a commentary on each scenario on pages 135–7.

Involvement in the steps of child protection

You should confirm your referral in writing within 48 hours and the social worker should confirm in writing to you that the referral has been made. It is important that you, or the designated safeguarding lead, keep alert to these steps and are ready to follow up if you hear nothing back from the social worker within a matter of days. As the source of the referral, you should be kept up to date with the process. Be ready to follow up, by telephone and written communication, if the social worker fails to contact you beyond the initial confirmation.

The social worker should be in contact for your contribution to gathering information at the different stages of assessment and investigation, as described in Chapter 1. The relevant early years practitioner should be invited to the child-protection case conference, or child-in-need meetings if it has been decided by the social worker that it is not an issue of child protection. It is an internal decision for a setting about whether the key person or the designated safeguarding lead will attend.

They should also be invited to on-going meetings if the child is managed under either section 17 or section 47 of the Children Act 1989.

It is good professional practice to prepare thoroughly for any meetings, either informal ones with the social worker or a child-protection case conference, child-in-need case conference or review meeting.

Act in advance by ensuring that you or the representative of your setting has a slot on the agenda. Talk with the chair of the meeting or lead professional (probably the social worker) if you have not been contacted to attend.

- Organise in advance the information you have to contribute and the facts underpinning any opinions that are expressed. You have to be confident in presenting the perspective and observations of your setting or service.
- In formal meetings, including case conferences, you are likely to submit a written report in advance. Be ready to contribute the main points from that report, sharing your knowledge of the child, young person and family.
- Arrive promptly for the meeting, dressed in a smart style, and allow enough time so that you are present for the full conference.
- Continue to pay full attention throughout the meeting, not only during your slot. Another professional may raise issues about which you can appropriately add your understanding. Do not break into their contribution; make yourself a note and indicate to the chair that you would like to add a comment.
- Use straightforward language and be ready to explain any terms that are specific to your area of work, including explaining what any acronyms mean. Be ready to request an explanation in your turn. It is important to establish common goals and raise any professional differences in approach or terminology that could influence the effectiveness of any plan to protect a child.

In order to help a child and family, practitioners need to know key points about an individual child-protection plan; what you will contribute and the ways that your involvement will complement other sources of support.

Step 1: Initial concern and referral

The aim of this section is to give readers an understanding of the whole process. There are differences across the UK in the detail of how the child protection system works, but also many common features. This section uses general terminology that should make sense wherever you work within the UK. In England, Wales and Northern Ireland a 'child', who could legally be in need of protection, is defined as under 18 years of age. In Scotland, the definition is under 16 years, but vulnerable 16–18-year-olds can be viewed legally as children, still in need or protection.

The flow chart in Figure 4.7 has been designed to support that understanding. You may find that national or local child-protection documents will have a more complex chart, or more than one chart. That description occupies the part of the flow chart here that is summed up briefly by 'Practitioners would have made appropriate information gathering'. Unless you specialise in working with vulnerable families, a high proportion of your concerns will remain at this lower level.

The child protection process is started when someone expresses concern about the welfare of a child, which can include disclosure by children or young people themselves. This concern may be expressed from one or more of the professionals and services listed on page 73. However, it is not always professionals who first voice worries about a child. Some child protection inquiries start as the result of fears for a child that have been communicated by members of the child's own immediate family, other relatives, friends or neighbours.

It is most likely that child protection concerns will be communicated to the local children's social care (sometimes still referred to as the social services department) or the local NSPCC. The NSPCC is more active in some local systems than others, but representatives of this national charity have 'authorised person' status because their inspectors protected children for decades throughout the twentieth century, when local authorities were not active in that role. The police would not usually be the first point of contact, unless the situation seemed dangerous for everyone. However, the local police may well become involved and should have a designated officer and most likely a unit for child protection.

Step 2: Initial inquiries and strategy

Any concern regarding the possible abuse of a child or young person has to be considered and an initial investigation made. The steps in the child protection process are intended to be steady as well as timely. The aim is

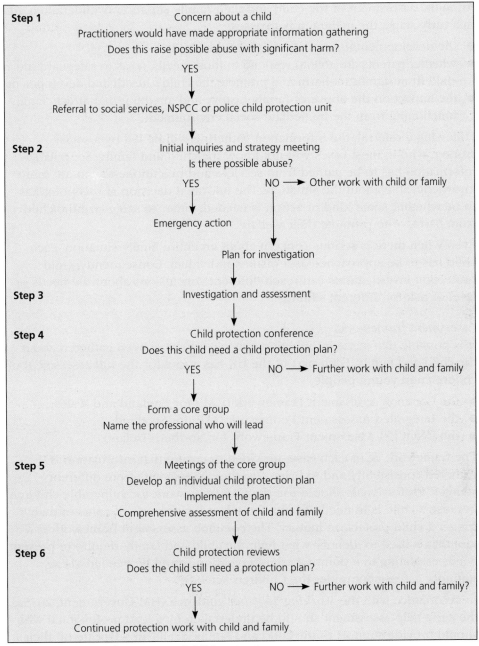

Step 1 Concern about a child
Practitioners would have made appropriate information gathering
Does this raise possible abuse with significant harm?
YES
↓
Referral to social services, NSPCC or police child protection unit
↓
Step 2 Initial inquiries and strategy meeting
Is there possible abuse?
YES   NO ⟶ Other work with child or family
↓
Emergency action
↓
Plan for investigation
↓
Step 3 Investigation and assessment
↓
Step 4 Child protection conference
Does this child need a child protection plan?
YES   NO ⟶ Further work with child and family
↓
Form a core group
Name the professional who will lead
↓
Step 5 Meetings of the core group
Develop an individual child protection plan
Implement the plan
Comprehensive assessment of child and family
↓
Step 6 Child protection reviews
Does the child still need a protection plan?
YES   NO ⟶ Further work with child and family?
↓
Continued protection work with child and family

Figure 4.7 Steps in the process of child protection

that any concerns are checked carefully, but that no further measures are taken unless this is judged necessary. At the start of any investigation, a decision has to be made about whether the inquiries will be made by the social services on their own or whether the investigation will be a joint one, also involving the police and possibly an NSPCC social worker.

An initial assessment of the child and their family situation is undertaken. At this early stage, the main aim is to assess:

- the developmental, or other, needs of the child;
- whether parents are able to respond to those needs, so as to safeguard the child from significant harm and promote the child's health and development;
- the impact on the above of family history and anything that affects family functioning from the immediate social environment.

Following a referral, the information gathering will be led by a social worker, who in most cases will not know the child and family. So, reliable information has to be gained from services and practitioners who are more knowledgeable about the situation. The informed decision at this point has to be whether some kind of action is needed, either to safeguard the child from harm, or to promote their welfare.

Even when there is serious concern about an entire family situation, each child has to be approached as a distinct individual. Consequently, child protection investigations can reach different conclusions about the needs or level of risk for different siblings.

Assessment frameworks

It is possible that some information may already have been gathered about the child and family. Each part of the UK has a tool for the full assessment of children and young people:

- the Common Assessment Framework (CAF) for England and Wales;
- the Integrated Assessment Framework (IAF) for Scotland;
- the UNOCINI Assessment Framework for Northern Ireland.

The framework is, in each case, provided to ensure that information is gathered consistently and to bring together assessments from different sources. Professionals should use the CAF framework for vulnerable children because a child is in need of help, though at lower levels of concern than trigger a child protection inquiry. The common assessment framework is a tool that is used to identify what help the child and family require to prevent needs escalating to a point where intervention would be needed via a statutory assessment under the Children Act 1989.

In accordance with the *Working Together* guidance (HM Government, 2015a), the early help assessment should be undertaken by a lead professional who should provide support to the child and family, act as an advocate on their behalf and co-ordinate the delivery of support services. The lead professional role could be undertaken by a General Practitioner (GP), family support worker, teacher, health visitor and/or special educational needs co-ordinator. Decisions about who should be the lead professional should be taken on a case by case basis and should be informed by the child and their family.

The approach of all the national assessment frameworks is to identify the needs of the children and any risks. However, an equal aim is to recognise strengths in the overall situation, including the child's family, that could work well alongside any professional intervention.

However, if at any time when completing a CAF it is considered that the child may be a child in need as defined under section 17 of the Children Act 1989, or that the child has suffered significant harm or is likely to do so, a referral should be made immediately to local-authority children's social care. This referral can be made by any professional.

The Assessment Framework is used in England and Wales for section 47 child protection processes.

Strategy meeting

If there is any concern about likely or actual significant harm, then there has to be a meeting between key professionals to plan any future investigation. A strategy discussion is convened by the Local Authority (LA) Children's Social Care to decide whether to initiate section 47 enquiries. At this point, there are three main possibilities:

- On the basis of the information available, it may be decided not to go further with the protection process for this child. This decision does not mean that any concerns are ignored.
  Sometimes, though not always, the decision will be that low-key support will help and that parents, or other key family carers, are willing to accept that support. At this point the social worker should communicate with the professional who made the referral.
- It may be decided that the case requires investigation on the basis of child protection concerns. Initial plans will then be made for an investigation and assessment.
- The third possibility is that the risk to the child or others in the same family is judged to be so great that steps must be taken immediately. The investigation and other steps in the process will also be undertaken, but the child is judged to be in serious and immediate danger, and action cannot be delayed.

Possible emergency actions

The principles guiding child protection stress that professionals must act in the best interests of the child, but not take more action than is necessary. If the child cannot be protected in the very near future, given all the facts of the nature of the risk (who, what, where, when, how), then the child is judged to be at risk of immediate and significant harm. A professional, who is most likely to be a social worker, then applies to the court for a relevant emergency court order, given the nature of the risk. It is judged too risky to wait for a meeting and the court order is a swift but temporary response to the situation.

Emergency legal steps might be taken at any point in the child protection process, because the situation suddenly changes. Such actions are not taken lightly and the key principles of the legal process are that:

- the welfare of the child must be the prime concern;
- professionals avoid and reduce delay that would leave children in a seriously unsafe situation;
- making a court order (emergency or other kinds) is clearly in the best interests of the child. Orders are not to be used as a matter of routine.

In England and Wales:

- An Emergency Protection Order operates to allow the removal or detaining of a child for their own safety, for up to eight days. The order will be granted if the child is not safe at home, the parent(s) will not permit the voluntary removal of the child and there is nowhere for the child to be kept safe with the parents' consent.
- The effect of an Emergency Protection Order is to compel a parent, or other relevant person, to produce the child and allow the local authority to remove them to a place of safety. The order can also be used to prevent the removal of a child by parents, or other persons, from a place that is judged to be safe for the child.
- The court can additionally issue a warrant authorising a police officer to assist in the removal of children, or in preventing their removal by the family. Alternatively, the police have the powers to remove the child to suitable alternative accommodation or to prevent the child being removed from a specific place: such powers last a maximum of 72 hours.
- It is also possible to apply for an Exclusion Order, under which a child stays in their own home and a named person, who is alleged to be the source of risk, has to leave the home or not visit, if he or she lives elsewhere.

In Scotland, application for emergency orders is made to a Sheriff.

- In a similar way to the process in England and Wales, a Child Protection Order may require a relevant adult to produce a child about whom there are serious concerns. Under the order a child can be removed to a place of safety, or the order can prevent the removal of a child from a place where he or she is judged to be safe.
- An Exclusion Order, like that used in England and Wales, deals with the alleged abuser so that children can remain in their home, unless their removal is the only safe option.
- In exceptional circumstances, when a Sheriff is not available, any person can apply to a Justice of the Peace for authorisation to remove a child or keep a child in a place of safety

In Northern Ireland:

- An Emergency Protection Order enables a child to be made safe.
- For longer-term protection of children at significant risk, one option is a Care Order, making a child the responsibility of the local Health and Social Services Trust.
- A Supervision Order places the child under the supervision of the Board but without assigning parental responsibility.

Developing a plan for investigation

The initial strategy meeting must plan the investigation, if it has been decided to proceed with a child protection enquiry. The details have to be decided on the basis of the information available so far, the strands that have to be followed and the other professionals involved with the family. It has to be clear who will be responsible for conducting the investigation and making contact with the child, family and other involved agencies. The strategy meeting basically assesses the evidence so far. It is possible that, at this point, the police representative might say that there is insufficient evidence to suggest a possible criminal prosecution in the future. Then the police will not be involved further in this process.

NOTE: Where the need is relatively low-level, individual services and universal services may be able to take swift action. For other emerging needs a range of early help services may be required, co-ordinated through an early help assessment, as set out above. Where there are more complex needs, help may be provided under section 17 of the Children Act 1989 (children in need). Where there are child protection concerns (reasonable cause to suspect a child is suffering, or likely to suffer, significant harm) local-authority social care services must make enquiries and decide if any action must be taken under section 47 of the Children Act 1989.

A section 47 enquiry is carried out by undertaking or continuing with an assessment in accordance with the guidance set out in *Working Together* (HM Government, 2015a) and should follow the principles and parameters of a good assessment. Local-authority social workers have a statutory duty to lead assessments under section 47 of the Children Act 1989. The police, health professionals, teachers and other relevant professionals should help the local authority in undertaking its enquiries.

A section 47 enquiry is initiated to decide whether and what type of action is required to safeguard and promote the welfare of a child who is suspected of, or likely to be, suffering significant harm.

Understanding the role of the police

The work of the police in the child protection process is rather different from that of other professionals. They can only justify their continuing involvement with a child protection case on two related grounds:

- That if the abuse is proven then the abuser(s) will have committed a crime. The alleged actions have to fall within one of the possible categories that define a crime under law.
- There has to be sufficient evidence that a prosecution is likely to succeed. In England and Wales the police who have investigated a case then pass on the evidence to the Crown Prosecution Service (CPS), which makes the final decision about whether to go ahead with criminal proceedings. In Scotland this decision rests with the office of the Procurator Fiscal and in Northern Ireland with the Department of Public Prosecutions (DPP).

In Scotland, the police have a general duty to investigate on behalf of the 'Procurator Fiscal', when they have reason to believe that a criminal offence has been committed. Each Procurator Fiscal is the local representative of the Lord Advocate, and can interview witnesses.

If the police withdraw from the child protection process, it does not mean they believe the abuse of this child does not matter, nor that they think someone is mistaken or lying. It means that either there is no identifiable crime, however powerful the information collected, or that the evidence collected is not strong enough to stand up in court. On other occasions, it is judged not to be in the child's best interests to attempt a prosecution (see page 240). Of course, some cases do go to trial and, for various reasons, do not result in a prosecution. It is important that you understand the limits placed on the police force, since you may support parents and children who have unrealistic hopes that a recognised abuser will definitely be punished in law.

It is important to realise, for yourself and in supporting parents and children, that very serious steps can be taken on behalf of a child at risk, regardless of whether there is an identifiable crime.

Step 3: Investigation and assessment

A full investigation has to be carried out after the initial meeting of key professionals and before the child protection conference. This investigation is carried out as part of the requirements under child protection legislation and is a necessary part of the later decision at the case conference (Step 4) whether or not to place the child's name on the child protection register in Scotland or Northern Ireland, In England and Wales the equivalent decision is that it is necessary to develop a child protection plan. From 2009, England and Wales ceased to have local child protection registers. Instead, children who are suffering or likely to suffer significant harm are made the subject of a Child Protection Plan.

However, the safeguarding process cannot continue without this prior investigation. Guidance has established that the prime tasks of a child protection investigation are to:

● Establish the facts about the circumstances giving rise to the concern.
● Identify whether there are grounds to consider that the child is suffering or is likely to suffer significant harm. If that is the case, then the investigation has to identify the sources and level of risks, and then decide on the necessary protective, and other, actions in relation to children.
● Secure by interview or medical examination the evidence from which a decision can be made regarding civil or criminal proceedings (the difference between these is explained on page 56).

At this point in the process, some children are judged to be 'in need' rather than 'at risk' of actual or likely significant harm. In such instances the process of investigation should identify the support services that would best improve the situation. Gathering information about the family would also include making an assessment of whether parents, or other significant family carers, would accept and work with a given service, or professionals who would visit the home on a regular basis.

The principles of an investigation are that it should:

- Always be child-centred and any procedures should be undertaken with the child's feelings and experiences in mind. Interviews or examinations should be explained and undertaken with consideration, avoiding further distress to an already hurt or confused child.
- Have due regard to the legal requirements. However concerned professionals may be about a child, they must act within the law.
- Fully assess the child's circumstances before any action is taken. It has to be clear, and properly documented, detailing how any decisions have been reached.
- Undertake interviews with an open mind, having regard to different childcare practices and cultural diversity, but with the welfare of the child as central. (See also Chapter 5 about equality practice and safeguarding.)

The investigation and assessment process should involve parents and carers, unless it can be clearly justified as prejudicial to the investigation. For instance, parents might be excluded if they continually disrupt meetings or intimidate the children. In that case the parents' views should still be sought and they should be given information. If parents refuse to co-operate in the investigation, a Child Assessment Order can be obtained in any of the four nations of the UK. This court order requires parents to allow an assessment to be made of a child at risk, when that co-operation is being withheld unreasonably. This order would not usually require the removal of a child from the home, unless obstruction from the family was such that professionals could not otherwise assess the child.

Guidance (for example, in *Working Together to Safeguard Children* (HM Government, 2015a)), makes it clear that the social worker leading this investigation should stay in contact with the professional who made the initial referral. Communication might be made not only for brief feedback on the progress of the case, but also for the appropriate involvement of that person and their setting or service.

Step 4: The child protection conference

Not all child protection concerns reach this stage. The whole point of initial inquiries and the investigation is that further steps are not taken unless there is genuine cause for concern. Some children are best helped by organising different kinds of family support services, when parents show that they are willing, perhaps keen, to address the problems that have given rise to concerns.

The child protection conference brings together any professionals who have relevant information to share and the family itself. The conference is attended by some, but not necessarily all, of the following people. Representatives from different professions are not invited unless they are involved with the family or have a direct contribution to make:

- A social worker will definitely be present, and this profession should be the lead professional on child protection.
- A practitioner who is directly involved with the child; this may be a residential social worker or foster carer, key person from early years provision or a child's class teacher (or possibly the member of staff with designated child-protection responsibility in the setting).
- In Scotland, the Children's Reporter.
- The police, represented by the liaison officer from a child protection unit or the investigating officer. In Scotland the police would usually represent the Procurator Fiscal.
- A medical professional, such as the family's GP or the school nurse.
- If relevant, someone from the Probation department.
- Perhaps a local NSPCC social worker.
- A representative of the local-authority legal department.

Studies of the child protection process have suggested that detailed co-operation between different professionals is most likely at the beginning of the process and at the investigation stage. Social workers are the most likely professionals to carry on with the work, and good practice has to ensure that all the relevant parties continue to contribute information and take action to safeguard in accordance with legislative and policy frameworks.

Involvement of parents

Law and guidance across the UK firmly stress that parents should remain a part of the child protection process. Parents – or another key family carer – must be invited to the case conference, unless it can be shown that there is a very good reason why they should not be there. These family members might be excluded if there is reason to suppose that they are likely to become violent or very disruptive. At the case conference, parents can hear the views of everyone else and they can contribute their own views. However, they do not participate in the conference decision making and they may not be present for the full meeting.

Any professional involved in a case conference needs to understand what the experience can feel like from the parents' point of view. It is very stressful, as is all the investigation. Parents can feel seriously outnumbered when sitting around the table and especially threatened if the police are present – as they will be if the suspected abuse could lead to criminal prosecution.

Family group conferences

Some local authorities have developed the use of family group conferences (FGCs) as a way to involve the immediate and extended family in steps to protect a child. The idea of FGCs originated in New Zealand. This meeting does not replace the child protection conference and any decisions have to be carefully considered, so that the child's well being is assured.

It is possible that an independent co-ordinator will lead the FGC and work with the immediate and extended family. The aim is to reach a plan for the safe care of a child or adolescent, to which the family, social care services and children themselves all agree. The FGC can work well when there are other family members who are able to take care of a child at risk. Sometimes there will be a clear agreement that a child will become the specific responsibility of a relative. A formal arrangement of this kind is called 'kinship care'. Such arrangements can avoid the situation in which a child or adolescent becomes looked after by the local authority. However, in FGCs, the term 'family' is interpreted broadly and can include people, such as previous foster parents of the child, who have taken a family-like role.

Find out more

NSPCC (2009) *Family Group Conferences in Child Protection. An NSPCC factsheet.* NSPCC
www.nspcc.org.uk/globalassets/documents/information-service/factsheet-family-group-conferences-child-protection.pdf

Involvement of children

It is expected that an older child or young person will also be invited to attend their own case conference. They can bring a friend or other person to support them, who does not have to be a relative. If an older child or young person does not want to attend the conference, then the professional most involved with them needs to make their wishes and feelings clear to the conference, and communicate the results of the meeting to them. The same pattern applies to family group conferences. Care plans will not work if a child or young person feels left out of the decision making or even opposed to the end result.

The child protection plan

In Scotland and Northern Ireland, the conference decides on the basis of the evidence whether to place the child on the local child protection register, which would mean that a child protection plan must now be developed. The register is maintained by the local social services on behalf of all the agencies involved in working with children who have been abused or who are judged as being at risk of abuse, and for whom there is a need for a child protection plan. It is also possible for the NSPCC to maintain the register on behalf of the local authority. In England and Wales, when a child-protection case conference decides a child or young person is at risk of abuse they are known as a 'child subject of a child protection plan'. The plan determines the contribution of the different professionals. A child protection plan is a working tool that should enable the family and professionals to understand what is expected of them and what they can expect of others. The Social Worker will be the lead professional as they carry the statutory responsibility for the child's welfare.

If you are working with a child who has a child protection plan you need to:

- know what the child protection plan says you have to do
- know who the key worker is and report any concerns to them immediately
- implement any policies and procedures that you would have used for children on the child protection register
- attend all child protection conferences and core group meetings with a progress report on the child and their family.

Serious concerns can be expressed at birth, or even prior to the birth of a baby. A pre-birth child-protection conference is called to make a decision about what should be done, given the capability of the pregnant woman and family situation. The conference can decide that the unborn infant, or a newborn, needs to be protected by a child protection plan. The key point is that babies or children are judged to be at risk of significant harm through abuse or neglect. The children may not necessarily have been harmed already, but all the information gathered for the case conference leads to a decision that abuse is a real possibility. For some children, there may be very strong indications that they have already been harmed.

Following section 47 enquiries, an initial child-protection conference brings together family members (and the child, where appropriate), with the supporters, advocates and professionals most involved with the child and family, to make decisions about the child's future safety, health and development. If concerns relate to an unborn child, consideration should be given as to whether to hold a child-protection conference prior to the child's birth.

The step of a child protection plan (or initial placing on the child protection register) can only be taken if the following criteria are met:

- There must have been one or more identifiable incidents that can be described as having adversely affected the child. These incidents might be something that was done to a child, or failures to act on behalf of a child.
- The professional judgement is that further incidents involving this child are likely to occur.
- The key areas of risk have to be identified from neglect, physical injury, sexual abuse or emotional abuse. In Scotland, a fifth category, that of non-organic failure to thrive, has to be considered. Also, in Scotland it is no longer required to give a category for the primary source of risk.

If a child protection plan is not judged to be essential, there may still be further work with the family. This intervention may be led by the relevant social worker or involve local family support services, including early years or school settings. The investigation will be written up in the family's file but no further steps will be taken within this child protection process.

Once a child protection plan is judged necessary (and in Scotland or Northern Ireland, if the child's name is placed on the register), other actions must follow:

- A core group is formed of the professionals most involved with the family. This group will not be very large and the aim is that it should not be unwieldy (see under Step 5 for more details).
- A named person has to take responsibility for this case and ensure that the necessary planning and further assessment are undertaken. This lead professional will most likely be a social worker.
- A child protection plan must now be developed specifically for this child. There are no off-the-shelf plans.

Usually, there is only one child protection case conference and the work is continued by the core group. Another case conference would only be called if there was evidence that procedures had not been properly followed. Another reason would be if it becomes clear that all the relevant information for the decision had not been shared at the time of the first conference.

Statistics about child protection

Statistics about the implementation of child protection are public information and data are gathered separately for England, Wales, Scotland and Northern Ireland. If you want to find out more, refer to the suggestions at the end of the chapter.

The NSPCC provides useful information on Statistics on Child abuse. See: www.nspcc.org.uk/search/?query=statistics

The main statistics record the numbers of children who have been placed on the child protection register, or now in England and Wales the number of children for whom there is a child protection plan. Statistics have been published for some time and there are some consistent themes:

- Across the UK there is what looks like a large total number of children and young people on the child protection registers or with a child protection plan. But this figure has to be put in context for the total child population: it represents two or three children per 1,000.
- The numbers on the registers or with a plan are not a final measure of child abuse or neglect. Not all children or young adolescents about whom there are concerns are necessarily judged to need a child protection plan. Considerably greater numbers of children and young people are referred to social care services. Some continue to the stage of initial assessment, but do not go beyond that point. They, may be stepped down to child in need processes and they, and their families, may still be receiving different types of support.
- The names on the registers do not remain constant. In many years, as many names have been taken off the register (de-registered) as have been added.
- In many cases, the child protection plan has worked to protect the children. However, concerns about some families do not go away: in some

years over a tenth of the names added to the register were for children or young people who had previously been registered.

Details of the child protection plan

In safe practice, professionals do not focus significant energy on identification and investigation of children at risk, but then let concerns dwindle. Children will be protected and helped through actions that follow. When faced with children at risk, the involved professionals have several options:

- They can start a child protection inquiry under the requirements set out in the relevant Children Act or Order. A comprehensive assessment of the child or young person will often prove to be important in identifying how best to help. The earlier investigation is made only to establish whether the child is being abused or at risk of abuse and to determine immediate actions.
- They can look at the possibilities within family support services. Each of the Children Acts and Orders in the UK is concerned with children in need as well as child protection. There are possibilities for support services covered in the legislation: Part III of the Children Act 1989, Part II of the Children (Scotland) Act 1995 and Part IV of the Children (Northern Ireland) Order 1996.

These options are not on an either/or basis. A child protection inquiry often leads to developing the use of family support services as the way to safeguard or promote the child's welfare. With younger children, the support services might include attendance with their parent(s) at a family centre, home support for parents or placement of children in a daily early-years setting, which can guarantee close attention to their development and well being.

Care proceedings

Early years, school and out-of-school practitioners are sometimes worried that a child protection investigation is very likely to mean that children will be taken away from their families. Parents can be very anxious that their children will be taken into care. However, in the great majority of cases, children and young people stay in their own home, even when concerns about abuse or neglect have been substantiated. Guidance is clear that children should remain with their family, unless there is clear evidence they can only be effectively protected elsewhere.

Emergency court orders are temporary measures and do not automatically lead to care proceedings. However, if children or young adolescents are assessed as being at serious risk, then more permanent steps will be taken. Social workers may apply for a Care Order, which starts the legal process of care proceedings: removal of a child or young person into the care of the local authority. If the order is successful, then children or adolescents have looked-after status: the local authority has assumed parental responsibility for them. Children may be placed in foster care or in a residential home. However, a minority of looked-after children remain with their own family, but under the close supervision of a social worker.

Families whose children are taken into care have long-standing difficulties, frequently from more than one factor. Problems that affect children's safety include serious mental-health problems, substance abuse, persistent domestic violence, a chaotic family lifestyle that leaves children consistently at risk, and an inability to cope with or control the child or young adolescent. Additionally, circumstances are such that it is very unlikely that parents, or other key family carers, will co-operate with support services. Sometimes a family may have received a great deal of support. Yet the circumstances for the children are no better and there is no prospect of improvement to ensure a child's safety and well being.

Pause for reflection

The need for everyone to understand how child protection really works was brought home in 2007, when a private family problem (in North Tyneside, England) became very public.

The predicament of Connor McCreaddie, eight years of age and weighing 14 stone, was reported in newspapers with headlines of 'Fat boy may be put into care' (*Sunday Times*, 25 February) and 'Mother's anger as obese boy, 8, faces care order' (*Guardian*, 26 February). Muddled reporting implied that removing children from their family was a prominent choice for social workers. *The Times* (26 February) went further, with the headline, 'Go on diet or be taken into care, 14-stone boy is told': a message that being taken from your family is used as a threat to children.

There was limited explanation of the significant role of family support within safeguarding, even in the briefer follow-up reports. The child protection conference, in North Tyneside, had decided that the best route was to continue to support Connor's mother and grandmother while he remained at home.

● Follow up this story on the internet, by typing Connor's name into a search engine such as Google. What do you think people who are not professionally involved at all in safeguarding may take away from these media stories?

● Connor's story became public property because his family decided to speak to their local newspaper, followed by GMTV, and to be filmed for the ITV programme *Tonight with Trevor Mcdonald* (broadcast on 26 February 2007). What do you think about this choice? What could be the impact on Connor himself, especially now that this child has a permanent presence on the internet, with images and YouTube videos?

Step 5: Meetings of the core group

The core group will consist of the lead professional (most likely a social worker) and other professionals directly relevant to this family. The group also includes the parent(s) and the children, if they are judged to be old enough to be involved. As with the child protection conference, there would have to be a very compelling reason for not inviting the parent(s). The core group meets on a regular basis (often about fortnightly) and should:

- meet after the initial child-protection conference if the child is the subject of a child protection plan;
- further develop the outline child-protection plan, based on assessment findings, and set out what needs to change, by how much, and by when in order for the child to be safe and have their needs met;
- decide what steps need to be taken, and by whom, to complete the in-depth assessment to inform decisions about the child's safety and welfare; and
- implement the child protection plan and take joint responsibility for carrying out the agreed tasks, monitoring progress and outcomes, and refining the plan as needed.

Assessment

Part of the child protection plan may be to make a comprehensive assessment of the child through the assessment framework used in this part of the UK. This action includes gathering information from all the agencies who know the child and family and can include a developmental and/or medical assessment of the child. Any assessment must also include the views and wishes of the children and young people themselves.

Any assessment directly involving the child must be undertaken with respectful concern for their physical care but also their feelings. This care applies to a developmental assessment, an interview or a medical examination. No assessment, at this stage or at the earlier investigation stage, should further add to a child's distress or feelings of being used or abused. Any collecting of evidence should always be balanced against avoiding further trauma to the child. Some public inquiries have made the specific point that children should not be subject to repetitive and long interviews, nor to repeated medical examinations.

Medical examinations would not always form part of the assessment of children at risk. This step would be undertaken for specific reasons, such as to:

- detect traumatic or infectious conditions;
- evaluate the nature of the abuse;
- provide evidence, including forensic proof;
- provide a developmental assessment that could constitute a benchmark on children's future health and development;
- reassure children who fear that the abuse has seriously damaged them physically and help in the process of recovery for an abused child.

A medical examination, including the use of technology such as X-rays, does not always produce clear-cut results, for instance about how an injury was caused or whether it is accidental or non-accidental, beyond reasonable doubt.

A comprehensive assessment is presented to the first-child protection review meeting or less often to a reconvened case conference. The core group is responsible for taking action on the basis of the assessment, always bearing in mind the child's wishes, feelings and perceptions.

Step 6: The child protection review conference

The purpose of the Child Protection Review conference is to:

- To review whether the child is continuing to suffer, or is likely to suffer, significant harm, and to review developmental progress against child-protection plan outcomes.
- To consider whether the child protection plan should continue or should be changed.

Children do not just remain with a child protection plan forever. The first review for a child is usually set for three months after the child protection conference, and then every six months. The point of the review is to assess whether a child protection plan is still necessary. This review involves all those with relevant information, including the parents and the older child or young person themselves.

The child protection plan is brought to a close (and the child's name is taken off the register) when the original factors that led to this high level of concern no longer apply. Specific examples include:

- The child or young person is still at home, but the risk is reduced through work with the family.
- The child is away from home and the source of harm.
- The alleged abuser – adult or young person – has gone from the home.
- Assessment and analysis show that child protection is no longer necessary.

In other cases the plan ceases if:

- The child has died of natural causes. If the death was suspicious, then there would have to be a child death investigation.
- The child and family have left the area and the area to which they have moved has assumed responsibility for the case.
- The individual who was previously at risk is no longer legally a child: they have passed their eighteenth birthday in England, Wales or Northern Ireland or their sixteenth in Scotland. Or they have married and are therefore viewed legally as an adult.
- A disabled young person might still need protection and support, but will now come under legislation to protect vulnerable adults.
- A review may decide that a child protection plan is no longer necessary. However, targeted support work can still continue with the child and family, involving whichever professionals and services are appropriate. The child and family may still need help, but the child or young person is judged to be no longer at risk.

Commentary on the scenarios

In each example, the commentary offers possibilities and suggestions. No commentary can act as detailed guidance for an actual situation that you face.

Sally (page 79)

It is good practice to listen to this mother's concerns and ensure that you understand what she is saying, including an invitation to 'say some more' about Sally's play with dolls. It would not be appropriate at this point either to agree or disagree with the perspective, nor to the mother's request. You should thank her for telling you her concerns and say that you will talk with your team.

Sally's mother has not made an allegation as such, but her worries need to be taken as seriously as if they were expressed by a practitioner in the team. There needs to be an internal discussion about the dynamics of the group room run by Richard and Jessica. Much will depend on whether there have already been concerns about Jessica's style with the children. It will be important to hear Richard's view before he leaves. If he has been silent about poor practice from his room colleague, then any nursery senior team should find out the reasons that Jessica's unacceptable style has not been challenged properly. Depending on the situation, this may be an occasion when supervision, clear direction, or even the early stages of disciplinary warnings may be necessary.

It is important that you get back to Sally's mother within no more than a few days. If there is an issue of poor practice, then this problem will not be resolved by moving one child. If you feel reassured that Sally's comments are not imitated from Jessica, then there may be reason to have a further conversation to help her mother consider the possible source.

Fazila (page 87)

It should be possible to join in Fazila's play through imagining 'what we can do' to make matters better for the doll. If Fazila makes the direct link to her own situation, then you can follow her lead.

Depending on your relationship with Fazila's mother, it may be possible to share this play as a way to highlight her daughter's feelings. If friendly support and suggestions for Fazila's mother fail to make much difference in the care of her daughter, it may be necessary to explore possibilities of family support that she would accept. If friendly persuasion does not bring any improvement, then you will need to explain to Fazila's mother that you wish to refer the family, because of your concerns about her daughter.

Olwyn (page 92)

As the practitioner, you are faced with a number of concerns, some of them vague. It is time to bring in the Designated Safeguarding Officer, and not only because Olwyn's teacher does not seem to be taking your concerns seriously. It is inappropriate to assume that any out-of-the-ordinary behaviour can be explained away by disability.

Olwyn's behaviour has changed in terms of her habit of masturbation, and the incident in the toilets raises concerns. You need to gather your thoughts, and make notes, with the help of the Designated Safeguarding Officer, including what, if anything, Olwyn said to you about what happened in the toilets today. If the boys have been involved in inappropriate activity, then their behaviour must also be addressed.

You need to untangle the strands around Olwyn's tendency to masturbate in the classroom and the conversations with her father. The Designated Safeguarding Officer should be able to support you as you think and talk through this aspect. If the behaviour were something different, for instance if Olwyn chewed her nails, do you think you would find the conversation repetitive rather than creating a sense of unease? Is there something about how the father speaks to you and, assuming you are female, in what way is the gender difference an issue? Is it a conversation that should happen out of the hearing of other children and yet this father starts talking in clear earshot of Olwyn's peers?

You need to be more specific about what feels wrong about the new driver. This unease and your other concerns need to be raised fully in a conversation with, ideally, both of Olwyn's parents. The Designated Safeguarding Officer will probably decide whether it makes more sense for you to take that meeting, with her or his support, because you are Olwyn's specialist teaching assistant (STA). The decision may be that the class teacher also needs to be directly involved, as well as informed about the next step.

Cameron (page 94)

It seems likely that something has happened to confuse and distress Cameron. It is tempting to consider his mother's new boyfriend as the source of risk. But Cameron has also recently spent three weeks with some of his mother's friends.

Cameron's mother seems unable to consider his emotional needs, so possibly he would not confide in her, or his worries might have been dismissed.

The school needs to tackle the issues with Cameron's mother. One issue arises from his refusal to go home with the boyfriend and this strong reaction needs to be addressed, with Cameron's needs to the forefront. Today, Cameron's teacher should telephone Becky and ask her to come for her son. It is almost certain that she is the only person who 'officially' can take responsibility for Cameron at the end of the school day.

Cameron's comment about people holding his 'willy' needs some exploration if he is comfortable to talk, perhaps with the male teacher with whom he has already raised the question. Another possibility would be to ensure that Cameron's class soon has a general session on appropriate touch, raising issues that concern Cameron, but in a way that does not put the spotlight on him.

The school needs to keep descriptive notes of Cameron's words and actions and of conversations with his mother that attempt to explore the situation.

Without reasonable reassurance from such conversations, the concerns about Cameron may have to be taken further. But so far the information is vague.

Kitty (page 97)

Any conversation with Kitty needs to be gentle and avoid leading questions. You could reflect back her comment with a question in your tone or add something such as, 'No more Grandad – is that a good thing, Kitty?' When Kitty scribbles over a figure, you could ask a non-specific question such as, 'Do tell me what you've done to your drawing.'

It is important not to assume that all of Kitty's play is related to the alleged abuse and to support her as you would any four-year-old. It will be appropriate to keep notes of Kitty's progress and careful descriptions of play and conversation. Much of this observation could be shared carefully with her mother. If the grandfather has been denied access to the family home, it seems likely that social care services have been involved. Depending on the current situation regarding child protection and Kitty, the designated safeguarding lead (or key person) might also need to continue to share relevant information with the social worker. Kitty's mother will understand that this careful professional communication will be ongoing.

Longmead Primary School (page 100)

The headteacher should take more seriously the consistent feedback from the children. It is a very negative message for children that their emotional distress about the swimming coach has been dismissed. Even if the coach proves to be no more than bad-tempered and insensitive, the children should be supported by the head in tackling his disrespectful outlook and actions.

The parents' concerns have also been dismissed and this is a poor approach to partnership. If the head insists on the extra coaching, it is likely that some parents will withdraw their children, out of appropriate concern, and the whole situation will sour school–home relations in a much broader way.

Ciaran (page 106)

Option 1. There are negative consequences to accepting the head's instruction, as passed on by the Designated Safeguarding Lead. There is a strong chance that Ciaran will stop confiding at all if he is blocked in this way. There is already concern about his home situation, so this possibility could raise, rather than reduce, the level of risk for Ciaran and his sister. In some schools, STAs are not shown the same respect as other team members and this different status may be a complicating issue here. But also the head may not understand that good practice in child protection shows respect for children's choice over disclosure.

There also needs to be consideration about contact with the parents. From Ciaran's comments there is concern that he and his sister could be at risk and that steps may need to be taken within child protection. But it could be very distressing for Ciaran, if the one person in whom he has confided is made inaccessible.

Option 2. Now there is a possibility that a more positive consequence could emerge for Ciaran. If you speak up rather than passively accept the instruction, you are behaving professionally as an STA and are keeping Ciaran's interests to the forefront. The Designated Safeguarding Officer/ Safeguarding Lead/Safeguarding Adviser needs to deal with the head's demand, explaining how she and you will work together. In the meantime, for Ciaran's sake it is important that you and the Designated Safeguarding Officer/Safeguarding Lead/Safeguarding Adviser find a way of working which respects Ciaran's choice. If a compromise is unavoidable, then perhaps ask Ciaran if the Designated Safeguarding Officer/Safeguarding Lead/ Safeguarding Adviser could be present for a conversation.

All team members should be enabled to deal with possible disclosures, so that a child is not 'passed on' from the person to whom they have chosen to speak. It is appropriate that adults explain to children when and why the information has to be shared with somebody else.

Monica (page 113)

It is respectful that practitioners follow the family diet. However, partnership with parents has boundaries set by your responsibility for children's well being. There are health risks when a diet removes many sources of nutrition, and young children have different nutritional needs from adults. Babies and toddlers have become very ill; some have died from extremely restricted diets.

It would be appropriate to attempt at least one further conversation with the mother. The childminder needs to get across that she is concerned professionally about the current and future well being of both children. But if there is no progress, then it would be necessary to see if the mother is willing to listen to informed advice from another professional, perhaps the health visitor responsible for the baby. If there is still no progress, it would be appropriate for the childminder to talk with the local childminding adviser about the situation.

If Monica's mother acts on her threat to find another childminder, this conversation should definitely take place. It is important that this family does not get 'lost'. If Monica's long-term childminder is rejected by the mother, that action raises the level of concern. The childminder and adviser might decide that a referral to social care services was the only safe way forward.

Sergio (page 114)

This kind of behaviour is not usual for a four-year-old and should not simply be dismissed. The team has coped by reducing Sergio's opportunities for inappropriate behaviour, but they have not dealt properly with his actions. The team has also generated a spurious cultural explanation that needs challenge. It is not acceptable for practitioners to stereotype any national or ethnic group.

Without further information, it is not possible to know how Sergio learned that it is acceptable to impose on women in this way. He may have observed inappropriate touching or heard adult conversations that are dismissive of women. At the moment, the concerned practitioner does not know. As a new arrival to the team, this practitioner needs to find the confidence to raise this problem, most likely with the Designated Safeguarding Officer/ Safeguarding Lead/Safeguarding Adviser for the setting. If that person is equally dismissive, then the practitioner should go to the manager.

There need to be firm boundaries set for Sergio's behaviour, with an explanation that is suitable for a four-year-old. The team needs to act in a consistent way to monitor whether his behaviour does change. There also needs to be a proper conversation with his parents about the behaviour, the legitimate concerns that it raises and how the setting is now dealing with Sergio's actions. Any further steps would depend on the parents' reactions.

Rory (page 114)

Rory's parents are fully responsible for him when he is at home and they should balance their home and work commitments in a way that keeps their son safe and happy. Rory's mother needs to be reminded that the nursery is responsible for tracking injuries to the children. It is also fair for Rory's key person to say that toddlers need careful watching and to be engaged in safe activities.

It may be possible to have a friendly conversation about work–life balance. But it is not for the nursery to be apologetic about their hours; Rory's parents accepted the time boundaries to the service. The family may need a different kind of childcare, probably a live-in nanny, if their work commitments continue at this high level. Depending on the relationship with Rory's mother, the key person might be able to talk around a greater involvement of Rory's father. But it is not the nursery's responsibility to sort out frustrations between the adults.

If Rory continues to have many minor accidents at home, this is a situation in which it would be very useful to be able to talk in general with an adviser or a social worker who will accept conversation without formal referral.

Yvette (page 114)

You may disapprove of Yvette's style of dress. But that is not club business unless her clothes are unsafe for play, in which case a conversation with her mother could be about practical clothes. An exception would be if Yvette's tops had an image or slogan seriously inappropriate for a young girl.

Yvette's comments about Martin would probably be at a lower level of concern without the incident with your male colleague. (Female readers should bear in mind that men are as alert to out-of-the-ordinary movements on their lap as females are to deliberate groping.) It is important not to link the two strands together by any assumptions about Martin. If something untoward has happened in Yvette's life, it is not certain that Martin is implicated. A conversation with Yvette's mother could include a comment that her daughter seems enthused about 'Martin' and imply a friendly question about his place in the family.

It would be wise to be alert to Yvette and notice if her behaviour suggests an inappropriate intimacy with male practitioners or boys in the club. If the same kind of incident is repeated, then the club team will need to talk with her mother about their concerns. Any further steps will depend on her reply.

School-age children do not stop wanting to be physically close to familiar adults. The value of a good after-school club for tired children includes the chance to snuggle up for a chat or a shared book. As children get older, some teams take the option of welcoming children to be close and enjoy a sideways cuddle. Older children sit next to a practitioner, but not on a lap. The comments about physical contact on page 207 allow for adjustments as children get older, without encouraging paranoia about touch.

Marsha (page 114)

It would be right to intervene in the play, following the lead of the other child. Marsha could be helped to comfort the baby appropriately and you could make non-critical comments about how careful everyone has to be with babies.

Since there has already been contact with the social worker, it would be appropriate to share this observation, either in the upcoming meeting or to integrate into the written report that the playgroup should contribute to the child protection inquiry that is underway. Everyone has to take care not to over-interpret children's play and conversations. But this incident has the look and sound of a child imitating what she has observed.

Summary

This chapter details the steps that should be taken if you have a concern about a child's welfare and the child protection processes that are followed in accordance with statutory policy guidance.

Anyone who has concerns about a child's welfare should make a referral to local-authority children's social care. For example, referrals may come from: children themselves, teachers, a GP, the police, health visitors, family members and members of the public. Within local authorities, children's social care should act as the principal point of contact for welfare concerns relating to children. Therefore, as well as clear protocols for professionals working with children, contact details should be signposted clearly so that children, parents and other family members are aware of who they can contact if they require advice and/or support.

Key texts

There is more information on mental health available from:

www.thesite.org/mental-health/self-harm

www.mentalhealth.org.uk

Marsh, P. (2009) *Family Group Conferences,* Highlight no. 248, London: National Children's Bureau

Street, C. (2011) *Self-harm and Children and Young People,* Highlight No. 263, London: National Children's Bureau

Department of Health (2014) *Closing the Gap: Priorities for Essential Change in Mental Health,* London: Department of Health. Available online at: www.gov.uk/government/uploads/system/uploads/attachment_data/file/281250/Closing_the_gap_V2_-_17_Feb_2014.pdf

Find out more

www.nspcc.org.uk/Inform/publications/publications_wda48207.html
The NSPCC offers useful fact sheets, such as 'An introduction to child protection legislation in the UK' and 'An introduction to the child protection system', at this webpage.

www.caeuk.org
Children Act Enterprises publish pocket-sized guides, mainly applicable for England and Wales.

www.nspcc.org.uk/Inform/policyandpublicaffairs/wales/guidance/guidance
Practitioners working in Wales can explore through the links provided here.

www.scotland.gov.uk
For information particular to Scotland, search by 'child protection' on the home page.

www.dhsspsni.gov.uk
If you want to know about Northern Ireland, search by 'child protection' on this site.

5 Equality practice and safeguarding

Introduction

Daily practice can bring situations that are not straightforward to resolve and which present competing priorities arising from concerns about equality. It is expected that the laws and guidance about child protection will be put into practice with active respect for all sources of diversity. However, concerns for equality and respect for traditions of any kind cannot overrule the obligation to protect children and young people.

This chapter discusses key issues for gender and disability, cultural background and faith, cultural traditions that challenge protection and the implications for effective safeguarding practice.

Key issues for gender and disability

Equality practice applicable to all groups in society requires that safeguarding does not rest on unacceptable or unsafe assumptions.

Male practitioners

Considerably more wariness and outright suspicion are expressed about men than women in paid or voluntary work involving children. Male team members are also, in some settings and services, given informal (if not official) job descriptions that differ from those of their female colleagues. There are some men working in early years who do not undertake any personal care of children. The rationale for this differentiation is sometimes that at least one parent has objected to a man changing a baby or young child. But sometimes the rationale is that men are more vulnerable to allegations of abuse, so, the argument follows, a different role is needed in order to protect this male practitioner.

On the basis of reliable statistics, sexual abuse is the only area of child abuse or neglect in which men predominate. Otherwise, the stance 'Most abusers are men, so ...' is ill-informed. Men do not outnumber women in terms of emotional or physical abuse or neglect. Furthermore, although most identified sex abusers are male, most men do not sexually abuse children or young people. The prosecution of Vanessa George in 2010, for sexually abusing young children in the Plymouth day nursery where she worked, was a sharp wake-up call for anyone who still insisted that the danger, if it came, would be from a male. The internet ring to which George contributed her images of abuse was led by a man, but included other women.

It is hard to see reluctance to employ men, or deciding to give them a different care role from female colleagues, as anything other than gender discrimination against males. It is an equality issue. Problems arise because an 'Everybody knows' atmosphere has developed in which parents may express unease about a male childminder, or male colleague, in a nursery or school team. Media reports also focus on the statistically less frequent dangers to children, such as abduction and murder by non-family members. Child homicides by parents tend to be perpetrated about equally by a child's mother or father. However, it is more often males who are responsible for the murder of a child, if the act is committed by someone other than the child's parents.

Effective partnership with families has to acknowledge any unease, but problems have to be resolved by reassuring parents about the checks made on all practitioners before they join a team, or are allowed to work as a childminder or foster carer. Good standards of care and personal contact with children have to apply to all members of staff. Nor can any individual parent's worry about men be resolved by creating a situation in which all practitioners keep their distance from children. Such a practice undermines children's well being (see page 207).

Some settings are concerned that male practitioners may be especially vulnerable to false allegations about sexual abuse from children, young people or their family. Again, it is hard to see how a different informal job description for men is the best response to unacceptable behaviour from service users. Poorly supported allegations are made about other kinds of abuse and neglect, against female as well as male practitioners. Settings and services need a robust approach to allegations that prove to be false, irrespective of whoever is accused (see page 189).

Family preferences

Issues about male practitioners in the team can also arise because a child's family feels strongly that females should undertake any personal care. This stance may be linked with the family's cultural tradition or faith, but is not limited to parents whose identity would be classified as minority ethnic group. Ideally, any team needs to have thought through this potential dilemma before they are faced with a direct request for a female carer. Settings have made different decisions, but our considered support goes to those who take a full equality approach.

The head or key person, if the child has already started in the setting, needs to explain that all team members have the same role. So it is not possible to restrict a male practitioner from appropriate caring contact with any child in the setting. Families can use the childminding service if, for whatever reason, they want to be sure that only a female will be involved in the personal care of their child. Otherwise, settings create problems for daily practice, especially if one family's request is granted, on the basis of faith or minority cultural background, but other families are deemed not to have a 'good enough' reason.

Disability and health of practitioners

Employment law requires that applicants for any job are not discounted as possible candidates on the grounds of disability or ill-health, unless there is good reason to argue that this person's condition means that they cannot fulfil key responsibilities in this job. The same requirement applies to people who are already in post and whose physical or mental health changes. Equality law requires employers to make reasonable adjustments when minor changes could enable a well-qualified candidate or existing employee to be effective in this job. Employers are not required to make disproportionate adjustments, although the boundary is not always clear.

Managers of group settings are responsible for ensuring that every team member is able to behave in ways that keep children safe from harm, as well as experiencing happy and productive days. Individual practitioners, in a team or working alone like childminders, share the responsibility to ensure that their mental and physical health is sufficient to ensure children's safety and well being. Practitioners should seek medical advice, and their manager make sure this happens, if prescribed medication could affect their concentration or overall fitness to take good care of babies or children.

The vulnerability of disabled children

Many people hope that disabled children will be relatively safe from abuse or neglect. It is often assumed that high standards for their care, and support for their family, will be available to safeguard children. Unfortunately, they can be more vulnerable than their peers for the following reasons:

● Children may need more personal physical care because of physical disabilities, or they continue to need help at an older age because of severe learning disabilities. Such care can, of course, be offered with respect and consideration. But disabled children are vulnerable to anything from poor standards to deliberate abuse of their need for intimate care.
● Unsupported and exhausted parents, or other carers, may snap under the relentless pressure of a very high need for care, with no respite, especially when their sleep is constantly disturbed.
● Intrusive medical procedures, necessary for some conditions, may leave children with an underdeveloped sense of their own privacy or bodily

dignity. Abusive behaviour by adults or young people may not appear to be out of the ordinary or worthy of complaint.

● Children can have a high number of carers because of their condition or because they attend different specialist facilities. The risk is then that children learn that intrusive attention by relative strangers is a 'normal' part of their life.

● Children may not have developed a conceptual framework for making sense of what is done to them: appropriate and inappropriate touch, a sense of personal privacy and their right to express preferences. Limitations may be less related to the actual disability than to how carers have shaped the experience of the child.

● Children can be made vulnerable in a situation where there is no key adult responsible for closely monitoring their overall care. Good practice guidelines for working with children and their families have regularly stressed the importance of a lead professional, as well as a child's committed parent, to avoid a patchwork of care and support. Good standards of practice in care will support disabled children just as much as their peers.

The impact of disability

The details of a child or young person's disability may complicate their ability to disclose what is happening to them:

● Children with learning disabilities may have difficulty in telling a trusted parent or carer that something is happening to them that is wrong.

● Children with severe communication disabilities may have difficulty in communicating that they are in physical pain, arising from non-accidental injury. There has been more general concern that profoundly disabled children may experience chronic pain that goes unrecognised by their carers. This situation complicates the interpretation of behaviour patterns that are explained as part of their disability, yet arise at least in part because the child is never free of pain.

● A high level of physical disability may literally make it harder for children to resist an abuser who ill-treats them physically or sexually.

● The care and education of some disabled children may mean that they are in a residential setting, perhaps some distance from home. They can be vulnerable to institutional abuse in a closed community, with very limited opportunity to disclose to family or other people external to the setting.

● When children's care and educational arrangements cause them to be isolated and less able to make friends easily, they can also be vulnerable to wanting to please their carers and less likely to object.

● Some forms of abuse may actually cause disability or serious ill-health, or worsen an existing condition. An abusive or potentially abusive situation may be difficult to distinguish from the child's condition.

Risky assumptions by adults

Parents, practitioners and other professionals may hold unchecked beliefs, some of them offensive, which put children and young people at greater risk.

- Adults may assume that nobody would abuse a disabled child, because they cannot believe that someone could be so cruel. In the case of sexual abuse, they may reject the possibility that anyone would want to become sexually involved with a disabled individual.
- Behaviour and communication that would usually raise concerns may be pushed to one side. The assumption may be that any 'odd' habits are part of the disability or that sexualised reactions are 'normal'.
- Adults may fail to communicate with children about appropriate physical touch, using a suitable vocabulary of words and signs (see also page 96). So children have little basis for judging and rejecting dubious behaviour from someone else. The mistaken assumption may be that children are within a protected environment, so abuse cannot possibly occur.
- When unacceptable practice has been allowed to grow, practitioners feel that maltreatment matters less and that disabled children are unaware or soon forget.

Consistent practice in safeguarding

Effective equality practice meets reliable child protection when the same basic procedures are followed for disabled children as for any individuals about whom concerns have been raised.

Key messages:

- Any assumptions arising from disability need to be checked rather than assumed to be correct.
- Appropriate support needs to be given to the children so that they can better communicate about their experience and express their wishes and preferences.
- Careful decisions need to be taken when a child needs an interpreter to support communication. The individual's specialist teacher or residential worker may appear to be the obvious choice. However, this is an unwise option if there are already concerns that practitioners may be implicated in the abuse, or are very reluctant to consider the possibility.
- Some disabled children cause trouble for their peers through physical bullying or inappropriate sexual activity. An environment of risk is created from mistaken beliefs that disabled children would not act in a bullying way, or could not become young abusers.

Helena

You run a holiday support group for carers of children with disability. Five-year-old Helena has recently started to attend with her childminder. Helena has mild learning and physical disabilities and her family is still distressed that their daughter is not 'normal'. Her parents seem to find it hard to place boundaries on her behaviour. Helena's childminder follows the family line that 'the poor little girl' can not be expected to behave like other children.

Helena has a soft voice and sweet smile, but you are beginning to think that she deliberately hurts other children under the cover of giving them a cuddle in play. A couple of incidents also make you consider that Helena is adept at 'setting up' other children, so they break the group rules and get into trouble. You want to address the situation, without overreacting. You want to be realistic about the ways in which Helena's disability may genuinely limit her understanding.

- What would concern you for the child in this situation?
- What might be complicating factors for practitioners to consider?
- What should probably be your first step now?

You will find a commentary on page 162.

Cultural background and faith

Practitioners are possibly most anxious about making a wrong decision when there are differences of ethnic group, faith or cultural background. Safeguarding depends on well-informed and reflective practice; complex situations can require tough decisions.

Awareness of and respect for diversity

All practitioners need a broad base of knowledge in order to make sensible and properly supported judgements. The idea of what is 'normal' is certainly not explained just by what you know from your own childhood experiences of your family or those of your friends. All practitioners, whatever cultural and ethnic background, have to make the effort to extend their knowledge of different family traditions and ways of raising children.

- An awareness of cultural diversity in approaches to childcare has to be part of a more general awareness that adults vary in how they deal with children and young people, in the family and other situations.
- Some parents may be less demonstrative than you in their dealing with children. Less overt affection does not necessarily mean that an adult cares less about a child; people have different ways of showing that they care. Alternatively, you may feel some parents are too emotional with their children for your taste and upbringing.

- None of these differences may relate to cultural traditions; some may be linked with particular families and their personal style. However, if you do not share a culture with a parent, or you know that you differ in religious beliefs, it is easy to assume that the different patterns arise from that group difference. This explanation may or may not be valid.
- Cultural tradition is a strong influence on how parents raise their children and treat sons and daughters. All families are affected by the social and cultural environment in which they live. Culture is not something that 'happens' only for people within minority ethnic groups or faiths.

Take another perspective

Think carefully about three or four families whom you know well and who share your own cultural background (or faith, if you prefer). These may be families you know through work or through personal contact.

- If someone from a very different background met these families, do you think it would be accurate to take them as representative of your culture (or faith)?
- In what ways could it be misleading to generalise from these families without further experience?

All professionals need a firm foundation of knowledge. Everyone must avoid believing 'I know all about … ' based on information taken from a very small sample. Knowing a few families with a particular cultural, national or faith background does not provide a safe basis for broad knowledge about this group. Practitioners whose national background is English or Welsh would be unimpressed by assumptions that they were much the same as people from any country picked from Europe. Yet people sometimes believe that contact with a few families from the continent of India is enough to be able to talk about 'Indian families'. There is tremendous diversity in culture, faith and social status within the large group of families within the UK who are of Indian origin. Practitioners are not helped by the slap-dash tendency in some written materials to talk about Africa as if it were a single, small country. In fact, Africa is a huge continent with many distinct countries that vary between, and within, themselves in ethnic group, language, cultural traditions and faith.

Make the connection with…

Behaviour under stress

A broad base of knowledge needs to grow from different sources. It is especially important to take care not to develop your beliefs about any culture or faith from contact with families who are under stress. When experiencing some form of crisis, families do not usually behave in the way that is normal for them in calmer times, let alone typical of the social group, culture or faith to which they belong.

Patterns of childcare

It is regarded as common family practice in the UK that mothers take the primary responsibility for children, although there is much more variation in this pattern than a couple of generations ago. There is also considerably more informal sharing of care than is often acknowledged, between friends and within families whose country of origin is the UK. However, in some cultures – for instance, families from a range of countries within Africa and the Caribbean – it is more usual that the care of children is shared between relatives, who are probably female.

Within these same cultures, it has been accepted practice to leave some or all of the children with the extended family, while one or both parents go elsewhere in search of work, sometimes at a considerable distance. This pattern was continued by some West African families in the UK who sought long-term private fostering for their children, within the UK, while they worked or completed studies. A reverse pattern is also accepted in some cultures, in which children are entrusted to a relative living in another part of the country or another country altogether. The aim with this arrangement is to offer a better life to the child, who leaves the immediate family home.

Case study

Natasha

Natasha is just four years old and her family came to England from Jamaica when her mother was still a child. Natasha lives with her mother and two aunts. Other relatives live within two streets of her home. You have become increasingly concerned because neither you nor Natasha ever knows who will pick her up from nursery class and some days it is up to half an hour after the end of nursery before anyone arrives. Natasha always recognises the person and seems content to go but has said to you, 'I wish Mummy or Auntie Tess would pick me up.'

This week the arrangements for Natasha have become even less predictable. On two mornings you found her in the main school playground when you came to work, an hour before any child should arrive. You spoke with the aunt who arrived in the afternoon and she said, 'I can't help it. I have to get to work and you're here anyway, aren't you?'

In the middle of the week, the school caretaker strikes up a conversation with you about Natasha. He recounts, 'They live three doors down from us. Poor little soul, nobody watches out for her. One evening she was wandering on the pavement in her nightie until one of them shouts out the window at her. A lot of weekends she knocks on the door to come in and play with our two and that's fine by us. So, the wife phones up and half the time Natasha's mum doesn't even know she's gone and the aunties think my wife's odd for calling anyway. These people don't know how to look after kids properly. Now my wife is home with ours … '.

- What are the main issues in this situation?
- What do you think should be the next steps?

You will find a commentary on page 163.

Delegating the parenting role across any extended care system depends on a high level of trust in the commitment and kind intentions of the substitute parent(s). If that trust is abused, then the child's family may not be close enough to realise the dangers. A long-standing cultural tradition within the UK, for some social groups, has been to entrust children as young as seven years of age to non-family adults for considerable parts of the year at a location sometimes far from home: the boarding school system. Some children seem to have enjoyed, or at least tolerated, their experience of residential care and education. But this practice has continued in some families despite children's protestations that they were very unhappy. Alternatively, some children have simply not spoken of their feelings about the separation, believing that there was no other choice.

Legislation and guidance about safeguarding children and young people do not specify the details of exactly how they should be raised. The laws set a template that requires respect for family life and parents' decisions, from whatever basis, so long as those decisions do not damage children's development and well being.

● It would be unacceptable for a practitioner to criticise a shared-care family system on the grounds that 'it should be the mother' who provides care. On the other hand, any way of organising family life must work for the safety and well being of the child. A shared-care system can fail children just as some mothers, or fathers, in sole charge have neglected their children.
● Any professional involved with families should be concerned about the quality of care for children in the extended family, any private fostering arrangements and also any kind of residential accommodation where children and young people live away from the family home for extended periods of time.

Keep the child in mind

The public inquiry led by Lord Laming reported on the events that led to the death of Victoria Climbié and made clear-cut recommendations. In section 16.10 of that report, it was clearly stated: 'The basic requirement that children are kept safe is universal and cuts across cultural boundaries. Every child living in this country is entitled to be given the protection of the law, regardless of his or her cultural background. Cultural heritage is important to many people, but it cannot take precedence over standards of childcare embodied in the law.'

One of many failures in professional contact with Victoria was an assumption by the social work team that the harsh behaviour of her great-aunt was 'normal' for the family's cultural background.

Find out more

Brodie, I. and Shaw, C. (2010) *Private Foster Care Highlight No 260*, London: National Children's Bureau

The Victoria Climbié Inquiry (2003) *Part Five: Working with Diversity* www.dh.gov.uk/en/Publicationsandstatistics/Publications/PublicationsPolicyAndGuidance/DH_4008654

www.nspcc.org.uk/search/?query=Culture
The NSPCC also provides useful resources about culture.

Pause for reflection

How will you make sure that you maintain a child-focused approach at all times and meet cultural needs, yet at the same time ensure that the child is safe?

Willingness to challenge assumptions

Careful attention to equality practice is part of general good professional practice across childhood. Effective safeguarding practice has to integrate a willingness to address unsupported assumptions, yet in ways that enable practitioners to reflect and rethink.

● It is unacceptable and inaccurate to assume that particular kinds of families are more, or less, likely to abuse or neglect their children. Reviews of child protection have made it crystal clear that damage, as well as safe upbringing and treatment, occurs in every possible social, cultural or faith group.

● It would be a racist outlook to dismiss a family's competence with 'These people don't take care of their children'. This stark view should be challenged by colleagues, senior staff or advisers. Such practitioners are expressing bigoted attitudes, regardless of their own cultural identity, or faith, and the specific identity of 'these people'.

● Good-quality practice for equality may be a particular struggle for practitioners when there is ill-feeling within a local neighbourhood on the basis of ethnic group, cultural background or faith. The necessary challenge of decent professional practice is to step aside from a poisonous atmosphere, however long-standing.

Practitioner outlook and anxiety

It is crucial to approach each child or young person and their family as individuals, alongside a commitment to understand more about this family pattern. Practitioners often need support in exploring their concerns when they do not share a cultural or faith identity with the family. In particular, some practitioners may be so anxious about an accusation of being racist that they fail to express even serious concerns. No practitioner should have to think through complex, sensitive issues on their own. A senior practitioner, the designated safeguarding lead or mentor (see page 104) should help you to reflect on the situation, including your own uneasy feelings, and the basis of your concerns.

The inquiry into the death of Victoria Climbié (Laming, 2003) raised the reluctance of some professionals to express concerns about a child when they did not share the same ethnic group identity and skin colour as the family. An atmosphere that creates such fears does not represent good equality practice and, in this specific case, was one of many contributing factors in the avoidable death of a young girl. The Laming report (Laming, 2003) also raised a different, although related, issue about the discomfort faced sometimes by professionals from minority ethnic groups. Practitioners may feel judged as unsympathetic to families with whom they 'should' have much in common and maybe 'should' protect against an ignorant majority community. The obligation of accurate knowledge, compassion and professional objectivity with detachment is a requirement for everyone.

Case study

Abbas

Abbas is 10 years old and attends your primary school, with his sister Nneka, who is seven years old. Both children appear happy, well cared for and attend school regularly. You and your colleagues have become aware that Abbas seems to carry a great deal of responsibility for Nneka. He accompanies her to school and home each day and deals with any messages for her class teacher. Abbas stays on the school premises if his sister has an after-school activity, but has declined chess club for himself, with the explanation that he has to get Nneka home and organise a meal. You have also heard through the parent grapevine that children who invite Abbas round to tea always have Nneka as well. There seems to be no option, even at the weekend.

You and your colleagues are concerned not to appear to criticise Abbas's parents, although you feel that he is carrying undue responsibility for a 10-year-old. There is no direct cause for concern about either child, although a few comments from Nneka have made you wonder if Abbas sometimes has sole responsibility well into the evening. This year Abbas will move on to secondary school and the transition will involve a much longer daily trip for him to bring Nneka to primary school. You wonder whether to raise the issue with his parents and in what way.

- Do you have any concerns about either child in this situation?
- What might be the complicating factors for practitioners to consider?
- What should probably be your next step?

You will find a commentary on page 163.

Genuine knowledge

Team leaders in any setting, as well as professions such as social work, need to be clear about appropriate experience and knowledge. For example, practitioners of Caribbean origin will not automatically be better equipped than a 'white' Scottish colleague to relate to a Somali refugee family. Practitioners whose country of origin is China will not speak the same language as every family from that very large country. It would be appropriate use of a team member's skills, if that person shares a fluent language with a parent otherwise ill at ease or limited in what could be expressed in English. However, practitioners need to speak up if they find themselves expected to have unrealistic levels of knowledge on the basis of culture, religion or simply their skin colour.

Make the connection with...

Reflective practice

Policy and procedures for child protection are not isolated from other aspects of your work. For instance, in full-day early years settings it is important that children get out with staff on regular local trips and that practical risk assessment (for each type of outing) ensures that children are safe. A nursery policy should be clear that children visit public places such as the library or the park but are never taken to a private home. But safe practice on outings also includes that the organisation of an outing has the child's interest at the centre. Practitioners should engage with babies and children; it would be bad practice if adults talked endlessly with each other or on their mobile phones (see also page 36).

Unchecked beliefs can be wrong and may put children at risk. Ill-informed assumptions might be bigoted on the basis of ethnic group or faith, but are not inevitably so. Any beliefs about a family need to be checked through discussion and support for practitioners in any setting or service. For instance, a practitioner might assume a lone parent will be without any family back-up. Yet some lone parents have an effective network of family and friends. In contrast, perhaps another practitioner assumes, without asking, that the struggling Indian mother will be fine 'because all Asians live in an extended family, don't they?' But this mother may be on her own without any possible family support, or feel for some reason that she cannot access help from family and friends.

- You need to be ready to ask yourself, 'What is my basis for assuming this?' or 'What makes me so sure?' and accept similar questions from colleagues, including support workers.
- The same process applies if concerns are dismissed with 'It's about partnership. We're respecting the faith of families who attend this nursery'

or 'I share this cultural tradition and you don't understand anything about it.' Concerns about a child's welfare are more important than adult sensibilities. It would be unprofessional if a colleague refused to discuss the issues.

● Professional dialogue is ready to consider 'What is the impact of this family's preference on the child's safety?' Timely discussion in the team can clarify how to explain concerns to parents, who may disagree that there is any problem. Colleagues have to be ready to answer, 'Please explain to me why I should not be worried about ...' .

● All teams, or confidential professional meetings, need an atmosphere in which colleagues have the mental and emotional space to backtrack in a constructive way. They should not have to choose between defensive silence or going on the verbal attack because their stance has attracted heavy criticism.

Find out more

Lindon, J. (1999) *Understanding World Religions in Early Years Practice*, London: Hodder and Stoughton
Lindon, J. (2012) *Equality and Inclusion for Children and Families: Linking Theory and Practice*, London: Hodder Education
The Victoria Climbié Inquiry (2003) chaired by Lord Laming, especially Part Five: Working with Diversity.

Cultural traditions that challenge protection

The 'handshake' between equality practice and safeguarding is a delicate balance. You should not reject other ways of child rearing because it is not your culture's way, but neither is a practice made acceptable because it is associated with a long tradition. Children from a wide variety of different cultural backgrounds can be, and have been, damaged by their family's actions or inaction. Some traditions are regarded as justified and necessary by those who follow them, despite the risks for children.

Hitting children

If you listen to everyday conversation, or discussion on radio or television, you will hear adults speaking who believe that it is fine to hit children. Some would rather avoid this action, but are puzzled about what else to do. Some adults express what sounds like enthusiasm and persistently link the right to hit children with the need for discipline. (Supporters tend to prefer the word 'smack'.)

The case against hitting children

There has been a long tradition within the UK, and in other countries around the world, of an adult's right to hit children. Beliefs run deep within cultures and are sometimes justified from tenets of a faith. A strong counter-tradition developed over the last decades of the twentieth century for professional involvement with children, as well as an approach to family life.

- The core of the argument is a moral stance. UK society does not approve of adults settling disputes and imposing their wishes through physical maltreatment of other people. In law, this behaviour against adults is called assault or domestic violence; it is wrong to treat young citizens in this way.
- The practical links are that there are respectful and effective alternatives to hitting when adults need to deal with children's behaviour. The same point applies when an adult is scared by a child's unsafe actions that put them in danger.
- Hitting gives children the clear message that physical means are an acceptable way to settle arguments or express anger and frustration. Adults are setting a bad example through their behaviour.
- Supporters use bizarre phrases such as 'a gentle smack' or 'loving tap'. But hitting children is rarely calm and gets easily out of control. A disturbing rationale underlies claims that hitting can be an expression of affection.

Adults, as parents and practitioners, need to consider their attitudes as well as their actions. Childhood experiences can muddle adult thinking, as people struggle to reconcile the fact that parents, whom they love, raised them in an era when it was socially more acceptable to hit children. Times have changed and some adults have to address their feelings of 'My parents smacked me and it didn't do me any harm!' The questions have to be: 'What good did it do me?' and 'Was there really no other way that I could have learned how to behave?'

Case study

Ann-Marie

This three-year-old girl has attended your nursery for nearly five months. Her parents were initially doubtful about the nursery's behaviour policy and expressed vague reservations based on their Christian faith. Her father has since made several comments that children need more discipline than the nursery provides; for example: 'You don't understand. Children need firm guidance and our daughter is very wilful.'

Ann-Marie came in last week with severe bruising to her bottom, which became obvious because she winced when she sat at the table to play. In reply to a gentle question, Ann-Marie said a few words about an 'accident on the stairs'. When you asked her father about the bruises, he confirmed that Ann-Marie had slipped on the stairs but was otherwise evasive, saying, 'I don't know, she was coming down too fast. We've told her so often to be more careful.'

$\Rightarrow$

Ann-Marie did not return to the nursery for three days, by which time she no longer seemed to be in pain. Today you notice red marks on Ann-Marie's palms and she is unwilling to explain what has happened beyond that she was 'very naughty'. At pick-up time Ann-Marie's mother is initially apologetic about an unspecified 'accident' to her daughter. Then she blurts out, 'Anyway, my husband says you should respect our beliefs and what we do in our own home.' Then she rushes off with Ann-Marie.

● What would concern you for the child in this situation?
● What might be the complicating factors for practitioners to consider?
● What should probably be your next step?

You will find a commentary on page 164.

The law and hitting children

Legislation throughout the UK has removed the option of using corporal punishment (hitting and other forms of direct physical discipline) on children in all public establishments and registered services.

National governments in the UK have resisted introducing the same legal protection against assault for children that exists for adults. Many other European countries have taken this legal step, alongside public education campaigns to create a climate in which adults guide children's behaviour in non-physical ways. An anomaly has remained for families in the UK because law in each of the four nations still allows parents, or other family members such as a step-parent, to hit children and adolescents. Informal carers or those running special classes, such as for religious instruction, are seen legally as having temporary parental authority (*in loco parentis*) and are covered by the same exception as children's parents.

Roger Singleton submitted a report to the Labour government in 2010, *Physical Punishment: Improving Consistency and Protection*, in which he recommended that the ban on any kind of physical punishment in schools should be extended to cover any kind of part-time educational settings or classes to which parent send children.

As discussed in Chapter 1, in 1991 the UK central government signed the United Nations Convention on the Rights of the Child 1989. Several of the articles within the Convention aim to secure children's rights to be protected from physical or mental violence. The UN Committee on the Rights of the Child (which monitors the Convention) has recommended prohibiting physical punishment in families and the active change of social attitudes that support it. The Committee has stated several times (1995, 2002 and 2006) that the UK government approach to limit, rather than remove, this parental right was a failure to comply with the Convention. No nation within the UK has taken this final step, although changes have included the following:

- The Criminal Justice (Scotland) Act 2002 provides the concept of 'justifiable assault' when parents, or others in a parental role in the family, hit under-16s. The Act lists various forms of attack that are not acceptable under the law. However, if parents hit their 17-year-old, it becomes the crime of assault.
- The Children Act 2004, for England and Wales, replaced the phrase 'reasonable chastisement' with 'reasonable punishment' and offered the alleged protection that adult actions should not be so violent as to leave a visible injury or create lasting physical or mental damage. In effect, parents are permitted to use physical punishment up to the level of common assault.
- A clear stand has been taken in Wales that children should be brought under the same legal protection against assault as adults. *Children and Young People: Rights to Action* (Welsh Assembly, 2002) sets out a commitment to lobby Westminster and use public education to guide parents to alternatives for discipline.
- The Law Reform (Miscellaneous Provisions) (NI) Order 2006 brought the laws in Northern Ireland in line with the legal situation for England and Wales.

Make the connection with...

Your own values and beliefs and your ground rules

Any setting will have a ground rule that nobody hits anybody within the boundaries of your 'territory'. Sensible teams, childminders, nannies and foster carers also support children to use words: to tell another child to stop or to resolve common problems that need negotiation within play.

Regardless of the legal situation about parents hitting children in their own home, practitioners can take a firm line of 'not here'. Even if a child has passed from your responsibility to that of their parent, or other family carer, you cannot ignore the situation if that adult hits, or otherwise roughly handles, a child within your hearing and sight. Doing nothing gives the message that you agree with the action, or are only confident to take children to task for hitting each other.

It is important, ideally right at the time, to go up to the adult and child. In a firm voice, you say something like, 'Stop now. Nobody hits anyone in this nursery.' You can immediately follow by saying something appropriate to the circumstances. It might be that you realise the parent is in a terrible hurry, or that the child was being rude and unco-operative. You are pleased to help now or later, but any hitting has to stop. Partnership means establishing a friendly working relationship with parents. So your message of fellow feeling about times of stress comes across as genuine. However, your professional role is also to be ready to discuss other ways of dealing with the same behaviour.

Female Genital Mutilation (FGM)

'FGM is child abuse and a form of violence against women and girls, and therefore should be dealt with as part of existing child and adult safeguarding/protection structures policies and procedures'

(HM Government, 2014)

What does it mean?

Female genital mutilation (FGM) 'comprises all procedures involving partial or total removal of the external female genitalia or other injury (procedure) to the female genital organs for non-medical reasons. It has no health benefits and harms girls and women in many ways. It involves removing and damaging healthy and normal female genital tissue, and hence interferes with the natural function of girls' and women's bodies. The practice causes severe pain and has several immediate and long-term health consequences, including difficulties in childbirth also causing dangers to the child'

(HM Government, 2014).

Female circumcision, in any of its forms, is illegal in the UK. In England, Wales and Northern Ireland, the practice is illegal under the Female Genital Mutilation Act 2003 (this offence captures mutilation of a female's labia majora, labia minora or clitoris), and in Scotland it is illegal under the Prohibition of Female Genital Mutilation (Scotland) Act 2005.

Under the 2003 Act, a person is guilty of an offence if they excise, infibulate or otherwise mutilate the whole or any part of a girl's or woman's labia majora, labia minora or clitoris.

It is also an offence to take girls aboard for mutilation.

FGM appears to have become established many centuries ago in parts of Africa, and the tradition remains strongest in some countries within that continent. FGM is also practised in communities within several countries in the Middle East and Far East (as described from a European perspective). FGM is a strongly held cultural tradition and has travelled with communities that have relocated elsewhere, including the UK. Many, but not all, of these communities follow Islam. Religious leaders of these social groups often insist FGM is a requirement of faith. However, considerable numbers of Muslims around the world reject the practice, saying there is no basis in the Qur'an for what is a cultural, not a religious, tradition. Some Christian communities (for example, in Egypt) are also committed to the tradition.

The cultural pressure is strong to perform FGM on girls before they become young women, because it is seen as the way to ensure that daughters are chaste and therefore marriageable. Families living in the UK have been able to find some doctors who are prepared to circumcise their daughters and some traditional circumcisers have operated illegally in this country. Otherwise, mothers or grandmothers have taken girls abroad to obtain the operation. The Female Genital Mutilation Act 2003 made it illegal for any residents of the UK to take girls to any other country for this purpose.

The practice of FGM is illegal in the UK. The procedure results in considerably greater mutilation of the female genital area than the usual circumcision procedure for males. Girls either have the clitoris cut, or suffer the removal of all the external labia, and almost complete sewing up of the vaginal opening (infibulation). The circumcision itself can be very painful, since traditional circumcisers do not necessarily use pain relief or sterile tools. Girls can bleed dangerously and be left with pelvic infections, gynaecological problems and later difficulties with childbirth.

The issue of FGM is one in which child protection concerns are in inevitable conflict with the wish to respect cultural traditions of a community. It is an important reminder that respect for any cultural practice must not override concern for children's well being. Nor is respect for cultural tradition a more important concern than that of equality: the procedure is judged as violence towards the girls, a matter of gender discrimination. Child protection teams who face this issue also need to offer support for those families and girls who wish to break with the practice. They are likely to face hostility from their community and pressure that the girls will no longer be pure for marriage.

Early years practitioners are less likely to encounter the practice, since girls from the relevant communities are most likely to undergo FGM between four and ten years of age. Any concerns about unexplained injury and pain should be dealt with as possible abuse, in line with good child protection practice. But it is also important that schools, and out-of-school provision, are very aware if girls talk about an impending 'holiday' in ways that suggest concern.

The term 'female circumcision' is actually anatomically incorrect and gives a misleading analogy to male circumcision.

Male circumcision is not regarded as an automatic child protection issue, since the procedure does not cause equivalent damage to boys. Male ccircumcision may be performed for:

- **religious reasons** – circumcision is a common practice in the Jewish and Islamic faiths, and is also practised by many African communities as a tribal or ethnic tradition
- **medical reasons**, although alternative treatments are usually preferred to circumcision.

There are medical advantages as well as disadvantages to male circumcision. See: NHS Choices, 2014. www.nhs.uk/conditions/Circumcision-in-children/Pages/Introduction.aspx

Legislation

Female Genital Mutilation Act 2003 as amended by the Serious Crime Act 2015

FGM is illegal in England and Wales under the FGM Act 2003.

'Section 5B of the 2003 Act introduces a mandatory reporting duty which requires regulated health and social care professionals and teachers in England and Wales to report "known" cases of FGM in under 18s which they identify in the course of their professional work to the police. The duty applies from 31 October 2015 onwards.

"Known" cases are those where either a girl informs the person that an act of FGM – however described – has been carried out on her, or where the person observes physical signs on a girl appearing to show that an act of FGM has been carried out and the person has no reason to believe that the act was, or was part of, a surgical operation within section 1(2)(a) or (b) of the FGM Act 2003'.

Home Office (2015)

The legislation requires regulated health and social care professionals and teachers in England and Wales to make a report to the police where, in the course of their professional duties, they:

- are informed by a girl under 18 years that an act of FGM has been carried out on her;

or

- they observe physical signs that appear to show that an act of FGM has been carried out on a girl under 18 years and they have no reason to believe it was necessary for the girl's physical or mental health or for purposes connected with labour or birth.

For the purposes of the professional duty, the relevant age is the girl's age at the time of the disclosure/identification of FGM (i.e. it does not apply where a woman aged 18 years or over discloses she had FGM when she was under 18 years).

What does it mean?

'The duty only applies in cases where the victim, a child discloses. If someone else, such as a parent or guardian, discloses that a girl under 18 has had FGM, a report to the police is not mandatory. However, in these circumstances disclosures should still be handled in line with wider safeguarding responsibilities and a referral made to children's social care.

'Complying with the duty does not breach any confidentiality requirement which might otherwise apply.

'Professionals should make the report immediately after the case has been discovered. Best practice is within one working day, but in exceptional cases there is a maximum timeframe of one month from when the discovery is made.

'If professionals fail to comply with the duty, this will be dealt with in accordance with existing performance procedures in place for each profession.'

(Home Office, 2015)

Policy and guidance

Procedural information related to the above can be found with the policy document: 'Mandatory Reporting of Female Genital Mutilation' (Home Office, 2015). This provides information for health and social care professionals, teachers and the police about their responsibilities under the female genital mutilation (FGM) mandatory reporting duty that came into force in 2015. It details when and how to make a report; next steps following a report; and failure to comply with the duty. Practitioners should be familiar with the policy guidance.

The NSPCC website also provides useful information regarding FGM and the legislative framework. Please see: www.nspcc.org.uk/preventing-abuse/child-abuse-and-neglect/female-genital-mutilation-fgm/legislation-policy-and-guidance

Multi-agency practice guidelines for FGM

Practitioners should also be familiar with multi-agency policy guidance regarding FGM. See: HM Government (2014) *Female Genital Mutilation: Multi-agency Practice Guidelines'*.

Find out more

www.forwarduk.org.uk
Foundation for Women's Health, Research and Development: An organisation supporting women and communities to resist pressures for female genital mutilation and forced marriage.

www.unicef.org
A range of papers and reports are also available on the UNICEF website.

Practice point: key messages

- As of 31 October 2015, it is mandatory to report FGM. The mandatory duty requires regulated health and social care professionals and teachers in England and Wales to report known cases of FGM in under 18-year-olds to the police.
- The **Female Genital Mutilation Act 2003** makes it a criminal offence for UK nationals or permanent UK residents to:
  - perform FGM overseas
  - take a UK national or permanent UK resident overseas to have FGM.

Safeguarding, culture and faith

Any hope that children would be automatically safe within faith communities does not stand up to the weight of evidence. Serious child-protection issues have arisen that have tainted a wide range of faith groups and religious leaders.

The NSPCC (2014) highlight that published case reviews indicate that professionals sometimes lack the knowledge and confidence to work with families from different cultures and religions. Sometimes a lack of understanding of the religions and cultural context of families can have the outcome whereby professionals overlook situations that may put family members at risk. It is important that practitioners take care to be culturally sensitive while not accepting lower standards of care, and that families' cultural and religious context is acknowledged when undertaking assessments and offering support. However, the rights and needs of the child need to remain the focus of interventions at all times, regardless of this context (NSPCC, 2014).

The NSPCC (2014) have identified the following risk factors for culture and faith in case reviews:

- Social and cultural isolation or fear of isolation
- Cultural and religious beliefs overriding self-interest (e.g. preventing people from seeking help)
- Cultural conflict within families
- Religion and culture as a distraction from a child protection issue
- Professional misconceptions, lack of confidence and lack of knowledge
- Challenge of children developing their own self-identity
- Converting to a partner's religion
- Belief in spirit possession
- Interplay between religion and mental health issues.

Significant risks arise when the well being of children and young people is judged less important than the reputation of the religious or community leader who is alleged, sometimes with very good reason, to be an abuser.

- Members of faith communities who feel under threat from people who do not share their beliefs can be especially keen to close ranks. Representatives of a range of different religions have insisted on dealing with any problems within their own internal systems, until pressurised to take a more transparent approach.

● Pressure has been put on children and their families to take the matter no further because of the likely backlash on the community. Similar risks have also arisen around domestic violence.

● Interpretation of faith values and key scriptures can be used to justify the chosen priorities and even to vilify the child. In some cases, serious cruelty and sexually abusive treatment have been justified on the grounds that the child (or young person) is sinful or evil.

● Such an atmosphere provides a safe haven for individuals who would abuse children wherever that adult lived, worked or worshipped.

● Involved professionals who share the faith or community allegiance can be forced into a choice between personal and professional loyalties. Professionals who do not share this source of identity may be anxious that they will be accused of ignorance or outright hostility to the faith or cultural group.

Scandals within the Catholic Church and the Protestant Church of England have arisen from the preferred solution of moving the alleged abuser to another parish, or to a post in which it is claimed he will have no contact with children. (The abuser always has been a male, in reports of which I am aware.) This option is an unacceptable response to the actual abuse of children or risky adult behaviour such as accessing child pornography. Additionally, the promised 'no contact' has sometimes failed to be upheld. See, for instance, the editorial news item about the Church of England in *Caring*, Summer 2007: www.ccpas.co.uk

Children and young people are at risk from any combination of a closed community, powerful social position and values that consider adults to be the more important individuals in an uncertain situation. The incidence of abuse or neglect within a given faith does not, of course, support the stance that everyone who shares the religious beliefs would tolerate ill-treatment of vulnerable individuals. However, concern cannot be brushed aside because the identity of a group is based on faith or a combination of cultural background and faith.

● All religious groups and leaders are obliged to address safeguarding of children and young people within their community as a whole.

● They should make proper checks on individuals who are responsible for activities for children and any form of religious education offered by the faith.

● Many faith groups, and separate sects within a world faith, have developed or accepted guidelines and clear policy about action that is needed to protect children.

Faith- or belief-based abuse

Some sects and church groups within the Christian faith believe that it is possible for children to become infected – possessed – by an evil spirit, or to become a witch. The accepted solution is to perform a ritual of exorcism that involves actions that are physically and emotionally abusive of the child or young person. This tenet of faith is strong in some Christian groups whose country of origin lies within parts of Africa. However, families who originated from the Caribbean and 'white' English families have also been involved in documented cases.

Some involved adults genuinely believe that what they are doing is mandated by their faith and in the best interests of the child, whom they believe to be possessed. However, the process is a welcome option for adults who dislike and resent a child, or regard them as unacceptably different in some way. Spirit possession offers a useful external explanation for what the adult insists is bad behaviour, and justifies abuse and neglect of the child. This dynamic was one of the many appalling events experienced by Victoria Climbié before her death.

To work effectively in addressing child abuse linked to faith or belief it is important that:

● Practitioners in all services for children are alert to injuries, unexplained accidents or fearfulness shown by children towards particular adults.
● Practitioners notice when children seem to be treated significantly differently from others in the family, or individual children seem convinced that they are 'bad' or 'unwanted'.
● Practitioners listen to own feelings of anxiety if a child about whom you are already concerned talks unhappily about an impending trip or holiday.
● Practitioners should be alert for any children going missing for a period of time, because some are taken abroad for the exorcism ritual, as well as for FGM.
● Services and professionals should share information on places of worship and individual faith leaders about which there are growing concerns. Effective local and national initiatives (such as that of the CCPAS; see above) have to make sustained contact with the groups in question, dealing with concerns about children while giving the very clear message about what constitutes a crime against children in the UK.

In 2012 the Government launched a National Action Plan to tackle child abuse linked to faith or belief (Department for Education, 2012). A National Working Group was set up and the Action Plan was developed through partnership between central government and local statutory partners, faith leaders, voluntary sector organisations and the Metropolitan Police. This action plan contributes to understanding the problem and should be used in conjunction with national legislation and policy guidance for safeguarding.

In addition to the above, the NSPCC (2014) conclude that the following issues need to be addressed to improve practice:

- Culturally informed assessments – as part of an assessment the practitioner should explore the impact of a person's culture on their life, including: spiritual practices, rites/blessings, beliefs and practices surrounding life events, dietary restrictions, personal care, daily rituals, communication, social customs and attitudes to healthcare and support. This will then help to meet the individual needs of the child while at the same time providing an opportunity to pick up on concerns.
- Taking into account families' cultural and religious needs – for example, consider gender issues where it may be culturally inappropriate for a member of the opposite sex to discuss certain issues with service users; and that some families may feel more comfortable working with professionals from a similar cultural background. It is also important that when children are taken into care their cultural and religious needs are given consideration. However, it is important that common culture or religion does not override other considerations, **especially not the child's safety**.
- Culture, faith and pregnancy – it is important that professionals always check the faith and marital status of pregnant women and discuss the impact that this may have on their parenting. Professionals should be aware of the increased risks around concealed pregnancy amongst single mothers' whose faith condemns sex outside marriage and abortion.
- Recording information – where applicable, professionals should record the ethnicity, culture and faith of children and families that they work with and share this information across agencies.
- Challenging parents – it is important to be confident in challenging parents who raise matters of race or religion to distract attention from the focus on the child.
- Improving relationships between professionals and different minority groups – it is important that the local community and professionals trust and understand each other.

It is also important to note for practice that it is not about challenging people's beliefs **but** where these beliefs lead to abuse this needs intervention in order to protect the child or young person.

Commentary on the scenarios

Here are possible suggestions for the scenarios given in this chapter.

Helena (page 144)

Disabled children can behave in ways that hurt or distress other children, as well as being secretive about their behaviour. A sentimental approach does not help children, nor does a reluctance to address their behaviour out of pity.

It is right to be careful about over-reaction, but observations made during the day should give you a firm basis for a conversation with

Helena's childminder, who is the key carer in the working relationship at the moment. You definitely do not want to label any child as a 'bully'. However, it is important to address Helena as a girl who may well need some clear guidance on how to behave. She will not be helped by a lack of boundaries, either now or in the future. Adults also have a responsibility to look towards what is likely to block Helena's friendships with other children. Her peers will become annoyed if she appears to 'get away' with actions that would be stopped if another child behaved in that way.

If Helena's childminder is open to considering another perspective, then the discussion and support might extend to including the parents. It will be useful for you to have information about appropriate support groups, but that step will depend on what happens in the short term.

Natasha (page 146)

There is cause for concern about Natasha, since the care arrangements seem to be unpredictable and potentially unsafe. All carers within her family need to understand that nursery hours are not elastic and that children must be handed safely to a member of staff. It also seems that the nursery team may have been too flexible in allowing a wide range of family members to pick up Natasha. The nursery teacher needs to talk urgently with Natasha's mother and be very clear about what is acceptable and what is unsafe regarding this four-year-old. If the school has a breakfast club, it may be possible for Natasha to arrive in time to join that facility. But any change must be properly discussed and no child must be simply left in the playground.

The information given by the school caretaker raises further concerns. The nursery needs to gain some idea of the reliability of this information before discussing anything with Natasha's mother. The lack of supervision, if true, is outside nursery time, but the staff can have the same concern that a neighbour might feel. If Natasha's mother is unresponsive to a careful conversation about her daughter's supervision, the nursery could look for a low-key conversation with another professional, perhaps in the social work team. It is unlikely to be at the stage yet for a referral.

It is appropriate that the caretaker should share information relevant to the children in nursery class or the main school. However, it is inappropriate for him to talk dismissively about 'these people'. His line manager, possibly the head of the school, needs to talk with the caretaker. Respect for families is a professional obligation and sweeping statements are unacceptable.

Abbas (page 149)

It is appropriate that the school team resists making judgements about Abbas and his family. Ten-year-olds can be very competent and, in many cultures, older children take safe responsibility for younger siblings. The staff may feel regret for Abbas that he cannot have an independent social life, but that would not be a basis for intervention. It would be possible to look at practical issues, such as whether Nneka could come to chess club as well, so that Abbas may enjoy this activity.

It would be possible for Abbas' or Nneka's class teacher to talk with their parents about making practical arrangements for Nneka when her brother goes to secondary school. Perhaps there could be a friendly offer to see about linking Nneka up with another family who walk in from the same direction. Such an arrangement would have to be a clear agreement between the families; the school team will have to be careful about not taking responsibility outside their sphere. An alternative might be possible if the primary school has a breakfast club.

The children appear well and healthy, yet there is a level of concern that Abbas may be responsible for his sister into the evening. The school does not know for sure; there may be other people in the home. The class teacher, after discussion with the Safeguarding Officer, might look for an opportunity to raise the issue within a meeting with the children's parents in the first instance.

Ann-Marie (page 153)

Neither partnership nor equality policy mean that settings should accept actions from parents that place children at risk. It is important that family faith is shown respect, but that does not extend to acceptance of cruel treatment of children, apparently justified through religious beliefs. The nursery team also needs to be aware that suspicions are not in themselves firm proof. If Ann-Marie's parents are hitting her, it is also important that nobody in the nursery assumes that their behaviour is typical of other families who follow their faith or sect within the faith.

The nursery needs to keep records of what has happened and the reactions of Ann-Marie's parents. Part of the written record will be to put in descriptive terms the reason that pain from bruising became 'obvious'. The team will be aware that UK law still allows parents to hit their children, within limits. If Ann-Marie's injuries are the result of being hit by one or both parents, such treatment has definitely left a visible mark – so their actions have gone beyond the bounds of 'reasonable punishment'.

It is not the nursery's task to try to work out the precise legal position. However, it is a professional responsibility to take a clear line with families that hitting is not necessary as a form of discipline and to share other ways of dealing with children's behaviour.

There needs to be a proper meeting with Ann-Marie's parents to express the serious concerns of the nursery arising from recent incidents, and listen to what the parents have to say. Unless concerns are put to rest, it a referral will need to be made Children's Social Care for further assessment.

Summary

This chapter has discussed the differences that need to be taken into account to safeguard all children effectively. Children with a disability are vulnerable to increased risk of abuse and this should be considered when working with a child who has a disability. The chapter has also discussed the extrafamilial and wider issues for safeguarding practice, including those related to faith and FGM.

Practitioners must at no time use culture as an excuse to allow abuse to continue.

Key texts

Elliott, M. (ed.) (1993) *Female Sexual Abuse of Children*, London: Longman

Lindon, J. (2012) *Equality and Inclusion for Children and Families: Linking Theory and Practice*, London: Hodder Education

Miller, D. and Brown, J. (2014) *Protecting Disabled Children from Abuse*, London: NSPCC: www.nspcc.org.uk/services-and-resources/research-and-resources/right-to-be-safe/

NSPCC (2003) *'It doesn't Happen to Disabled Children.' Child Protection and Disabled Children*. Available at: www.nspcc.org.uk/inform/research/findings/itdoesnthappentodisabledchildren_wda48257.html (accessed 2 August 2011)

The briefing papers on child protection statistics: http://www.nspcc.org.uk/preventing-abuse/child-protection-system/england/statistics/

6 Policies, procedures and best practice

Introduction

An effective safeguarding process depends on clear policies and linked procedures for daily practice with children. Policies and procedures matter, but a guidance document, however well written, cannot actually do the safeguarding job. Best practice requires people to behave in ways that protect. This chapter is concerned with safeguarding in practice and the nature of the policies and procedures that should guide the practice of safeguarding. It also addresses safety and security and the importance of documentation and record keeping.

Policies and procedures for safeguarding

Laws define the legal framework for safeguarding, and guidance explains how practitioners and services need to operate in order to implement the legal requirements (see Chapter 1). Settings and services are expected to have written policies on key aspects of good practice, and child protection is definitely one of those areas.

A written policy is usually a statement of commitment. Then the separate document about procedures will describe the steps that enable policy to be put into practice on a daily basis: actions to take, with a sequence to order those actions, when that makes sense. The document will also clarify any details about what should *not* be done. Local policies and procedures should, however, be written in accordance with national guidance and the Local Safeguarding Children Board Procedures.

What does it mean?

Policy: a policy lays out the key principles and values that guide this aspect of practice.

Procedures: provide details of what will be done, or steps that will be followed.

Key issues for practice

Some documents for safeguarding combine a policy statement followed by more detailed procedures. It is, however, useful to distinguish between the different aims of a policy and procedures.

Your policy should make a succinct statement and should ideally fit a single side of A4, certainly no more than two pages, and state:

- who you are: the name of your organisation or kind of service and the main aspects of what you offer to children and families;
- the importance of safeguarding and protecting the welfare of children and your safeguarding responsibility, with brief reference to the main laws and guidance for your part of the UK;
- the responsibility of everyone within a setting or service to be active in safeguarding and the prevention of abuse or neglect;
- in broad terms how you will meet that obligation – for instance, through safe recruitment to the team or active support for children and families;
- that the safeguarding commitment works together with other policies, such as those on equality, on behaviour and on partnership with parents.

Your procedures will be longer, although it is unwise to create such a lengthy document that people rarely read it. The procedures make clear your responsibilities, as an individual or member of a team, and that everyone is accountable for their own actions. Procedures have to be clear about the following points:

- The obligation to respond appropriately, and in a timely way, to any concerns, whoever raises them. Some procedures include a brief summary of signs that should concern practitioners, or refer to a guidance document.
- The steps that should be taken when there are concerns, perhaps with a flow chart (similar to Figure 4.7).
- Shared responsibility for child protection across the team and the particular role of the designated safeguarding lead (see page 104).
- Details of the agencies and service(s) – name(s) and telephone number(s) of those who should be contacted or consulted locally
- Some procedures build in specific guidance about how to behave if a child discloses an abusive experience.
- How child protection is supported by other procedures, such as written records or dealing with allegations of abuse or malpractice.

Effective safeguarding includes helping children to learn skills of personal safety. A school, for instance, might make commitments linked with the curriculum, whereas childminders or an after-school club might explain their ground rules around internet use, for slightly older children.

Putting good intentions into practice

No procedure, however well drafted, will make every decision for you. The most experienced professionals in child protection still need to make carefully considered judgements. There will always be a level of anxiety when dealing with concerns about the well being of children, so good teamwork and easy opportunities to discuss work issues are an essential support for practice in child protection. Practitioners who work alone, such as foster carers and childminders, need easy access to a fellow professional (see page 107).

It is also important to recall that the 'team' of people who have responsibility for the same child can be an extended system. Some disabled children cannot reach services, or get home again, without the driver of their special transport. The 'school run' by local taxi firms is necessary in many areas where pupils live beyond the reach of public transport. Some families are judged in need of this kind of extra support to ensure school attendance.

Case study

Heather

You have recently joined the staff of a small private nursery school. Heather is nearly four years old and has been attending the school for six months. She is an articulate girl and has started to talk with you about what she has done at the weekend or the previous evening. In a conversation with you yesterday, Heather described a film she had watched on television that you know did not start until 11 pm. You said to her, 'You were up very late, Heather. Did Mummy know you were watching that film?' Heather replied, 'Oh, Mummy was with John. They were in the bedroom, doing ... well, you know what.'

Today, you notice that Heather is playing with Jack in the home corner. When you look more closely, you realise that Heather is sitting astride Jack and bouncing up and down. She is making grunting noises that sound very like orgasm. At that moment Heather's key person goes into the home corner and lifts the child off Jack, saying, 'None of that, Heather. Don't be silly.' In a coffee break later, the other practitioner explains, 'I should have told you. We have to watch Heather. She tries that sort of stuff with the little boys. Poor kid, it's not her fault. Goodness knows what she sees at home. But we can't have it here.'

- As the new arrival to this team, what is your impression of their approach to child protection?
- What are your concerns about the children in this situation?
- What would be a sensible first step?

You will find a commentary on pages 201–2.

Policy and procedures need to be easy to understand for all the team, including any volunteers. Details must be shared effectively with all the adults involved in the setting or service, not only those practitioners who work directly with children. In any setting there needs to be a whole-team approach, inclusive of support and administrative staff.

Part of the induction for a new team member must include a proper discussion about child protection policy into practice. However, it is essential to continue to talk around safeguarding issues within an established team. Everyone needs to be sure about 'This is what we mean by confidentiality.' If you are drafting a policy for the first time, it is a good idea to set a date for review that will take place a few months ahead. You will need a full discussion about whether all the procedures are clear to everyone and if there have been unexpected confusions or consequences. Childminders and foster carers are expected to have simple policies and practical procedures for child protection. Helpful discussion for these practitioners often arises within their professional support network.

Communication with service users

Parents and other family carers need to understand that you have an obligation to address serious concerns about children. Open communication about the policy is not only an issue for early contact. A written policy and procedures should continue to be available for parents, or other adults with family responsibility, to read on request.

Written policies or procedures should ideally be available in the main languages spoken in your neighbourhood. For some settings, this task may be straightforward, but if you work in a diverse area that has many languages and written scripts, the translation task will be daunting. Some parents or carers will not be literate or may be very reluctant readers; the same issue may arise with some practitioners or volunteers.

Practitioners should be ready to explain the key points of policy in straightforward spoken language, and more than once, when necessary.

It is essential that:

- Every team member, or the individual childminder, has a commitment to children's welfare and safety. Part of that responsibility is an obligation to follow up any concerns about a child.
- The preferred route will be to discuss any worries first with the child's parent or other family carer. In the same way, the setting would welcome that parents directly raise any concerns they have with their childminder, the child's key person or class teacher. In a group setting, parents can talk with a senior team member or the safeguarding lead, if they prefer.
- Private family matters are kept confidential. However, if there are concerns about children's well being or safety, early years practitioners are obliged to share information with other professionals. When concerns are serious, they have to make a referral to social care services.

Pause for reflection

Gathering examples

Gather some examples from local public material about services for children. Look at the ways in which different leaflets, brochures or websites for settings cover the ideas in this section:

● How does the material explain child protection to users of the service?
● What words and phrases are used? Do they appear clear to you? Discuss your examples with friends who do not work in your profession.
● What meaning do they take from the materials?
● Are there any phrases that might be unclear to anyone outside the profession?

Childhood memories of practitioners

Memories of personal experience of childhood abuse or neglect, which may include a practitioner's own distress or that of a sibling or close friend, can be revived by working with an abused child and family, or through training workshops on child protection. A proportion of early years and out-of-school practitioners are still in their late adolescence or early adulthood. Deeply unhappy memories may still be fresh and perhaps undisclosed to anyone so far. The Safeguarding Lead in a setting or a college needs to be aware of this real possibility, but the situation can also apply to practitioners who are mature in years. All professionals have to consider, preferably with support:

● in what way their own difficult experiences (not just abuse) are relevant to their work;
● to what extent details are shared, with whom and how;
● how they will seek help for unresolved problems or distress that could otherwise affect their work.

It is appropriate in professional practice to raise personal issues within supervision, in confidence with a link worker or childminding adviser. Anyone can use a helpline, such as that of the NSPCC (0808 800 5000), to talk about troubles arising from abuse. The following points can help, whether you offer support or are yourself working through memories of childhood abuse:

● Practitioners who themselves experienced childhood abuse or neglect should not be regarded as either too close to the subject to help a child or as better informed because of their own experience. There should not be an automatic decision in either direction.
● If your feelings about your own experience are still raw, especially if you have not disclosed your experience until this time, it would be professional to accept generous support as you work with a particular child and family. In a setting, there would be a good reason for the safeguarding lead to take the lead in this situation.

- If you have strong and unresolved feelings about your own abuse, then the professional step is to seek help appropriate help and access, for example, counselling services. A colleague, manager or safeguarding lead will not be in a position to offer proper counselling, if that is what is needed. Students should be encouraged to access the college or university counselling service.
- If you were given support as a child and your abusive experience is now a part of you (an unhappy memory but resolved in some way), then there is no reason why you should not continue to be the key person with this child and parent.

Sorting out personal from professional

In any helping relationship it is crucial to keep your own experiences in perspective. Practitioners' personal experience of abuse (or of bullying) does not give them a shortcut to insight on this child's experience now. You have some understanding of how this child, or parent, might be feeling. But it is never wise to say, 'I know exactly how you feel,' because nobody can.

- Any discussions about possible action must focus on the individual child and family. Do not be tempted towards a particular course of action because it helped you, or because you wish somebody had taken that approach in your own situation.
- Supportive discussion with parents needs to be open and not run to swift conclusions. Just because your own child had a very unpleasant experience with a sports coach does not mean that the uncertain problems of this boy are related to his attendance at a sports club.
- It is very unlikely to be appropriate to let a parent know about your personal experience, whether in the past or more recently. The risk of any kind of personal disclosure, not only about a sensitive issue like abuse, is that a supportive conversation may easily lose its focus on the other person and become a discussion about what happened to the practitioner.
- You might decide to make a personal disclosure with colleagues because you feel your knowledge could help them understand the current situation. However, bear in mind that the consequences of sharing a highly personal experience can be unpredictable.

Owen

In a conversation over lunch at your centre, three-year-old Owen is talking about the new baby that will soon be born. Owen is talking with affection: 'I pat the baby in Mummy's tummy. Her tummy's very big and knobbly. I see it in the bath.' Your colleague asks Owen with some surprise, 'Do you and Mummy have a bath together?' He replies, 'Oh, yes. We have wet cuddles in the bath.'

You have never been concerned about Owen or his family but your colleague talks with you later. She says, 'Don't you think we should report this? People shouldn't have baths with their children. It isn't right.' She shudders and looks very uncomfortable.

● Are you concerned about the child in this example?
● Do you have any other concerns and if so, what might you do?

You will find a commentary on page 202.

Safeguarding children and safer recruitment

HM Government (2015a) states that all organisations providing services for children and young people should work together to 'take a co-ordinated approach to ensure effective safeguarding arrangements. This is supported by the duty on local authorities under section 10 of the Children Act 2004 to make arrangements to promote co-operation to improve the well being of all children in the authority's area' and 'In addition, a range of individual organisations and professionals working with children and families have specific statutory duties to promote the welfare of children and ensure they are protected from harm'.

Section 11 of the Children Act 2004 places duties on a range of organisations and individuals to ensure their functions, and any services that they contract out to others, are discharged having regard to the need to safeguard and promote the welfare of children.

Organisations should have in place arrangements that reflects the importance of safeguarding and promoting the welfare of children and this includes safe recruitment practices for individuals whom the organisation will permit to work regularly with children, including policies on when to obtain a criminal record check (DBS checks, see page 174), barred list checks and prohibition checks.

It is vital that organisations who provide services for children create a culture of safe recruitment and, as part of that, employ recruitment procedures that help deter, reject or identify people who might abuse children.

Organisations and services are obliged to make official checks (vetting) on anyone who will be in a position, paid or unpaid, that brings them into close contact with children on a regular basis.

The level of DBS certificate required, and whether a prohibition check is required, will depend on the role, responsibilities and duties that the practitioner will undertake. In education settings, for most appointments, an enhanced DBS certificate, which includes barred list information, will be required as the majority of staff will be considered to be engaging in regulated activity.

Regulated activity

The full legal definition of regulated activity is set out in Schedule 4 of the Safeguarding Vulnerable Groups Act 2006 as amended by the Protection of Freedoms Act 2012. HM Government have produced a factual note on Regulated Activity (Department for Education and DHSSPS, 2012).

Regulated activity includes:

a) teaching, training, instructing, caring for (see 'c' below) or supervising children if the person is unsupervised, or providing advice or guidance on well being, or driving a vehicle only for children,
b) work for a limited range of establishments (known as 'specified places', which include schools and colleges), with the opportunity for contact with children, but not including work done by supervised volunteers. It does include schools, children's homes, childcare premises.
   ● Work under (a) or (b) is regulated activity only if done regularly.
   ● Some activities are always regulated activities, regardless of their frequency or whether they are supervised or not. This includes:
c) relevant personal care, or healthcare provided by, or provided under the supervision of, a healthcare professional:
   ● personal care includes helping a child, for reasons of age, illness or disability, with eating or drinking, or in connection with toileting, washing, bathing and dressing
   ● healthcare means care for children provided by, or under the direction or supervision of, a regulated healthcare professional.

Regulated activity still excludes family arrangements; and personal, non-commercial arrangements.

What does it mean?

Vetting: the process of making a series of checks to ensure that someone can safely be allowed to do something.

Barring: the process and agreed basis by which someone is not allowed to do something.

Regulated activity: the specific involvement, paid or voluntary, that is covered by this vetting and barring process.

The Disclosure and Barring Service

The Disclosure and Barring Service (DBS) helps employers make safer recruitment decisions and prevent unsuitable people from working with vulnerable groups, including children. It replaces the Criminal Records Bureau (CRB) and Independent Safeguarding Authority (ISA).

The system operates to vet applicants by name through checking that they are not on a database of individuals who are barred from contact with, or taking responsibility for, children or young people in any role, paid or voluntary. Individuals may be barred for two main reasons:

- They have come to the attention of the police for behaviour that makes them unsafe to be with children. Examples would include the use of child pornography, inappropriate conduct of a sexual nature or behaviour that put a child at risk of physical harm. Individuals may be barred not only because of specific criminal convictions but also for being cautioned over relevant offences.
- Their conduct in a job was seriously unacceptable and led a service or organisation to submit their name to the relevant authority to be placed on the relevant database.

The vetting and barring process is similar across the UK. Each system checks whether a named person has behaved in ways that mean they are barred from 'regulated activity': in this case, close contact with children. The process removes a negative; it cannot tell a potential employer whether the person is suitable for the job or voluntary support. Vetting works alongside, and not instead of, a thorough process of recruitment. Additionally, the vetting process is not a check for identity fraud, since it accepts the personal information given in order to run a name, or names, through the databases.

The vetting and barring scheme

During 2007–08 the vetting and barring system in England and Wales was overhauled, following the Safeguarding Vulnerable Groups Act 2006: a new law passed in response to recommendations from the Bichard Inquiry. The law applies to England, Wales and Northern Ireland. The Scottish Parliament also took account of the Bichard Inquiry and passed The Protection of Vulnerable Groups (Scotland) Act 2007.

The aim has been to create a single list of named individuals who have been barred from working with children and young people, and to align the new database with one relevant to working with vulnerable adults.

- The Independent Safeguarding Authority (www.isa.homeoffice.gov.uk) was established for England and Wales and works with Access Northern Ireland. Referrals from early years or any other settings about incidents or suspicions of abusive behaviour should be made to ISA.
- The Protecting Vulnerable Groups (PVG) Scheme is run by Disclosure Scotland and they make decisions about who should be barred from working with children or other vulnerable groups in Scotland.

All the contemporary legislation aims to make it easy to share information appropriately about unsafe adults across the UK and to address the risks that arise from both the mobility of individuals and inadequate data sharing.

Recruitment and induction

Vetting checks can only highlight individuals whose past behaviour has brought them to the attention of the police or who have been reported for professional misconduct. Thorough recruitment procedures are therefore crucial and the basics for any service include the following:

- Use application forms for everyone, including volunteers. A prepared, standard form ensures that the same questions are asked of everyone. The application process also then links properly with the interview.
- If applicants have difficulty with literacy, then they can seek appropriate help. Under some circumstances, that may be offered from within your service. But it is non-negotiable that a written record is created for any application.
- Take up at least two written references and follow them up by telephone. Explore any doubts about the people whose names are given as referees: what they say or how you are required to contact them.
- Many people legitimately use a mobile phone for their work. But you need to make an independent check, most likely through a landline, to be reassured that applicants hold the position, or previously worked for the organisation, that has been claimed.
- Look carefully at the curriculum vitae of any applicant and reassure yourself about any unexplained gaps or swift changes of job. Verify any qualifications by asking to see original certificates.
- Ask for proof of identity, preferably something that contains a photograph, or request a National Insurance number.

An effective recruitment process is only part of safe practice to ensure that adults are safe and supportive of children and young people day by day in their practice. All settings and services should have an introductory process, usually called 'induction', which eases new staff or volunteers into what good practice means here.

- Policies and related procedures are discussed in terms of what they mean in practice, and not left simply as a task of 'Please read through these.'
- Friendly conversation also invites a new team member to ask questions along the lines of 'Does that mean that ... ' or to check: 'In my last job, I was told not to ... How do you handle that situation here?'
- Such exchanges can be useful because a reflective colleague can revisit key policies. Questions from a new member of staff also sometimes reveal a misunderstanding established within the existing team.
- Paid staff should have a written job description, but that will not cover every single detail. Everyone needs to be consistent and clear about guidelines on good practice – for instance, about taking a positive approach to children's behaviour, their physical care or trips out of the setting.

- Staff should know how they will be offered continued support, whether through informal conversation as well as regular supervision, and that it is good practice to ask rather than assume, when you are uncertain. Anyone involved in your service or setting needs to recognise that unacceptable practice will be challenged, as indeed 'good' practice should be acknowledged and encouraged.

What does it mean?

Induction: the process of introducing someone new in a setting, service or specific role to the details of their work.

Students and volunteers

The induction process is usually organised for paid staff. Such support is sometimes overlooked for regular helpers like parents or for students on work placement. It is unlikely to be appropriate to take non-staff through a full induction process. But everyone involved with children has to keep within the good practice boundaries. It is irrelevant for children that someone is volunteering or present only for a short placement.

- Students, parent helpers and other regular volunteers should be given an explanation of what they are expected to do and the limits to their responsibilities.
- Clear support may be necessary to explain what is legitimate discussion and what is gossip or breaking of confidences overheard in the setting.
- Volunteers can be welcome and may be crucial for the running of some community settings. But no setting should ever tolerate bad practice from a volunteer on the grounds of 'We can't make a fuss, she's giving her time.'
- Unacceptable practice from volunteers will not always be abusive or neglectful. Team members may need to explain, for example, that it is not all right to insist on table manners that are culturally very specific.

Vetting is not judged necessary for irregular support such as accompanying a group on outings or helping out at a concert or fête. The key difference is that for such activities the volunteer or parent helper will not have close, unsupervised contact with children.

Ground rules for other adults

Many services have a range of adults who legitimately visit the setting or premises. Recent safeguarding legislation has not changed existing good practice for protection and basic security for everyone.

Some regular adults are, of course, parents or other family relatives of children and young people who attend the provision. The result of effective practice in partnership with families is that practitioners get to know parents and other family carers as individuals. Safeguarding practice certainly does not require you to return to a suspicious attitude towards parents with 'Not beyond this point!' notices. A friendly yet working relationship will mean that practitioners should be aware if there are any family members (adults or adolescent siblings) who have problems, such as drug or alcohol use, which mean they could pose a risk.

Other visitors to a setting, such as a medical practitioner or an educational psychologist, may have a professional reason for their presence and it is reasonable for a setting to assume that their professional organisations have undertaken proper checks. Other people have a legitimate involvement in your practice, for instance, members of the management committee or school governors. Any visitor, however well known, should co-operate with standard security, such as signing in and out and wearing a visitor's badge. Even regular visitors of this kind should not have unsupervised access to children.

Settings may also receive requests for other people to visit – for instance, to learn about innovative practice. It is good practice, and respectful of children and young people, that you keep a record of and limit the number of visitors. It is very encouraging when people are keen to find out more about how you work. With prior warning and discussion, the young users of any facility can be involved in making the visitors welcome. However, team leaders and practitioners must not lose sight of the needs of children and that the setting is also their nursery, school or club. A steady stream of visitors, however well meaning or peaceful, is a disruption of daily life.

Safety and security

High-risk people in the neighbourhood

The system for vetting and barring works to reduce significantly the possibility that unsafe adults gain a position of trust with children. However, risks may also arise from people who live in their local neighbourhood. Good practice for protection means that older children and adolescents steadily learn, with sensible practical support from adults, how to keep themselves as safe as possible (see page 215). But there are also limits placed on the free movement of people who have been convicted of serious sexual offences against children or young people.

Individuals who have previously harmed children can be judged a continued risk when they leave prison. Their names will be on the sex offenders register, which means they will be required to notify their local police when they move into an area and to keep the police up to date with any change of address. Some individuals may be required, on release, to live for a period of time under supervision in a hostel for people who have served their sentence but are assessed as still posing a risk. Sex offenders cannot, of course, undertake any kind of regulated activity. But they may also have other restrictions on their behaviour – for instance – that they do not go near any services for children, including public facilities like an open-access play area.

Local panels operate with the police to manage information about known sex offenders who pose a risk to children or young people. In England, Wales and Scotland this panel works with MAPPA: the multi-agency public protection arrangements. In Northern Ireland the panel works within MASRAM: the multi-agency sex-offender risk assessment management system. These panels, like the police, can decide to disclose information about a sex offender in order to safeguard children. The obligation for child protection over rules the privacy of the individual on the sex offenders register. Thus discretionary disclosure may be made, for example, to the head of a primary school because a person known to target children is now resident in the neighbourhood.

The child sex-offender disclosure scheme enables parents, carers and guardians to ask their local police to disclose if someone who is becoming close to their family has a record of sexual offences against children. The aim of this scheme is to allow ordinary members of the public to ask for a check, when they have good reason to enquire. An example would be a lone mother who had become uneasy about a new partner. The details of the national scheme are explained on: www.gov.uk/guidance/find-out-if-a-person-has-a-record-for-child-sexual-offences

In the second half of the 1990s, several frightening, and sometimes tragic, incidents raised awareness that some mentally disturbed individuals target settings with children. Nurseries, pre-schools or primary schools cannot turn themselves into fortresses and it is important to realise that incidents such as the murders at Dunblane primary school, in 1996, are very rare. A realistic, everyday balance has to be found between access and sufficient security.

Pause for reflection

Practitioners are responsible for keeping children physically safe. It is good practice to reflect on questions such as:

● Have we (or I, if you work alone) achieved the right balance between security and friendly access to the setting or service?
● Who are the security systems protecting? Have we explored the right balance between genuine protection of children and anxiety about allegations against staff?
● Do we use opportunities to enable children to take an active, age-appropriate role in keeping themselves safe?

Who is here today?

Any setting that takes responsibility for children needs to have an efficient system of registering who is present today and what happens when a child who is expected does not arrive. Completing a register does not have to be a tedious process. It can be a combination of self-registration, by children and parents, followed by a thorough adult check to complete the written record.

However, safety also includes adult alertness, plus secure physical boundaries to a setting, that mean babies cannot crawl nor young children wander off the premises without anyone realising they have done so. Settings for children have to manage the personal aspects of transition times. Children must pass explicitly from the responsibility of a parent to the practitioner and then the reverse. You want to welcome parents and children, yet avoid making it easy for people to access your setting or home when they have no good reason to be there.

When parents first come to your setting with their child, explain to them how you handle security. Stress that taking care over fastening gates and closing doors properly is for the safety of their children – a shared responsibility – and that adults who have legitimate reason to be in the building must still enter via reception or the office.

Closed circuit television (CCTV)

Some group settings such as nurseries and schools consider whether to install CCTV. This system may offer additional protection if your neighbourhood has problems arising from adults who are under the influence of alcohol or drugs. Alternatively your setting may be in an area with a high burglary rate. Cameras for security against intruders are likely to be positioned close to the entrances to your buildings, not in group rooms. However, some companies now promote an internal CCTV and webcam system as part of child protection for nurseries. Serious issues are raised by the practice of recording children and staff on a continuous basis. Please use this section as a basis for discussion, whether or not you work in a setting that uses the technology.

It is said that cameras will provide greater protection to children, because it will be possible to see, or to dissuade, adults who mean harm. However, if abusive adults get through proper checks, it is very unlikely that they will be so foolhardy as to ill-treat children in front of the CCTV. Note:

- The system cannot be secret; any setting is obliged to inform everyone who uses the premises, including staff, parents and visitors, by a clear notice that CCTV recording takes place here.
- It is risky to delegate the protection task, even partially, to technology. A good manager contributes to safeguarding by walking about the setting rather than watching the screens.
- It is claimed that the recordings will avoid false allegations of abuse, because a setting will be able to prove that nothing untoward has occurred.

- It is possible that a parent might be reassured by a video recording, when there has been a specific misunderstanding.
- However, parents who are convinced their child has been abused within the setting may not have a particular incident in mind. They may assert that anything happened off camera, or that someone has tampered with the recordings.
- All recordings must be stored in a secure place and not be held indefinitely. Settings would need a very good reason to keep recordings for more than three months, and so the system cannot counter accusations about less-recent events.

Keep the child in mind

In the previous edition of this book, Lindon (2011) comments: 'I have yet to encounter any company marketing this kind of CCTV that discusses the impact on children, other than to assert that being watched by camera is for their own protection. Guidance is unclear about the rights of children to know they are being watched remotely and also recorded. However, the Information Commissioner's Office (ICO) has stated that school pupils, and not only parents, should be informed and consulted over the use of fingerprinting technology for borrowing library books or cash-free lunch purchases. Any setting that installs this kind of CCTV needs to conform to laws about data protection. For example, some equipment enables a watcher to zoom in on individuals. This system generates personal data and the user will have to register with the ICO'.

Pause for reflection

Look at one or two websites of companies that promote the use of CCTV and webcams. You will find advertisements in early years magazines.

- Look carefully at the claims for what the technology will achieve.
- To what extent do promotional materials address the questions raised in this section?
- Do any websites acknowledge the issue of children's right to privacy?

Webcams

Similar issues of privacy and lack of informed consent for young citizens are also sidestepped when the CCTV monitoring is linked to a webcam facility for use by parents of children attending a nursery.

These systems are marketed to early years settings as a way to reassure parents that their children are safe and happy. Parents are given a password that enables them to log onto the website and the rationale is that parents can join in their child's day while at their own place of work. However, parents are not spending time with their children; they are watching a screen. Parents are best reassured by practitioners who welcome them – sometimes at short notice – and who share the child's day through conversation and generous displays of photos.

There is nothing in the webcam system to ensure that parents watch only their own children. There is no protection of confidentiality to prevent them talking about what they see of another child's frustrations or difficulties. Intermittent watching is unlikely to provide the context, and parents should not be informed about the private life of other families so that they can make sense of what they viewed today. There is no way, other than asking for responsible behaviour, to ensure that a wider circle of adults (for instance, parents' work colleagues) does not watch the webcam images.

Case study

Happy Days Nursery

This private nursery and others within the same chain have promoted access to the nursery webcam facility as a way for parents to join in their child's day. The baby-room team has reached an awkward position with one parent.

Darren's mother uses the viewing facility a great deal. She phones several times each day from her office to instruct Darren's key person that his nap is being allowed to continue for too long, or he is not being given enough attention, compared with other toddlers. At pick-up time this afternoon she comments on the behaviour of another toddler, whom she has watched, and seems to expect to hear an explanation from the practitioner. Another parent, also in the room, comments sharply, 'Excuse me! My son is none of your business. The point is to watch your own baby.'

- What issues arise from this situation? Do you have concerns of any kind?
- What would be a sensible next step?

You will find a commentary on page 203.

Find out more

https://search.ico.org.uk/ico/search
For more information about codes of practice for CCTV use.

Use of photographs

Computer technology and digital photography may be very useful for those working in a nursery setting or at home as a childminder. Photographs that have been taken using a digital camera can be displayed on a laptop at the end of the day, or very soon after the images were taken.

However, practitioners are sometimes confused about the use of photos because, during their training, some were told not to use images showing a child's face in their student portfolio. This situation is different from visual displays within a group setting or in your home as a childminder.

There is usually no problem with images that remain in the setting and document in a visual way what a child or young person has done.

- It is appropriate that you involve children in choosing between photos and in taking photos as well. It is a matter of respect not to insist on an image that, for any reason, a child does not want on display.
- If you work for services that operate from shared buildings, you should not leave photos on public display. You could use a photo album, large scrapbook or room dividers, all of which may be locked away when the service is not operational.
- Photographs should not leave your setting, except to go home with children, unless parents have given their informed consent. Photographs or other visual images such as video recordings are personal data and so their use is determined by laws on data protection.
- You should not put images of younger children on a website. If images were to be used the composition of the photograph should exclude their faces. Children's faces should be obscured in photography in a natural way; blanking out their features gives a bizarre message. Consent should be obtained from the parent and child to use the image, making it clear that the child's face will not be recognisable.

Pause for reflection

Some nurseries, schools and after-school settings have developed their own website as a means of giving information about the setting and promoting their services. You need to consider carefully what materials are put on the site.

Check on both the formal or informally understood guidelines in your setting or service about the use of photos, whether for a website or in general.

Look at this source. What ideas could apply to your own practice?

- Briefing paper from the NSPCC (2013) 'Using photographs of children for publication: An NSPCC Fact Sheet' NSPCC. Available online at: www.nspcc.org.uk/globalassets/documents/information-service/factsheet-using-photographs-children-publication.pdf

Mobile telephones

Mobile telephones are part of daily life for many people. A clear statement about personal mobile telephones should now be part of the safeguarding policy of any setting. Under no circumstances should practitioners be chatting or texting on their mobile while they are working with the children. For that reason alone, it became more usual for group settings to make it part of standard professional behaviour that personal mobile phones were placed in practitioners' lockers during working hours.

The actions of Vanessa George in a Plymouth day nursery showed the risks from abusers who used the camera function that is part of many mobile telephones. George took photos of her sexual abuse of young children and put the images online. She was jailed in 2010. Then, in 2011, Paul Wilson, who worked in a Birmingham day nursery, was found to have recorded his abuse of children, including some at the nursery, on his mobile phone.

Any group setting should have one or more workplace mobile telephones for practitioners to carry when they take children on local outings. Any photos should be taken on a workplace camera and be loaded onto a workplace laptop. There are no circumstances under which practitioners in a group setting should be using their personal equipment.

Dealing with allegations about practitioners

Any group setting, daily or residential, should have clear procedures for dealing with allegations, from whatever source. Childminders and foster carers also need to be clear about the steps they must take in response to allegations. The key point is that allegations must be treated formally as concerns about child protection. They must not be treated as a more general issue about establishing what has happened, nor can allegations be treated exclusively as a disciplinary matter.

Listen, hear and understand

When you first hear an allegation, your main focus should be:

- Listen carefully to what you are told by a child, a parent or another practitioner. Ensure you understand the details but do not leap to conclusions. The key point, as always, is to show that you take seriously what you have been told.
- The allegation may be about your own actions or the behaviour of another practitioner or volunteer. Childminders or foster carers may hear an allegation arising from their own behaviour or that of family members who also live in their home.
- Discuss the matter with appropriate people who are more senior than you or in a position to help you find a sound perspective on the matter. A practitioner working in a setting should speak with the designated safeguarding lead. If the allegation is about someone else on the team,

then the Designated Safeguarding Lead should discuss the matter with the practitioner or the volunteer in question. They should fully inform the manager of the setting. Childminders or foster carers need to contact their adviser or link worker promptly.

● Follow the procedures set out by your setting and ensure that anyone involved – parent, practitioners and other professionals – realises that you are acting in accord with agreed guidelines. Steps will include writing up the allegation and what is done at each stage of the process.

Sometimes there will have been a misunderstanding and a parent, or other adult, accepts there is a credible explanation for the behaviour that they questioned. However, they will be confident as long as the nature of their concern was properly acknowledged. Parents should feel that their concern or challenge about a practitioner has been taken with the same level of seriousness as if the nursery had been concerned that something untoward had happened in the family home.

Simple details should be entered into the written record in the same way that you would write up a parent's account of a child's injury when the matter was satisfactorily explained.

Who needs to know

Unless there really has been a complete misunderstanding (and still write this up), the details of an allegation of abuse or neglect must not be kept within the setting or service. Procedures should make clear for the Designated Safeguarding Lead who should be told about the allegation within line management and other relevant bodies, such as a management committee or school governors.

Allegations about practitioners, or any aspect of practice in a setting, must be passed to the relevant body that inspects and regulates provision in your part of the UK. This body has to be told of any issue that could affect the validity of your registration, including if a child protection investigation, started by a social worker, raises doubts about the behaviour of any member of your team. The same obligation to inform will arise if the allegation, or an investigation, raises questions about the safety of your premises. Other than these circumstances, it is not appropriate for the inspection or regulatory body to be told about child protection concerns; the referral and the responsibility belong to social care services.

It would not be advised practice for a visiting professional to report a concern (for instance, to the social work team) without first speaking with the practitioner or setting manager. The only exception would be if this individual genuinely felt a conversation would put a child at risk and that the situation was therefore an emergency. Nor would it be advised practice for the local education department, or similar body, to deal with an allegation without informing the setting or practitioner who had been accused. Apart from the right to defend oneself against serious allegations, the manager of a setting, with the Designated Safeguarding Lead, needs to make their own investigation of what is alleged to have happened.

However, anyone can make a referral independently. If your manager or safeguarding lead does not agree a referral should be made and you have concerns then you can still make your own referral to children's social care.

Whistle blowing

What does it mean?

Whistle blowing: raising serious concerns about actions or methods in one's own setting or service; it is not always about safeguarding issues.

Some concerns could be expressed by practitioners who are part of the setting or service, or temporary members of the team, such as students or volunteers. The term 'whistle blowing' usually means taking steps beyond talking with the person or people directly involved. The reason whistle blowers feel obliged to take their concerns up the hierarchy, or even outside their setting, is because they believe that ordinary procedures of expressing concern have not worked or have been ignored.

Whatever the level of concern, most practitioners are understandably reluctant to allege that something is dubious about a colleague's behaviour.

Practitioners registered with the NMC must follow the *Raising Concerns Guidance for Nurses and Midwives* (NMC, 2015).

Other regulated professionals must also follow relevant guidance provided by their regulatory body.

The following key issues are important:

- Feelings of loyalty mix with fears of the consequences: 'What if I am wrong?' Guidelines on whistle blowing often state that the focus needs to be on the well being of children: 'What if I am right to be worried and I do nothing?'
- Practitioners feel in a difficult position if their concerns arise from something they were told in confidence. Again, the key issue is whether it is right to keep that confidence. What is the likely impact on the well being and safety of children?
- It is better to express a concern at an early stage. Then it may be more straightforward for appropriate action to be taken. Any concerns about what worries you, in what way and for what reasons need to be expressed clearly.
- Keep a note of whom you told and the date. This personal record will be especially important if you feel your concerns were belittled and nothing then happens.
- Practitioners may be concerned about possible repercussions, especially if the team member is of a higher status or apparently more experienced.

Unfortunately, even junior team members can be regarded as culpable at a later date if they saw bad practice and failed to say anything – even if they were not directly involved in abusive or neglectful actions.

● Be prepared to raise your concerns again; either that the situation has worsened, or that the practitioner in question has not kept a commitment to change the actions or approaches that were challenged.

It is the responsibility of senior practitioners, managing or governing bodies and any involved advisers to ensure that whistle blowers are not put at a disadvantage by their actions. No team member should believe that loyalty to colleagues or the actual setting over-rules safeguarding. If practitioners victimise the whistle blower, then their behaviour should become a disciplinary matter.

Pause for reflection

The serious case review following the arrest of Vanessa George pointed to significant failings in the safeguarding system at the Plymouth day nursery where she worked. The report describes an isolated setting, whose manager failed to comply with requested improvements. The nursery continued with lack of proper safeguarding policy or procedures, an informal approach to staff recruitment and lack of any staff supervision system. Both the manager and staff showed evidence of blurring the boundaries of their personal and professional lives.

The conclusion of the serious case review is that these factors of poor practice created a situation in which Vanessa George was able to sexually abuse some of the children and record that abuse on her mobile phone. Some of her colleagues were uncomfortable about George's sexualised behaviour at work, such as crude language and showing indecent images of adults on her mobile phone. However, they felt unable to challenge her. George was seen as close to the manager and trusted by her, and came to occupy a position of power within the nursery.

The staff had poor knowledge of child protection and lacked confidence to question why George chose to change children's nappies in a different cubicle from all her colleagues. Unsupported practitioners were unlikely to whistle blow on a forceful practitioner, favoured by the manager, who was the safeguarding lead in the nursery. The manager's strong community links also appear to have contributed to the inadequate safeguarding and general poor practice, since some other local professionals failed to act about expressed concerns.

Read the overview report (Plymouth Safeguarding Children Board, 2010) online and discuss the key issues with fellow students or colleagues.

Take appropriate steps

If there is clear evidence or serious reason to suspect abuse or neglect, then procedures for dealing with an accused practitioner have to follow the same pattern as that of suspected abuse by any adult.

The manager has two main responsibilities. The first is to ensure that children and anyone else are safeguarded in an effective way. The second responsibility is to behave as a responsible employer: of the practitioner who is the focus of the allegation but also of practitioners who passed on, or made, the allegation. Unless the allegation is about the manager, she or he should undertake a swift and brief gathering of the main information and promptly contact the designated safeguarding officer for the local authority. That external person will support the manager with the next steps.

Take another perspective

The policy perspective

Practitioners should follow clear policies that are in line with national policy and the Local Safeguarding Children Board for dealing with allegations against people who work with children.

An allegation may relate to a person who works with children who has:

- behaved in a way that has harmed a child, or may have harmed a child;
- possibly committed a criminal offence against or related to a child; or
- behaved towards a child or children in a way that indicates they may pose a risk of harm to children.

HM Government (2015a: 54) in the *Working Together Guidelines* state that:

- 'County level and unitary local authorities should ensure that allegations against people who work with children are not dealt with in isolation. Any action necessary to address corresponding welfare concerns in relation to the child or children involved should be taken without delay and in a co-ordinated manner. Local authorities should, in addition, have designated a particular officer, or team of officers (either as part of multi-agency arrangements or otherwise), to be involved in the management and oversight of allegations against people that work with children. Any such officer, or team of officers, should be sufficiently qualified and experienced to be able to fulfil this role effectively – for example, qualified social workers. Any new appointments to such a role, other than current or former designated officers moving between local authorities, should be qualified social workers. Arrangements should be put in place to ensure that any allegations about those who work with children are passed to the designated officer, or team of officers, without delay.
- Local authorities should put in place arrangements to provide advice and guidance on how to deal with allegations against people who work with children to employers and voluntary organisations. Local authorities should also ensure that there are appropriate arrangements in place to effectively liaise with the police and other agencies to monitor the progress of cases and ensure that they are dealt with as quickly as possible, consistent with a thorough and fair process.

- Employers and voluntary organisations should ensure that they have clear policies in place setting out the process, including timescales, for investigation and what support and advice will be available to individuals against whom allegations have been made. Any allegation against people who work with children should be reported immediately to a senior manager within the organisation. The designated officer, or team of officers, should also be informed within one working day of all allegations that come to an employer's attention or that are made directly to the police.

- If an organisation removes an individual (paid worker or unpaid volunteer) from work such as looking after children (or would have, had the person not left first) because the person poses a risk of harm to children, the organisation must make a referral to the Disclosure and Barring Service. It is an offence to fail to make a referral without good reason.'

> ### Case study
>
> #### Joan
>
> A practitioner in your children's centre has been suspended following complaints. There are claims that Joan regularly humiliated and threatened children. Colleagues objected to her use of harsh punishments, such as shutting one child in a cupboard and making another child stand out in the rain.
>
> This afternoon you watched a group of children play out what seem to be some of their experiences. The child who played Joan was shouting insults at the others and threatening, 'It'll be the wooden spoon for you!' The game came to a close when the other children all leapt on 'Joan' and shouted, 'You're going to prison now.' A letter was sent to the parents, explaining in brief that the member of staff had been suspended, pending an investigation. But there has been no conversation with the children.
>
> - What should catch your attention about this situation?
> - What should probably be your next step?
>
> You will find a commentary on page 203.

Depending on the severity of the accusations, a practitioner would almost certainly be suspended while further enquiries were undertaken. Colleagues may find the allegations hard to believe; and everyone has to remember that suspicions may be unfounded. Depending on the nature of the allegation, childminders or foster carers may have their practice temporarily suspended and children will be transferred to other carers.

Any investigation should be undertaken promptly for the well being of a child. However, it is also unacceptable for practitioners to spend weeks, even longer in some cases, with a serious allegation hanging over them. Childminders and foster carers can feel especially isolated under these circumstances. However, practitioners working in a team may be placed on leave of absence, or in a large setting given duties that do not involve contact with children. This disruption cannot be allowed to drag on indefinitely and the practitioner should be kept informed of the progress of the investigation. If allegations prove to be unfounded, then equal effort should be made to ease the practitioner back into work and to reinstate the practice of a childminder or foster carer.

Unfounded or false allegations

Unfounded allegations may arise because of a misunderstanding or a premature leap to an unsupported conclusion about behaviour or an event. However, some allegations can be called false because there never was any basis for the claims.

What does it mean?

False allegations: claims about the behaviour of someone that prove to be untrue when the factual evidence is fully explored.

Malicious allegations: false claims made with the intention of causing harm and distress as a direct result of what is said.

A high proportion of adult fears underlying anxiety about physical contact (see page 207) arise from false allegations about abuse. The fear is also sometimes about malicious accusations. Strictly speaking, the two are not the same, although 'false' and 'malicious' can become entangled in practice and create a poisonous atmosphere, sometimes leading to personal tragedy. Everyone needs to know that allegations, like disclosures, are taken seriously. But, equally, it is necessary that everyone also knows that false allegations made by adults, children and young people are not simply brushed aside. Evidence of malice, defined as the desire to vilify or take revenge on another person, is an example of reprehensible behaviour that needs to be tackled in its own right.

False allegations from children or families sometimes draw attention to serious problems that need to be addressed. However, appropriate support has to be offered alongside actions – whether serious conversations with a child who is old enough to know what they have done, or documented meetings with parents. It must be made very clear that it is unacceptable to use accusations to gain attention or attract family support.

When fellow professionals make allegations that prove to be unfounded, a great deal depends on the details of the case. It is crucial not to discourage an expression of serious concern, nor to punish genuine whistle blowing.

Note:

- It is one situation when a practitioner turns out to be mistaken but expressed concerns appropriately and behaved professionally while the matter was being investigated. However, even under positive circumstances, the manager and designated safeguarding lead will need to work hard to re-establish trust and team working.

● It is a different situation if a practitioner has ignored appropriate confidentiality or shows a pattern of poorly supported accusations against one or more colleagues. The manager needs to consider disciplinary steps for anyone who excuses unprofessional behaviour with 'Better safe than sorry'.

Disciplinary procedures

Allegations of serious bad practice by a practitioner become part of the case in a child protection investigation when there is evidence that the person has:

● behaved in a way – by action or inaction – that has harmed a child or made it very likely that harm could result;
● committed or possibly committed a criminal offence against a child or young person, in which case the police would also be involved;
● shown such a poor standard of practice that this person is unsuitable to work with children.

Serious misconduct would lead to dismissal but, whatever the details of the situation, proper procedures have to be followed for disciplinary matters. This aspect of the process is separate from the child protection investigation, and will wait until that investigation is complete. The local authority Designated Safeguarding Officer will guide the manager on timing and steps. It will never be satisfactory to use dismissal as the only way to deal with practice that has put children at risk. Likewise, voluntary resignation is certainly not the end of the matter if a practitioner's actions have been abusive or neglectful. If a practitioner's behaviour has been unacceptable, then their contract of employment may be terminated, or conditions be attached to continued employment, as the result of the child protection issue. In that case, the manager must inform the relevant body for vetting and barring (see page 174).

Addressing unsatisfactory practice

You might be reassured that a practitioner's actions have not been as serious as abuse or neglect, but that their practice falls short of acceptable standards. Senior team members should address relevant issues promptly: through supervision or broader staff discussion. Examples of situations that need to be challenged are:

● A practitioner has been lax in informing parents about incidents between children in the club that led to injury, and failed to mention a child's accident.
● Two nursery practitioners working in one room have already been told not to use their mobile phones while they are on duty. A parent has questioned why a student was left alone with the children while both members of staff were in the corridor, each talking on their mobile phone. (More about mobile phones on page 183.)

- The key person did not check properly whether this mother had given permission for her child's photo to appear in a feature about the school in the local newspaper. Apart from the fact that it is for parents to give or withhold such permission, some parents are in hiding from violent partners.
- A parent's comment reveals that a practitioner does personal shopping during trips with children and drops bags at her home on the way back to the centre.

Clear directions about a practitioner's behaviour should be written up after the supervision session in the practitioner's file. If practitioners do not heed warnings and persist in bad practice, then they might eventually be dismissed. However, proper procedures will have to be followed to avoid accusations of wrongful dismissal. A senior practitioner may, for instance, have to ensure that a certain number of clear verbal and written warnings have been given to a practitioner. Check out your own procedures; they will be relevant whatever the unacceptable practice, not only alleged child abuse. A similar written process should be followed if childminders or foster carers need to address their less-than-good practice with the childminding adviser or link worker.

Communication with children

When children have been ill-treated by practitioners or volunteers, it is important that their experience is recognised. They need to know that responsible adults took notice and have taken action on the children's behalf. They might be reassured that the behaviour of a volunteer was wrong and this person will not be allowed to come to the centre any more. If there has been long-term or organised abuse in a setting or service, children may need specialist input, supported by the care of practitioners whom they know and who were not involved. Children need to be reassured, more than once, that they, or their peers, have been tricked by adults whose behaviour was wrong.

Communication with parents

It is better to be ready to talk with parents when there has been a problem. The local parent grapevine operates at speed and dealing properly with questions is the only way to increase the chances that accurate information is passed around.

In the early stage of an investigation, staff might be told to say that complaints have been taken seriously and are being thoroughly checked. It is important that practitioners do not allow themselves to be drawn into gossip. If a practitioner is dismissed, then it is wiser to give an explanation, otherwise parents will naturally speculate about the reasons. The head or manager should consult the management committee, school governing body, or other line management, about how best to phrase any communication, spoken or written by letter.

Case study

Aaron and Greg

Aaron

Aaron is three years old and attends the community drop-in session that you organise within the local children's centre. On his left hand he has an extra finger, which is loose. Aaron does not seem to be worried and his childminder has explained in the network support group that the family is waiting for surgery to deal with the problem.

You have noticed that a childminder, new to the drop-in, seems to avoid being close to Aaron and has visibly shuddered when she looked at the boy's left hand. Last week you thought this adult deliberately ignored Aaron's outstretched hand when he asked to be helped to jump down from the climbing frame. Today, you overheard the same childminder talking with a parent, another regular at the drop-in. The childminder looked across at Aaron and said, 'It's horrible. That floppy thing gives me the creeps.'

Greg

You have heard an increased amount of noise from the room next to the one in which you work with your group of children in a day nursery. A student on work placement appears to have taken a dislike to one of the children. She always calls him 'Gregory O'Connor', although he is known as Greg to everyone else and children in this setting are not usually addressed by their first and family name. Over the last week most of her shouting appears to have been aimed at Greg and you thought you heard her mocking the child's accent with, 'Can't understand you – talk properly!'

Your colleague next door has been showing the student how to complete a developmental record on children. As you passed the door of that room you saw the student propel Greg into a chair and say, 'Right, Gregory O'Connor. Let's see all the things you can't do.'

Today the two rooms have joined together for lunch. You are chatting with Greg. The student ignores you, leans over to Greg and shouts very close to his ear, 'You shut up, Gregory O'Connor! No talking at mealtimes!' You say to the student, 'I was talking with Greg,' and she just stares at you. The practitioner responsible for this room looks across but he says nothing.

Consider the following questions. If possible, bring together the views of your colleagues or fellow students.

● What would concern you about these situations?
● In each, what should probably be your first step

You will find a commentary on each scenario on pages 203–4.

Safeguarding and written records

The importance of good-quality records for child protection runs alongside what should already be careful and attentive standards. When concerns are raised from outside a setting, practitioners should be able to make an informed contribution from their knowledge and descriptive records of the child's physical well being, development and patterns of behaviour.

Make the connection with...

Personal information

Vulnerable children especially need attention to the detail of their lives and this cannot be achieved without keeping records in residential and foster care. Items such as a birth certificate and informal documentation of the kind that would usually be held by a child's birth family need to be stored carefully. Looked-after children (and young people) need good care to be taken of their personal information and keepsakes, with their involvement.

Children can experience many changes and part of the whole safeguarding process is that adults create a safe place for items of personal value that might otherwise get lost forever. When children do not have a family to keep a record of childhood events, then someone else needs to respect and store photos, drawings, certificates from school, birthday cards and all the other items that are very important later for adolescents and adults who have spent time in care.

When child protection becomes a possible issue, then good standards in written reports apply in the same way as any recording. The following guidelines for reflection apply to most kinds of records. The basic questions to consider are:

- what you need to record;
- the reasons why you are recording this information;
- good practice in how you record;
- issues of confidentiality of reports and of appropriate access to them.

These general issues apply to all kinds of records: log book, diary, accident book, serious incident book, medication records, descriptive record of a child's progress, diet or health, and so on. Any record needs a full date for each entry and a clear signature of who has written this entry, even if you work alone as a childminder or foster carer. Children move on to another setting or form of provision and earlier records may need to be accessed, read and understood. Separate individual records need to be kept, even for siblings. Otherwise, it can be hard to track clearly what has happened to a particular child or young person.

Different kinds of information

In terms of writing up child protection concerns, it helps to distinguish the following kinds of information.

i Directly observed evidence

What you can honestly describe as events you saw and words you heard. This information is in the first person: your own observations. In making it clear and writing it up accurately you still need to take care in keeping distinct what you observed and the sense you make of it – your supported opinion and interpretation.

ii Evidence from reliable sources

Some information is relevant that you did not hear or see for yourself; you judge the person(s) describing an event or concern to be reliable. You may trust them because they are fellow professionals, but that would not be the only standard. Another child or a young person might be reliable from your experience, whereas an individual fellow professional, or any adult, might have an outlook on events or people that unsettles your view of them as reliable. So you need to be clear about the grounds for judging somebody as a reliable source on this occasion.

iii Opinion

The important theme running through good written records is that they are honest, distinguish the source of what is presented as factual and explain the reasoning and support for professional opinion. Some practitioners are still told that reports must only be 'factual' and that they must not write about their 'opinions'. This ruling is neither helpful nor workable.

Well-supported opinions are of value for professional discussion as well as written records. But there always has to be the sense of 'for these reasons ... ', 'because...' or 'from my knowledge of ... '. Opinions are potentially dangerous if they are mixed with directly observed evidence and the boundaries are unclear. Can you give a straight answer to the question, 'In what way(s) does my opinion add to my factual description and help to understand what has happened?'?

iv Hearsay

The key points in the definition of 'hearsay' in the *Shorter Oxford Dictionary* are: 'founded upon what one has heard said, but not within one's direct knowledge' and 'report, rumour, common talk, gossip'. Hearsay might include comments such as, 'Of course, she hits the children. People are always hearing screams from that flat.' Hearsay can come with an aura of certainty, but reliable details are hard to distinguish from rumour because of the sense that 'Everybody knows ... '.

Hearsay information should not be immediately dismissed as unreliable gossip. There will be important factual content in some hearsay, but it has to be identified. If the content of hearsay raises concerns, there would need to be some exploration, for example, of who is included in this 'everybody'. What has happened to build this certainty? Can anyone contribute a more direct 'I saw' or 'I heard' or even 'So-and-so told me that ... had happened to her'?

v   A clear narrative

It can help to hold four basic questions in your mind: Who? What? Where? and When? These are sometimes called the four 'W's and are useful shorthand. The examples in this list use 'I' and 'we' but practitioners need to follow the style of writing requested for their own records. Sometimes, the preferred style is to step back from the personal; for example: 'Mrs Singh told (practitioner name) that ...' or 'In the conversation with Tania's elder brother, it was made clear that ...', with the information of who the named practitioner was who had that conversation.

vi   Clear source of information

Sometimes you will write up what someone else has told you, perhaps a parent or concerned older child. You should make it clear in your report that you are documenting what somebody else says they saw or heard. Only quote somebody else's words if you are sure that this is accurate. Certainly, do not edit a child's words, or those of an adult.

If you are uncertain, show that you are recording the broad message. If what was said is open to more than one interpretation, then this ambiguity has to be left in an honest way. For example, you may not have direct experience that 'Emma's parents are having awful rows.' More accurately, what you are reporting is that 'Emma's next-door neighbour (name) spoke with me on (date) to say that he is "very worried" because he hears "all these screaming matches" through the wall between his home and the Davisons'.'

vii Description of events and concerns

Does your concern focus on a pattern of behaviour or changes in a child's more usual reactions? Then what have you seen or heard, and when? Support your observation with an explanation of your reasons for concern. For example, perhaps an older brother has been seen to hit and drag the younger sibling he picks up from nursery. Who saw this incident? When did it occur? What happened before the blow was struck? Where were the siblings when the elder struck the younger one? Has there been more than one similar incident? What action did you, or anyone from the nursery, take?

If a child's physical well being is in question, then be specific about your observations. It would be inadequate to state simply, 'Fazila's parents neglect her.' A professional report has to offer full description, arising from, 'We have been concerned about the standard of Fazila's care from her family because she wears the same clothes, including underwear, for over two weeks at a time. Fazila has become distressed because other children do not want to sit next to her and say that she smells. Fazila is in regular pain with her teeth, which we have mentioned on three occasions (dates) to her mother. To our knowledge the child has not yet (date) been taken to the dentist. Fazila is usually very hungry on Monday mornings and eats several helpings at breakfast. Her hunger seems to lessen as the week goes by ... '. And so on.

viii Intuitions and feelings

It is good practice to include in your written record details of how you reached a conclusion, not simply the judgement itself. If you know you frequently use words like 'obviously', then get into the habit of answering the questions, 'What is so "obvious" to me?' and 'Why am I making that link?'.

Sometimes it will not be easy to put your finger directly on what concerns you. It is important to pursue strong feelings of unease, and a colleague may be able to help you identify an observational basis for an intuitive feeling (see page 108). This observation can then be written into the report. If you cannot identify the factual basis, then you should not write vague comments such as 'Nobody in Liam's family seems to care about him.'

Sometimes your uneasiness may be fuelled by what does not happen. For instance, perhaps a child's mother rarely seems to react to situations; she shows neither happiness when the child is excited nor sympathy if the child is distressed. You would not conclude from this pattern that the child was necessarily subjected to deliberate emotional abuse. An equally possible explanation is that the mother is severely depressed, which is a cause for concern in itself. The child is 'in need' and the problem requires appropriate family support services.

ix Visual facts of injury

If a child has injuries, then make an accurate record of the nature and extent of the bruises, cuts or other marks. Use the body outline figure (Figure 4.3) to sketch the location of any injuries. Do not draw any conclusions that you are unable to support, especially guesses about the possible cause of any injury. For example, you might write that 'there were four bruises on Aled's upper arm and one under the arm'. You should not claim that the marks are probably from a fierce grip on the child's arm, unless you directly observed that physical attack. A series of small, round, inflamed marks on Aled's back might be cigarette burns. But what independent evidence do you have? Unless you have some basis for this statement – for instance, that the child told you – then do not go any further than a factual description of the injury in your report, with the area marked up on the body outline.

- Do not feel under pressure to go any further than is appropriate, given your role.
- Practitioners should use only the body outline and a written description; you should not be asked to take photographs.
- Assessment in a child protection inquiry sometimes involves photographic evidence, gained later and within the investigation. But everyone who is part of such an inquiry must be highly aware of children's dignity and their right not to be subjected to intrusive or unnecessary investigation.
- Practitioners will not always be in a position to see children unclothed. Babies and very young children need a level of personal care that involves changing their clothes. Some disabled children continue to need a high level of adult support with personal care.

- School-age children may have reason to change for games. But some early years and out-of-school settings do not have routines that make it likely practitioners will see a child in less than lightweight summer clothing.
- You would not, of course, pressure a child to remove clothing. But you might ask a question if a child rubs her leg, as if in pain. If children tell you that something hurts, it is wise to say, 'Can you show me where the pain is?' or 'Please point to where it hurts.' Younger children do not always have accurate words for parts of the body and a word like 'tummy' is often non-specific.

Documentation and record keeping

Details of an explanation

Write down, as literally as possible, any explanation that the child gives about the injury. Use the words and terms that are familiar to the child or young person. If their words for parts of the body are unusual, then put the correct term in brackets afterwards.

After a conversation with parents and other family carers, make notes of your conversation, even when what they say reassures you. For example, your observation of a minor lacerated area on a child's leg might be supported with the note that 'Sian and her father both said that the family dog bit her on Saturday evening. Mr Evans told May (key person) that he took Sian to A&E that night. The doctor cleaned the wound but said that no stitches were necessary.' On the other hand, it is appropriate to express a professional concern through a description characterised by inconsistent explanations of the same event, or changing stories.

Professional written style

Records and reports need to be legible, accurate and professional:

- Correct spelling, appropriate punctuation and basic grammar really do matter. The spellchecker on a word processor is useful, but you still need to read a draft carefully. It is a common mistake to have a word correctly spelled but it is not the word you intended to use.
- If you do not work with a pro forma, then try to make it easy for anyone to follow the flow of your report. Ensure any narrative about a child or family goes in the right order, with dates or times next to the incident in question.
- Use headings and consider a series of bulleted points for a series of incidents or concerns. This layout is easier to absorb than a long, unbroken paragraph.
- More experienced practitioners should be ready to help colleagues improve their style. Feedback needs to be constructive, so avoid non-specific criticism, such as 'Your report is far too muddled.' Any help given needs to focus on why this draft is 'muddled'. For instance, the practitioner needs to be told, 'You have identified that you have three main concerns about Tom. But the report is hard to follow because your concerns appear in bits throughout the report. And your descriptions are often separate from the dates you give. Let's start with your worry about Tom and the games he tries to play with Shoshana.'

Keeping a record of accidents

Parents will probably be used to your normal practice of keeping a record of any accidents that happen while their child is in your care:

- Each accident should be written up promptly, with details of the child on a separate page of the log or on a separate sheet that will then be placed in the accident record file.
- The record should include the date, time and location of the accident, any equipment that was part of the event and a description of what happened.
- There should also be a clear description of any immediate action taken to care for the child and any issues arising, such as a risk assessment about time or place.
- There will not always be significant issues; sometimes accidents just happen. Often the appropriate action will be to remind children about 'one at a time on the slide' or similar ground rules.
- The form should be signed by the practitioner who observed the accident or who was first to go across to the child. The form should be shown to the child's parent that day and that adult also signs the form. On the same day, the information goes into the accident file.
- A similar system can operate using a form to complete for 'accident on arrival', when a parent or other family carer lets you know that the child has a bruise or sore spot arising from an incident at home.
- However, it is important that if there are concerns about significant harm at any time when caring for children, a referral should be made to children's social care. Do not wait to gather more information.

Take another perspective

There are advantages in also setting up an appropriate spreadsheet. (Thanks to Buckingham's Nursery School in Leek for this explanation of their spreadsheet system.) The information is entered under different headings: date and time of day, the base room or class of the child, where the accident happened and any equipment, the sex and name of the child, the practitioner involved and whether a risk assessment followed. The type of accident is also entered under a small number of possible categories, for example: TSF (trips, slips and falls), HC (human collision), CSG (cuts, scratches and grazes) and HI (head injury). More serious incidents, such as breaks or fractures, will need other categories. The spreadsheet technology then enables a senior practitioner or manager to look for patterns, such as how often an individual child has accidents or whether there are more problems at particular times or places.

Timely recording

You should write up your notes about children as soon as possible after your observation or conversation, preferably the same day. If a situation with a child or parent has become very emotional, then it may be more sensible to make brief personal notes right after the event. Give yourself time to calm down, especially if the incident happened at the end of a day or shift. But return to the notes and write them up for a proper report no later than the next day.

In general, the longer you leave it to make your written record, the greater the chance that you will forget details. Another real possibility is that you start to lay your own interpretation over events. Prompt recording is especially important in child protection. Risk to the child may unfold quickly in some situations. But also, if the case reaches court, then professionals giving evidence are often asked to be specific about exactly when they made their notes. Records written up days after important events are far less credible than those promptly recorded.

It is very unlikely to be appropriate to make notes while you are talking with a child or a concerned adult. Writing down becomes a channel of communication that interferes with listening, looking and talking. It is also very likely that a child would feel a practitioner was more concerned about a written record than attending to what is being said. How do you feel, as an adult, if you consult your doctor, and he or she makes notes in a file or directly onto the computer screen at the same time as you are talking?

The most usual situation for disclosure (see page 98) would be that you take the first opportunity to note down what you have heard. A possible exception may arise with older children, most likely those who are already looked after and have a general understanding about how such matters work. Alternatively, in a lengthy conversation with a parent or practitioner, you might ask if it would be all right to make notes now. You would explain that you want to ensure that you have grasped all the details and do not want to have to trust your memory for this long and serious conversation.

Professional notes

It is accepted that practitioners sometimes need to make more speculative notes – for instance, about ideas for how to help a child, or information that is of uncertain relevance for the moment. Check whether your setting or service has a specific guideline about professional notes. General good practice is that professional notes should be kept in a safe place and must meet the standards for good-quality records. Such notes are not a justification for unsupported speculation or offhand remarks about a child or family. Professional notes must not be used as a means of maintaining a secondary or secret file and they should not last indefinitely. After a maximum of two to three months, the notes should either be integrated into the main file or shredded.

Confidentiality and information sharing

Generally speaking, children and their parents have the right to expect that information about them does not leave this setting or service, either through written or spoken communication, unless they have given their permission through informed consent.

What does it mean?

Informed consent: when anyone, child, adolescent or adult, is given sufficient information to be able to make a genuine decision to say 'yes' or 'no' to a request.

This obligation needs to be revisited when anyone – adult or child – shares a confidence with you, or you become aware of a situation that could put children at risk. Wherever possible, you gain that person's consent to talk with another professional or service. If that permission is refused, then you need to be sure about the compelling reasons that mean you cannot follow the refusal of consent. For instance, possible reasons would be that the impact of a serious family problem, the actions of practitioners, what is happening to this child or a child's behaviour towards a peer mean that your silence will place children at risk. These will be times when practitioners need to talk with someone else for a second opinion, within their own setting or in a careful way outside those boundaries (see page 107 for possibilities).

Children's wishes should be treated with the same level of respect as those of an adult. It is also good practice to record the reasons for your decision: to share information, and whether this step is with informed consent, or not to share information at the moment.

Access to records

Parents should have straightforward access to the records of their own children and adolescents (usually up to 18 years) in childcare, educational, health and other family services. However, parents do not have right of access to their child's file when a child protection investigation is in progress, and not necessarily once the work is complete.

In general, it is good practice to share with older children and young people what is written in their own files. This sharing will be through conversation and young people signing some of their own records in residential care. It is expected that any under-18s should be able to see their own records so long as access is not likely to harm someone else and they can, or can be helped to, make a written request, if that is required by this setting or service.

Find out more

www.ico.gov.uk
Data protection is the responsibility of the Information Commissioner's Office. The website gives the regional offices around the UK.

Information Sharing (HM Government, 2015d) Available at: www.gov. uk/government/uploads/system/uploads/attachment_data/file/419628/ Information_sharing_advice_safeguarding_practitioners.pdf
Also make sure that you are familiar with the national policy guidance.

Contributing to an assessment

The quality of your reports are important and should support your professionalism and show social care services that you have a vital contribution to make to the process of child protection.

At some point you might have to present a summary of your report on a child to a group of other professionals, perhaps at a case conference. In a meeting, it is not usually appropriate to work your way through the written report; a copy will have been provided as part of the papers for the meeting. Practitioners who attend case conferences need to be ready to talk through the main points of a child's record or the report. You will cover the following:

- the nature of your concern about the child, placed in the context of development;
- information supporting your concerns, if you have them;
- what you have done in your setting with the child and parents;
- any changes, for better or not, that you have observed in the child;
- the contribution of any practitioner is not going to be the final word on whether a child is being abused. Your input will be part of informal early enquiries or a more detailed investigation. Your contribution may support the need to worry about a child, or may place isolated concerns in a more positive context.

When there are concerns about a child, or plans are already underway for family support, your knowledge will contribute to the detailed assessment undertaken by professionals such as social workers. Each part of the UK has a framework for assessment that is to be used under these circumstances. It is possible that the designated safeguarding lead of a setting might contribute directly to this assessment but individual practitioners would work through and with the designated safeguarding lead.

Pause for reflection

Print off the assessment framework relevant to your part of the UK. Look at the summary triangle and consider what kind of contribution you could make from your professional knowledge.

Commentary on the scenarios

Each commentary offers some possibilities. You and your colleagues may raise other ideas and perspectives.

Heather (page 168)

Heather's conversation and pattern of play are not usual for a four-year-old girl. A new member of staff needs to raise her concerns, ideally first with Heather's key person. If that conversation stalls, then the issue needs to be taken to the designated safeguarding lead. It is not sufficient to deal with the situation just by telling Heather to stop. Practitioners may be concerned about family privacy, but the child's words and actions have brought her home life into the nursery. Other parents may also become aware of Heather's play when their own child says something.

The designated safeguarding lead will need to deal with the immediate situation and with the apparent confusion in the team about how to react to out-of-the-ordinary behaviour from children. Heather's key person, or the designated safeguarding lead has to speak to Heather's mother. It may help to start with an opening sentence such as 'I feel uncomfortable raising this matter,' followed by 'But I need to talk to you about what Heather sometimes does in her pretend play.' The opening sentence helps you get into the conversation and is not a distracting apology – see page 110.

It is possible that Heather is imitating what she has seen and has not been sexually abused through direct contact. But it is irresponsible for adults to behave in such a careless way that they are highly likely to be observed by children. Responsible adults stop sexual activity if a child wakes up and wanders into the bedroom – as they do in a family home. Also, if Heather is poorly supervised late in the evening, she may watch inappropriate material on television.

Heather's mother may accept that she has been irresponsible. If there are changes for the better, then Heather's key person should be able to track those improvements. If the situation does not improve, or events suggest that Heather is more directly involved, the designated safeguarding lead should make a referral to social care services.

The nursery team, led by the designated safeguarding lead, needs to consider whether to speak with Jack's parent(s). If something is said, it would be along the lines that a child in the nursery makes inappropriate physical contact with other children. Jack did not seem distressed, but the practitioner is aware that he may mention the event.

Owen (page 172)

Some parents have baths or showers with their young children and Owen is only three years old. This pattern may seem odd to anyone whose family style is less intimate in this way. Owen seems perfectly happy and there is nothing in what he says that raises concerns, given other knowledge about the family.

Your colleague's reaction does need some exploration in a confidential way. It is possible that her family was more reticent about bathing. But her words and the shudder raise the possibility that she experienced inappropriate or abusive attention around bathing routines as a child. Practitioners need to use opportunities for support so that personal experiences do not overwhelm their professional judgement about risk and protection.

Happy Days Nursery (page 181)

Partnership with parents means forming a close liaison about childcare and care of babies. Staff should make efforts to ensure continuity between home and nursery, especially for the care routines. However, parents need to trust the staff in this shared-care arrangement. Directing operations through the nursery webcam facility is not a feasible way to run this relationship. Darren's key person needs to talk with his mother about boundaries and trust. A warm welcome can be given for her to spend real time with her child in the nursery or to arrive early to pick him up on some days.

The mother's comments about other children in the room with Darren raise one of the serious issues about nursery webcams. It must be made clear to this parent that the team respects the privacy of each child and family. They are pleased to talk about parents' own children but will not respond to detailed questions about other babies or toddlers. This situation may well give food for thought to the nursery team about the webcam facility and privacy for all the children.

Joan (page 188)

There needs to be a conversation about Joan with the children, and observation of their play is a natural opening today. The group needs to be reassured that Joan's behaviour was wrong and that she will not be allowed back. It may feel right to apologise to the children for the fact that nobody has had a 'proper chat' with them about what happened. Perhaps this observation adds further details about Joan's bad practice and should therefore be written and added to the relevant report.

Depending on the details and timing of the incidents, it may be that children need a chance to talk about the events. Alternatively, they may deal with their feelings effectively through the play. Within reason, the children should be allowed to play out their distressing experience. Practitioners could look for ways to be part of this sequence, which could reassure children through the pretend play.

Aaron (page 192)

A practitioner responsible for a drop-in, even an informal session, should challenge poor practice. You need to talk with this childminder and express your concerns. If the practitioner feels uncomfortable about Aaron's disability, it is her task to deal with those feelings. It is not acceptable to show distaste and certainly not to be offensive in a child's hearing. This practitioner needs to understand why her reaction was emotionally cruel and her comment to the parent was unprofessional. There needs to be a clear commitment that she will change her behaviour towards Aaron; it is irrelevant that she is not his childminder. If she belittles your concern, you need to talk with the local childminding adviser, telling the practitioner that you will take this step.

It would make sense to raise the issue with Aaron's own childminder, to clarify if she has been aware of the situation. If so, then what has stopped her from saying anything? A possibility might be to raise the issues in the childminders' support group: both how to deal with difficult feelings about children and addressing the practice of a fellow practitioner.

Greg (page 192)

This student's behaviour is unacceptable and needs to be challenged. She appears to have taken a dislike to Greg and her behaviour is emotionally abusive and offensive. Additionally, she seems not to understand good practice about developmental records or the importance of a social mealtime.

You need to talk promptly with your colleague who is responsible for this room. Why has he apparently said nothing to this student? Ideally, you would like him to speak now with a senior practitioner, with your support if that will help. If your colleague believes there is no problem, you need to disagree and explain that you now feel obliged to talk with the designated safeguarding lead or the head of your setting.

All group settings need an atmosphere in which team members can express concerns to a senior practitioner. In this case, a senior practitioner needs to deal directly with the poor practice and communicate with the student's tutor. There appear also to be issues of confidence for the practitioner, who should be guiding this student and has failed to address poor practice.

Make the connection with...

Reflective practice

Effective practice in safeguarding and protecting the welfare of children and young people has to be reflective. Practitioners are dissuaded from being reflective when they believe, or are told, that they have no choice about a specific 'do' or 'don't' in practice. Any advice from a fellow practitioner or advising professional should be received with courtesy and taken seriously. However, it is important to recall that such advice is often at the end of a long filtering process.

All practitioners need to find the confidence to ask for the rationale behind a specific 'do' and certainly to ask, 'Which law?' when they are told that a specific 'don't' is 'illegal' or 'against the law'. Children are not well protected if practitioners, who deal with them day by day, feel they cannot ask questions after a blunt announcement of 'It's child protection policy.' Every trainer, adviser or writer will not reach the same conclusion about some of the dilemmas that are hard to resolve within child protection.

Practitioners have to be professional, bringing any inconsistencies into open discussion and not hiding behind comments such as 'We were told to ... ' or 'You can't win; everyone says something different.' See the example about physical contact on page 207.

Summary

This chapter has discussed how effective practice is underpinning by policies and procedures. Local policy should be in accordance with the evidence for effective practice and in-line with national policy. Practitioners should be familiar with local policy and procedures within their setting or practice area, and how to access them. Practitioners should know who to contact when they have concerns and should be supported when raising concerns whether they be about a child or a practitioner. Communication and information sharing is essential and effective safeguarding practice is supported by documentation and effective records. Records should be timely, contemporaneous and factual.

Effective safeguarding practice is also supported by opportunity for reflection and supervision.

National policy guidance has underpinned this chapter and readers are asked to ensure that they are familiar with safeguarding policy and guidance for practice.

The next chapter will discuss how to support a child's well being through effective care.

Key texts

The Bichard Inquiry Report http://dera.ioe.ac.uk/6394/1/report.pdf
Keeping Children Safe in Education 2015 (which replaced *Safeguarding Children and Safer Recruitment in Education* (December 2006) *and Dealing with Allegations of Abuse made against Teachers and Other Staff* (2012)), available online at www.gov.uk/government/uploads/system/uploads/attachment_data/file/447595/KCSIE_July_2015.pdf

To find out more please see the Disclosure and Barring Service Website: www.gov.uk/government/organisations/disclosure-and-barring-service

The Office of Public Sector Information at www.legislation.gov.uk provides information (full texts and shorter explanatory notes) about legislation in all four nations of the UK and Bills that are in process.

7 Well being and effective childcare

Introduction

The younger generation will not be raised in safety to adulthood exclusively through the steps of a child protection system. The term 'safeguarding' is useful because it includes a wide range of supportive adult behaviour. Practitioners, as well as parents, need to ensure they promote a child's physical and mental well being and ensure safety without overprotection. Part of that task is to support children (and later on, young people) as they learn steadily how to take care of themselves. This chapter discusses how a child's well being and welfare can be promoted through effective childcare. It addresses physical care and nurture, safety and troubled relationships between peers.

Physical care and nurture

Care really matters within the experiences of children and young people. They need to feel confident that familiar adults will meet their personal care needs and that those adults are pleased to be close, physically as well as emotionally.

Care-full and not care-less

Physical care routines are a vital means of communication with babies and young children and continue to be important for older children and adolescents with disabilities that mean they still need help. A personal, communicative experience enables children to feel they merit time and attention. Rushed, disrespectful care undermines emotional well being, but also puts children at risk from more than inadequate nurture. Children may then be less able to distinguish abusers – physical, sexual or emotional – who are keen to exploit children's uncertainty about their own worth.

Babies and children should be able to get to know the small number of people who offer physical care. In group settings, the key person should do most of a baby's or child's personal care, supported by the back-up key person (Lindon, 2010). Children should not start to believe that any adult can appear and deal with their needs, regardless of whether they like, or really know, this carer. Consistency of care can be a serious issue that should be properly addressed when settings have a large staff group or depend on agency staff. Even if everyone's care is of a high standard, a young child or a disabled older child can experience a long list of people who attend to intimate care needs.

Practitioners responsible for the physical care of a child will inevitably get to know how their body usually looks. You will notice whether a mark, bruise or other sign of injury is new since you last helped this child with personal care. You become familiar with individual children. But it is also important to realise, if you have not yet met the situation, that some distinct differences on the skin are not a sign of physical abuse.

Children of African, Caribbean, Asian and Mediterranean origin sometimes have patches of darker skin that occur naturally: the medical term is 'congenital dermal melanocytosis'. The darker areas are benign skin markings, but unfortunately can look like bruising to the inexperienced eye. These areas are a consistent slate-blue in colour, unlike genuine bruising that varies in shade and changes over a period of days. However, the similarity has sometimes raised concerns of non-accidental injury. Open communication will give parents, and their children, the opportunity to tell you that these differences in skin colouration are permanent.

Some children, from a range of ethnic groups, have areas that are without melanin and so have no pigmentation. The condition is called vitiligo and may not be noticed in lighter-skinned children until they have been in the sun. The permanently pale areas of skin are more noticeable when children have a dark skin colour. Practitioners who are unaware of the condition may possibly worry about old injuries. Vitiligo is not in itself a problem for health, except that these areas of the body have to be protected by sunblock. Children may, however, feel self-conscious when the different skin tones are obvious.

Dilemmas around physical contact

In recent years, many practitioners across different settings and services have become uneasy about touch within their daily life with children. There has been concern over whether there have to be limits to physical contact on the grounds of child protection. Any problems and dilemmas must be resolved in ways that genuinely safeguard the younger generation.

Law, guidance and policy

Practitioners sometimes justify actions that severely limit touch by, 'We're not allowed to ... it's the law,' or 'We have to ... it's child protection policy.' However, all relevant legislation across the UK places the well being of the child or young person at the centre of the safeguarding task. None of these laws, nor any national or official guidance, has banned physical contact between children and practitioners in the relevant services and settings. Problems arise through interpretations of parts of guidance, conflicting directions from advisers, trainers and writers, and sometimes misunderstanding of that advice by practitioners or students. The main issues seem to stem from anxiety about what is 'inappropriate' contact and fear that caring touch, or direct physical contact to keep a child safe, could be misinterpreted as abusive.

Some, possibly many, schools have a policy, which may be either formal or less obvious, of 'no-touch' between children and staff. Early years provision on a school site is sometimes told to follow the same ruling. Statutory guidance for schools in England requires that all education staff need to know that inappropriate behaviour with or towards children is unacceptable. It is also unacceptable and an offence for an adult in a position of trust to start a sexual relationship with a student. However, there are no examples that ban a reassuring pat to a distressed young person, or accepting the hand of a child who wants to walk around the playground with you. It is accepted that it is not realistic to suggest that teachers should never touch students.

It has been heard by Lindon (2012) that some practitioners are using the words: 'You have to watch your back.' This phrase demonstrates the level of anxiety about allegations in some settings. However, no-touch rules do not prevent this situation, nor resolve adult fears. Individual practitioners and teams need to take a thorough, problem-solving approach that focuses on children's well being and not just on avoiding unpleasant situations for adults, which may never occur. Otherwise safeguarding policy and daily practice are led by protection of staff (losing the 'child' in 'child protection') and paranoia. Worries and questions have arisen around several aspects of daily practice, which are now discussed in turn.

Case study

Meadowbank Nursery

A division has developed between staff in a large nursery about different approaches to the physical care of babies and toddlers. Two practitioners feel that very young children should be given time and attention for their personal care routines. The other two practitioners who work with the youngest children argue that everyone is supposed to focus on adult-organised activities to 'get children to learn' and that changing and feeding time is 'just care'. A situation has now developed where toddlers vote with their feet and go to the more caring practitioners to be changed and when they want any personal attention. Their colleagues now say that the children are spoiled and should not be able to exercise this kind of choice.

● What do you judge are the main issues around practice for this setting?
● What should happen now?

You will find a commentary on page 225.

Friendly physical contact

Touch is part of friendly and full communication with familiar children and young people. Touch that is accepted from, or offered to, children is a way to express welcome, friendliness, shared excitement about a project or comfort and reassurance.

Young children need touch, yet when Lindon (2012) ran child-protection training courses, she encountered a few nurseries that felt impelled to establish a cuddling policy or an age limit – for example, that children older than two or three years should not to be allowed to sit on laps. On the other hand, some teams and individuals have a responsible approach to child protection and an equally strong focus on the full developmental needs of babies and young children. For many practitioners the answer to the question 'Can we cuddle?' is a confident 'Yes'.

Occasionally, it is possible to track the source of rules about limited physical contact. Sometimes, practitioners have misunderstood appropriate suggestions about the personalised care of babies or young children. For instance, it is not good practice to pat all toddlers to sleep, regardless of whether that is their preference. On the other hand, there are situations in which practitioners have specifically been told not to cuddle young children, or have been given training in how to pick up young children in ways that minimise physical contact. Some have definitely been given rules about sitting children on cushions on an adult lap, or that a child must never face inwards with their legs around an adult waist.

One reason given for unworkable, and occasionally bizarre, guidelines is that physical contact may be misinterpreted as inappropriate sexual touching of children. Nobody can work effectively in an atmosphere where practitioners assume that parents, or young children themselves, are poised to claim abuse at the slightest excuse. A second reason given is that adults who want to abuse children sexually may gain access to provision. Of course, services need to be alert to this possibility but effective safeguarding cannot build on worst-case scenarios. Checks on recruitment must be thorough (see page 175) but, if dubious adults gain access to children, they will certainly not be dissuaded by a cushion rule.

The most pressing argument against restricting touch is the impact on the young children themselves. What sense can young children make of adults who pull back or look uncomfortable through their body language and facial expression?

● Children do not think, 'Never mind, it's their child protection policy.' They take it personally: 'She doesn't like me' or 'Nobody cares about how I feel' (and, in reaction, the emotion could be 'excited' just as much as 'upset').
● Children who are persistently deprived of affection can be emotionally at risk. The need for affection does not go away, so children are vulnerable

to anyone who offers personal attention. They are then doubly at risk, because they have not built an understanding of how safe adults behave.

When children have experienced relaxed and generous physical contact within their early years, they make sense of the reduced level of touch that is likely in primary school. However, children may still be fond of their class teacher. Playground support staff can be important to children, and children will be hurt, if an adult withdraws a hand that the child clearly wants to hold, or shifts away on a bench when the child has moved in close. During middle childhood, children themselves choose to limit touch to peers and adults with whom they have a close relationship.

Of course, at the same time, practitioners should be guided by children; it is inappropriate to demand affection or particular kinds of expression.

- Wise adults redirect a young child, or a child with learning disabilities, who is still finding out about respectful touch and the private areas of other people's bodies. The same kindly guidance is needed if a child's sense of boundaries has been distorted by experience that was genuinely abusive.
- Children whose families tend to kiss on the mouth (hello or goodbye) can be offered kissing on the cheek, on the hand or blowing a kiss. Otherwise, germs can pass round at lightning speed.
- Older children's emotional well being will be under threat if practitioners are denied even a light touch to the hand or shoulder. Another option is to sit next to an older child and put an arm round the shoulder, known as a 'sideways cuddle'.
- Physical contact will be necessary for safety during some lively activities and games. Respectful ground rules are established when adults say what they are going to do, in order to help or to demonstrate. There should be no need to touch a child in intimate areas of the body.

Take another perspective

Some schools and nurseries have explored the possibilities of simple massage. Heather Piper and Ian Stronach (2008) have pointed to the irony that, at the same time as a panic about touch, there is great interest in a more organised pattern of contact. Massage by adults of infants and younger children can be very positive and relaxing for both adult and child. Careful introduction of massage as something children of four to five years of age and older can do for each other has worked well. Massage sessions, explained and initially led by a practitioner who has been trained, can be an enjoyable addition to the day. However, touch should not be seen exclusively as something that is organised in a special session and involves expert training.

Residential and foster carers are professionals whose role has to include a large element of parenting. It makes sense to discuss thoughtful guidelines about contact that meets the needs of vulnerable children and young people. Practice can still recognise that abusive experiences mean that some individuals may misinterpret touch or allege that practitioners have been inappropriate. Residential teams have ground rules that are genuinely needed to protect everyone, such as keeping the bedroom door open when a practitioner is talking with a child or young person. Foster carers might adjust routines, such as a story before bedtime, so that this enjoyable event happens on the sofa and not in a child's bedroom.

Physical care of children

Misdirected anxiety about child protection has led to decisions in some settings that a practitioner must never be alone with a baby or child while attending to physical care. This ruling is achieved either by leaving the bathroom door completely open, locating the changing area in a main room, or imposing a rule that there must always be a second adult present. All these options, especially the second and third, raise the important issue of privacy for children.

The obligation to have a witness for intimate care routines in early years provision is presented as necessary by some trainers and writers on child protection. Yet this requirement needs to be challenged precisely on the grounds of safeguarding. An adult has been withdrawn from the other babies and young children, whose safety and need for friendly company has now been compromised. The assumption is also that practitioners will be in a group setting; the requirement is obviously a non-starter for most childminders.

Most children in primary school are likely to be able to deal with their own toileting needs. However, it is part of normal life through middle childhood that girls and boys will occasionally have a toileting accident. Some schools have a ruling that staff do not help children at all, even those of nursery age, under those circumstances. Children have to wait until their parent or other family carer arrives to change the child. Families are told, 'We are not allowed to change children,' with the implication that powers outside this particular school have forced them to leave a child, often distressed and embarrassed, in wet or soiled underclothes.

This approach needs to be challenged when applied to children in primary school. However, some early years settings follow the same rule, adding 'It's child protection policy' to the claim that they have no changing facilities or expect that children are reliably toilet-trained, so the problem should not have arisen. There are also teams who have been told not to help children in the toilet, although three- and four-year-olds often cannot manage to wipe their own bottom.

There is nothing in any of the relevant legislation or guidance that justifies refusal to help with ordinary, basic physical needs. Any service that accepts responsibility for children should have the proper facilities to deal with normal events, including toileting accidents. There is no legitimate justification from child protection, and writing this ruling into a policy does not make an unjustified stance immune from challenge. Furthermore, such rulings are discriminatory, since a proportion of disabled children will not be continent in childhood.

Early years, school and out-of-school practitioners will probably experience contradictory recommendations from different trainers and writers on safeguarding. Advice may say something along the lines that practitioners should avoid conduct that would lead any reasonable person to question their motivation and intentions. The big question is, of course, the outlook and professional knowledge of this 'reasonable' person. Lindon (2012) challenged the notion that a reasonable person should question (without additional concerns about the behaviour) offering cuddles to young children or helping them in the toilet, as part of normal, safe practice. Early years practitioners should not adjust good practice because they are anxious about misinterpretation by (unknown) people who are ignorant of ordinary life with babies and young children.

Make the connection with ...

Family life

There is very good reason to challenge any behaviour from practitioners that would raise serious concerns if those adults were within a child's own family. Practitioners have a duty of care as well as obligations about genuine child protection.

How would you judge parents whose normal practice was to:

- leave a child in wet or soiled underclothes for long periods of time?
- expect a child to deal with their own scrapes or bumps, to be handed a plaster without any contact and denied a hug or touch, even if they were very distressed or shaken by a fall?
- Would you consider that the parents or other key carers in the family were safe, caring or responsible?

Minor accidents and intervention for safety

Anxiety about touch has also extended to reluctance to take care of children after accidents. Some primary school teams refuse to administer any kind of first aid. The excuse sometimes given is that children may be allergic to plasters or antiseptic first aid preparations. But this situation should be resolved the same way as any allergy: all the team know that particular children need different first aid treatment. Similar reluctance has been expressed about helping children with suntan lotion, which leaves them open to the health risks of sunburn.

Practitioners need to use close physical contact when children plunge into an unsafe situation, or because they will not stop hurting each other unless an adult intervenes. Refusal to use touch could well be seen as neglect, a failure in the duty of care. It would also be irresponsible if practitioners let a child continue with a successful escape bid from the school grounds. On outings, a child who does not respond quickly to firm words cannot be allowed to run away because practitioners fear to use physical contact.

Pause for reflection

Think about what would happen if some settings were honest with families about the unspoken rules. Parents would then read a policy that said something like:

'We are very anxious that you will accuse us of sexual or physical abuse of your children. We have decided to solve the problem by not touching them at all, not helping them directly if they have accidents (toileting or otherwise) and leaving them to get into danger or be hurt by other children. Rest assured we will not touch your children under any circumstances.'

How would that be received? How many parents would want the problem that worries teams to be solved in this way? When it is put this starkly, what head or manager would persist in this approach?

Of course, practitioners must use their greater strength wisely:

- Physical intervention is not the first option every time. For instance, it would be unacceptable to seize hold of a child because they did not immediately comply with a request to pick up a dropped item of litter. Firm words or an uncompromising look enable many children to redirect themselves.
- Physical contact to stop children and keep them safe needs to be the minimum necessary: a touch rather than a grab, a containing hold rather than rough handling. Your use of physical adult strength has to be proportionate to the situation and to this child.
- The safety of a familiar adult's arms is accompanied by the words that communicate 'You are safe in my arms,' or 'I will not let you hurt yourself.' Your informed judgement may be that this child prefers to calm down from an outburst in a cosy corner, aware of your kindly and watchful look from close by.

Practitioners who work with volatile older children need training in the techniques of safe physical restraint. Poorly understood, or wrongly applied, techniques of restraint can injure children or adolescents, especially when more than one adult is involved in the restraint situation. Adults can also sustain injuries themselves. This situation is especially pressing when children live with severe emotional and behavioural disabilities, as they may not respond to lower levels of physical intervention. Children whose experience has damaged their ability to cope with ordinary life may react unpredictably or become increasingly violent – to themselves or to others.

It is good practice to write up in an incident book whenever you have needed to use physical means to intervene, physically guide in a firm way or restrain a child or young person. All teams need to discuss the minimal level of intervention that could be seen as 'restraint'. For instance, daily life with babies and very young children is full of times when you gently remove little fingers from poking someone, or carefully untangle a couple of wrestling bodies. However, with both younger and older children there is good reason to keep an accurate note of out-of-the-ordinary interventions. Records also help to judge whether your strategy to guide behaviour is actually working; for instance, have you intervened less often this week to stop a child who bites when thwarted?

Undoubtedly, there are problems for practitioners when guidance about 'physical intervention' is written from the perspective of dealing with older children. The Welfare Requirements for the Early Years Foundation Stage (for England) fail to acknowledge the daily situation with babies and very young children, where good-quality care and basic safeguarding require wise use of physical contact and guiding on a regular basis.

Take another perspective

Children spend many hours of their life in school and they need staff to create a friendly social atmosphere. Then the younger members of this community feel confident to resolve some difficulties themselves. Children will sometimes use physical intervention: a warning touch on the arm or actually holding back a peer who is displaying extreme emotion. It is important that neither child protection nor behaviour policy prevents this kind of conflict resolution. There are serious problems if schools label all physical contact as 'unacceptable behaviour', whether from adult to child or between children themselves. The resulting atmosphere is nothing less than institutional; it is hard to see how normal community life can develop under such a definition.

Keeping safe

The adult responsibility for safety is two-fold. Over early childhood, practitioners and parents have to keep babies and young children safe. They cannot be expected to understand and anticipate risks themselves. The early years are not a time of total protection by adults, because three-, four- and five-year-olds can have learned a great deal about taking care of themselves within a familiar environment. As children move into middle childhood, the adult role has to include active help for children to learn how to take good care of themselves: in terms of personal safety as well as other life skills.

Safety without overprotection

Part of safeguarding is that responsible practitioners ensure that the physical environment for children is free from hazards and that children do not have accidents that could have been avoided. However, children need to enjoy their childhood, need opportunities to stretch themselves and, steadily, need to recognise and manage their own risk. Children are not, in the end, well protected if adults are so anxious about something going wrong (and about themselves being blamed) that they remove all interest from the play environment. The atmosphere becomes what Tim Gill (2007) describes as 'risk averse'. Practitioners (and parents too) decide it is better not to take any chances; they create a nominally safe, but very boring, day for children. The adults have overlooked the greater risk that lively children will find their adventures out of adult sight and, eventually, older children and adolescents will move about independently.

Adults should take responsibility for keeping children physically safe. Yet the practice of overprotection is, rather like any no-touch policy, much more about adult protection than about good basic safeguarding. Lord Young's report, *Common Sense – Common Safety* (2010), recognised that it is inappropriate to treat low-hazard environments such as schools and other places for children as if they are much the same as a factory. The advice also confirms the move that many thoughtful teams have made to well-rounded risk–benefit analysis rather than an exclusive focus on risks. In early years provision this means being aware of the benefits to children of particular resources, equipment or outings. Any discussion and brief written assessment is then focused on 'How do we make this valuable opportunity safe enough?' (Lindon, 2011).

Learning about personal safety

Responsible adults need to support children to learn about how to keep themselves safe. A key point is neither to wait until something happens nor to focus only on those children whom you believe to be more at risk. Learning how to keep themselves safe and being confident about what to do in doubtful or emergency situations are part of growing up through childhood. Helping children learn is a continuing process over the years, certainly not something that is 'done' after using a story with nursery-age children or one session at school about road safety.

Whenever possible, supporting children in personal safety should be a joint responsibility between practitioners and families. Like any other aspect of your work, parents have the right to be informed and consulted about your aims. Some conversations will appropriately be shared, with a child's involvement, because, 'This is an important subject that your mum/dad will want to discuss with you too.' It may also be important to ensure that parents understand subtle messages that you wish to communicate. For instance, you do not tell their children to be rude to every adult, whether strangers or familiar people. You explain that grown-ups do not deserve politeness, if they behave in ways that upset, worry or frighten children.

Older children and young people will begin to move about independently, starting with being at a slight distance from their responsible adult. Safety messages need to be considerate. Children can be unnerved when they gain the idea that danger lurks behind every bush and corner. It is irresponsible to make children or young people so anxious that they dread making even the simplest of outings on their own or with friends. It is equally risky to create a situation in which some children or adolescents decide that adults make a huge fuss about things that never happen. These individuals stop listening to anything that adults say.

A safe perspective on 'stranger danger'

When children go missing, the news media tend to focus on abduction by strangers, with lurid headlines around 'every parent's nightmare'. Any avoidable death of a child is one too many, but abduction and murder by a complete stranger is very rare; it is this fact that makes the event so newsworthy. When children do not survive their childhood, it is far more likely that they have died from accidents (road or domestic) or the diseases that, despite medical advances, still sometimes kill children. To acknowledge these facts does not reduce the terrible loss for families who have been struck by a statistically unlikely tragedy. However, there are serious consequences when adults try to build rules for everyday life on the basis of rare events.

Prominent news items require practitioners and parents to admit that some adults intentionally harm children. But an honest message is that most adults are kind and caring. There is sometimes concern that honest conversation undermines the 'innocence' of childhood. But, of course, children are not innocent in the sentimental way presented in some media discussions. Children are ignorant in the most positive sense of the word; there is so much they do not know. Children are learning about the world and they need an accurate framework in which to make sense of events.

Children are statistically more at risk from people they already know. However, the younger generation won't be supported by safety campaigns that make everyone afraid of their own family and neighbours. The vast majority of parents and practitioners will protect children and some have placed themselves in direct physical danger in order to keep children safe. The genuine risks to children are best met by steadily coaching them in personal safety and life skills. In a similar way, the real dangers to child pedestrians and bike riders are met by teaching children how to be safe near and on the road.

Safety from a strong sense of self-worth

Personal safety is supported by children's conviction of their right to feel and be safe. Children learn in an atmosphere of respect and trust: here their concerns are taken seriously and not dismissed as 'silly'. A great deal of supportive work with children arises through daily experiences, which are not in themselves a source of trouble or worries.

- When children are treated with affectionate respect, they learn about personal space and their rights over their own bodies, including a right to say 'No'. Over time, you can talk about 'comfortable' touches, what makes children uncomfortable, 'happy' sitting distances and 'private' areas of the body.
- Children need to develop trust in their own feelings about appropriate behaviour. This confidence develops from positive experiences around touch and physical care routines. Older children then have a strong sense of 'not OK' when someone infringes on their wish for privacy, for instance when changing their clothes or taking a shower.
- Care over first aid, trips to the dentist and other health needs are further opportunities to build children's confidence and bodily awareness. Any health professional should talk with children, not over their head to the accompanying adult. A doctor should explain what is about to happen and definitely not claim 'It doesn't hurt' when any procedure clearly does cause pain.
- Slightly older children can grasp the idea of 'good' and 'bad' secrets. 'Good' secrets, perhaps better called 'surprises', are enjoyable because they will give pleasure to someone else ('What we've bought Mummy for her birthday'). 'Bad' secrets make children feel uncomfortable or unhappy. They feel they should say something, yet someone has pressed them to remain silent against their wishes.

Children learn confidence through experience, including affectionate and trusting relationships, and respect shown for their feelings. You affirm children when you listen to their intuitions or 'gut' feelings about people. You would not encourage unreasonable criticisms, but children's view that somebody is 'not nice' or 'creepy' is usually based on their observations. You can have an open-ended conversation with 'In what way "not nice"?' or 'What does she do that you find "creepy"?' Sometimes the explanation will be innocent; perhaps a child has not understood that her uncle leans close because he is hard of hearing. But there are still alternative ways to solve this problem that avoid the uncle sitting closer than the child wishes.

Materials to support your messages

You need to remember that supporting the skills of personal safety extends over childhood and adolescence: avoid trying to cover too much at one time or getting too complex for young children. Just as with any other aspect of how you support learning, make sure that any planned experiences or activities will connect in a meaningful way with what children already know and understand.

- Stories, told from books or played out with dolls or puppets, may be a way of communicating simple points to younger children.
- During middle childhood many boys and girls relate well to storytelling that works with a 'pause' in the story to enable discussion of 'What might they do next?' You can also use a 'rewind' that goes back to 'What if ... ?': what if the characters had made a different decision at this choice point? It is wise to ensure that such narratives do not suggest life is continuously risky, whether for these story characters, the familiar puppets or anyone else.
- Sometimes the storyline of a children's television programme – actors or animation – naturally provokes a conversation about safety and risk.

So long as you keep it simple for young children, by middle childhood girls and boys are more able to talk around fictional scenarios. Sensitive contributions by an adult bring in the perspective that it is not just 'stupid' people who get themselves deep into a risky situation. It helps children to identify, in the plot, what made the character think it was safe enough to make this unsafe choice. Were they embarrassed to say no to something, concerned that peers might make fun of them, or were they too trusting for too long of someone who seemed 'nice' at the outset?

Rules to guide keeping safe

It is unwise to set up a 'Don't talk to strangers' rule that is never discussed for possible exceptions. Older children, let alone teenagers, will start to move around without an adult, either on their own or in the company of friends. Situations will arise in which they need to feel able to ask a stranger for help. An equally unfortunate consequence of the focus on stranger danger is that it has made some people, especially men, wary of offering help to an unknown child or young person who is lost or in distress. Caring adults need to consider how they offer assistance. But children are at an unnecessary additional risk if potential helpers walk away for fear of being accused of attempted abuse or abduction.

Children old enough to be allowed to move from an adult's side and hand may become separated from a school group or their family in a large space such as a museum. Children need to feel confident that they will not be left behind, and proper checking systems in a group must ensure that their trust is never shaken on this matter. Children need to be told, more than once with a clear visual explanation, about going to the person at the reception desk, or how to recognise a member of staff in public places, such as a library or large supermarket.

Adults have to follow rules too

You need to establish safety guidance in ways that do not put children at risk. For example, it is potentially unsafe to tell children that they must be polite to any adult or to insist that grown-ups are always in the right.

Keep the child in mind

By all means, encourage courtesy and consideration. However, children need to be reassured that grown-ups are responsible for behaving well. Unacceptable adult behaviour removes any adult right to expect politeness.

Children who are encouraged to follow adult requests need to understand that this guideline does not apply when what is asked seems wrong or makes the child feel very uncomfortable.

Children need to know that dubious people, such as sex offenders, look 'just like anybody else'. They do not all wear dark overcoats and have menacing expressions. Children need to gain the confidence to go by how adults behave. Children also need to be reassured that rules for proper adult behaviour hold regardless of whether the children were involved in any misbehaviour; for instance, having wandered off from their nursery or school group on a trip. Rules for adults still apply even if children have accepted gifts from the adult or much older adolescent. In fact, the older person is in the wrong for putting pressure on a younger or more vulnerable person. Children are right to be wary of adults, or persuasive young people, who knowingly increase the pressure to behave in ways that would definitely concern their own family.

There is a breath-taking array of information on the internet. Over middle childhood, boys and girls need to learn appropriate search and study skills to gain the benefit of this huge resource. However, the same technology that enables access to reliable materials has also created space for some loathsome websites. It is good practice in a setting or home to keep the computer in a communal area, so that adults can be watchful, without being intrusive. Practitioners in any setting or service need to share the interests of children and be ready to query something on screen that looks dubious. Adults need to install reliable software to block inappropriate access but also realise that the results are rather hit or miss.

This book focuses on early childhood, so you will be at the first stages of building safety skills with children for their internet use. The resources that follow offer options for readers who are involved with older children, and who would like to understand more about what can happen down the line when children have not been protected.

Troubled relationships between peers

Children need the experience of adults who handle their behaviour in a positive way, without using threats, verbal humiliation or physical forms of intimidation or punishment. Your setting or service should have a clear policy on how you deal with behaviour, and the ideas and approaches should be shared with parents. A positive approach is underpinned by values that view adults as having responsibilities towards children, not just a set of rights over them. The accompanying supportive approach builds on the rights of children to be heard and experience fair treatment, alongside their growing responsibility for the consequences of their own actions.

Dealing with bullying

Some children are abused and neglected by adults. However, a proportion of the troubles for the younger generation arise from each other. Bullying is a pattern of persistent ill-treatment, by an individual or group, that is intended to hurt the individual(s) on the receiving end, physically or emotionally. You will read material in which very young children are labelled as bullies, but I challenge the idea that under-fives are developmentally capable of the deliberate planning that characterises genuine bullying.

Troubles between young boys and girls should be taken seriously and adults should help children, who cannot yet resolve their own disputes. However, it is recommended by Lindon (2012) that the term 'bullying', describing a specific form of unacceptable behaviour, should not be applied until children reach middle childhood. This section is written with that stance in mind. Readers who spend time with older children will find more material in Lindon (2009) and other suggestions at the end of the chapter.

Bullying is not about trivial wind-ups or temporary troubles and indeed Tim Gill (2007) argues that children are poorly supported by responsible adults if they insist on stretching the working definition of bullying to include fleeting problems. Bullying behaviour between children, or young people, includes:

- physical attack or intimidation through the threat of attack;
- taking another child or young person's possessions or ruining them;
- persistent verbal and emotional cruelty to peers, including direct offensiveness and spreading rumours through conversation, or by using the possibilities of technology – text messaging or other forms of cyberbullying.

What does it mean?

Bullying: persistent ill-treatment that is intended to hurt the person on the receiving end, physically or emotionally. Bullying is also referred to as **peer abuse**.

Cyberbullying: a campaign of ill-treatment using words or images through the technology of mobile phones, email or the internet.

Signs of possible bullying

You need to be attentive to changes in a child, without, of course, assuming that any change is evidence of bullying. You will notice that many of the signs of ill-treatment by bullying are similar to those that could indicate possible abuse or neglect by adults. The common factor is that a child is being ill-treated and needs appropriate protection:

- Children may tell a trusted adult directly that they are being bullied or answer a friendly question of 'Is something the matter?'
- Alternatively, they may let you know in a more roundabout way – for instance, by saying they do not like school or club any more. They may say they do not want to attend a leisure or sporting activity that they previously enjoyed.
- Children may have injuries for which they give odd or evasive explanations; their clothes may be torn, their possessions missing or broken, or they may inexplicably run out of their lunch or allowance money.
- A child's behaviour may change, such as a loss of confidence or fear of particular children. Children may regress in development, for instance, bedwetting, or experience sleeping difficulties or nightmares.
- Children may show serious over-concern about their hygiene or weight, because they have been targeted as 'dirty', 'smelly' or 'fatty'.
- Children on the receiving end of bullying can show the effects in their physical and emotional health. They may appear depressed, express feelings of hopelessness and in extreme cases resort to self-harm, even suicide.

Why might children bully?

The work of Kidscape (see Further Resources) has demonstrated that there are different reasons underlying bullying. Adults who genuinely want to help need to keep an open mind about what is happening and why. Reasons are not excuses and responsible adults can still be tough on bullying. But efforts need to be directed in an informed way, given a better understanding of what probably underlies the bullying pattern on this occasion.

- Some children bully because they have no conception that they should limit their demands. Michele Elliot (2002) points out that such a child can be a 'spoiled brat' who uses harassment to get what he or she wants.
- Children who have not been indulged by their families may still have learned through life experience that intimidation of others makes them feel good and is a quick route to getting what they want.
- Some older children or young adolescents are essentially 'victims-turned-bullies'. They were bullied when they were younger, nobody helped them and now that they are bigger it is 'payback time'.
- Some children have very poor self-image and confidence, despite the appearance of being strong and forceful. They have learned to use bullying, physical or verbal, to boost themselves and feel powerful.

However, it is an inaccurate cliché that all bullies have low self-esteem.

● Some bullies are part of a group that intimidates others. The less-enthusiastic children feel reluctant to object. The activity is part of the group identity and they will have to find new friends if they refuse to be part of bullying. They may also fear, on the basis of reliable experience, that refusal will lead to their becoming the new targets.

Helpful adult responses

Children who are being bullied need reassurance that adults in whom they confide will take them seriously and help them to resolve the situation. They want adults to understand the situation from their perspective, and they do not want thoughtless action that only makes matters worse.

● Listen carefully to what is said by the children on the receiving end. Take what they say seriously; it has upset or frightened them, even if at first hearing the events seem minor to you.

● A child who has been bullied may not want you to tackle the children who have done the bullying. It is important to listen and certainly not to take sudden action. But you may need to explain your responsibility to keep people safe, which means that you cannot simply ignore what has happened.

● If the bullying is happening within your setting or family home, then find an appropriate opportunity for a calm, yet firm, conversation with the accused child or group.

● Avoid adult behaviour that is bullying in its turn. Check out what has happened and listen to what the accused children have to say.

● Challenge children who claim 'He said we could have his bag' or 'It's just a joke!' You need to communicate that real jokes are shared by everyone involved. These boys or girls did not stop when the child they were harassing was upset and frightened. So this was not a piece of fun at all.

● Reach an accurate view of what happened. Impose consequences where appropriate; these may include an apology (but there is no point in insisting on a 'Sorry' that will be insincere) and the return of anything 'borrowed'.

● You need to consider, with your colleagues in group settings, what further action needs to be taken beyond this incident.

● Children who have been bullied need support, as appropriate. Affirm that they were right to tell and work to help boost their self-confidence or skills of assertiveness if this focus might help.

● Consider what you could do to redirect the children who did the bullying. In some cases they may need continuing support, in order to meet their legitimate emotional needs in less harmful ways.

● Less keen participants within a bullying group may need help to establish other friendships. Adults can make headway, so long as the local culture has not become violent as the norm.

- In some cases, there may be a need for more general discussions to take place, in order to mobilise the power of bystanders, exploring how they felt unable or unwilling to tell or help.
- Does this incident raise more general issues for your setting? For example, have children let you know about times of the day, parts of the building, or outdoor space that need better or different adult supervision
- Do you all need some new ground rules, discussed with the children and young people themselves? You may well say that hitting must not be children's first reaction here. But they need to be able to raise their voice to a peer who is harassing them, without being told off by an adult for 'shouting'.

Children who abuse peers

Some ill-treatment between children (or adolescents) of a similar age goes well beyond the examples given so far. High levels of cruelty, whether emotional or physical, or where there are sexual overtones to harassment, raise questions that need to be explored. At root, what has happened to this child that their behaviour is so far outside normal range for their age? As always, it would be unprofessional to jump to conclusions, but serious questions have to be asked in the team if the behaviour of a child, or a bullying group, would be regarded as abusive if an adult were involved.

Cases of serious attack, or murder, perpetrated by children attract media coverage that can border on the hysterical. The murder of two-year-old James Bulger in 1992 by Jon Venables and Robert Thompson was a shocking example of what children could do to a very young child. In 2009, two brothers (10 and 11 years of age) launched a series of attacks on children in Edlington, where they lived with foster carers, reaching a head with extremely serious assault and torture of two other boys (9 and 11 years old). Nothing excuses or justifies such violence, but sober analysis of the attackers' background reveals blighted childhoods and ineffective intervention by the authorities.

Take another perspective

It is important to note that a bully is a victim as well as a perpetrator and will also require appropriate support, referral and interventions.

Young sexual abusers

Disclosures about bullying sometimes reveal that children or adolescents have a distorted idea of how to relate appropriately to peers because of their own experience of sexual abuse. This section offers a perspective that stretches beyond middle childhood, to enable practitioners to place early childhood and the first part of middle childhood into context.

Clearly, practitioners and parents have to keep a perspective, drawing on their knowledge of development and judging the details of any situation. Every instance of curiosity about private parts is not evidence of abusive activity by children. But nor must practitioners swiftly assume that activity is consensual, especially if that message arises from only one of the involved parties. It is not wise adult practice to decide easily that intimate contact between children or young adolescents is simple, ordinary experimentation. The behaviour of siblings and step-siblings, as well as unrelated children, sometimes goes far beyond a game that children say is 'just a bit rude'.

Adult judgement over concerns needs to draw on issues of relative power between children and levels of discomfort of either child in the play.

- In the case of children, the problem is much better described as sexually inappropriate behaviour rather than labelling a child as a 'sexual abuser'.
- Older children and young adolescents have a broader grasp of what is unacceptable, although the whole point is that some boys and girls have had that understanding distorted through sexually abusive adult behaviour towards them.
- Foster and residential carers sometimes have to cope with vulnerable siblings whose experiences have distorted their understanding of boundaries and led them into sexual activity with each other.

NCH (now Action for Children) was one of the first national charities to address the experiences of young sexual abusers and was part of the 1992 Committee of Enquiry into children and young people who sexually abuse other children. The work identified underlying patterns in this kind of abuse. The key points still apply:

- An adult sexual abuser may coerce a child or young adolescent into inflicting abuse in their turn. This activity can be part of sexual satisfaction for the adult.
- Abused children can become very sexualised in their behaviour: meaning that they seek to make physical contact with peers in intimate ways that are outside the normal range of behaviour for this age group.
- Children may seek sexual encounters with peers because this is the only way they have learned to make close contact, to express commitment and affection.
- Children may act in a sexual way to a younger or weaker child, more as an exercise of power. The abused child has been made to feel powerless and may be trying to feel powerful in his or her turn.
- Not all young abusers have been sexually abused through physical contact. Some have been exposed to pornographic material or exhibitionist adult sexual activity. The child's judgement of normal behaviour has been distorted.

Young abusers can experience a mix of emotions when they abuse others and they do not necessarily experience sexual satisfaction. They may feel:

- very angry at the time they sexually abuse others;
- excited by the sense of power and secrecy;
- temporarily relieved of their feelings of worthlessness through sexual contact with younger children;
- guilt and fear that they are becoming like the person who abused them.

The professional approach has to include support for the young abuser, and safeguarding guidance is clear that there should be two separate child-protection investigations. One investigation and assessment should focus on the child or young person on the receiving end of this abusive activity. But another investigation must focus on the young abuser. Their actions must be curtailed but the approach to this child or young person must not all be punitive. Practice is sometimes confused by steps to control the abusive actions of an older child or adolescent. In some cases, individuals have had their name placed on the sex offenders register yet received minimal support for their own trauma.

Commentary on the scenario

The commentary offers some possibilities. You and your colleagues may raise other ideas and perspectives.

Meadowbank Nursery (page 208)

Safe practice with very young children is shown by attention to their personal care and giving time. There is no 'just' about care or personal care routines and young children's learning can only be supported in an emotionally warm atmosphere. The current situation needs to be resolved on a team basis and with proper leadership from the head of centre. Thorough discussion is needed within a room, and maybe also a staff meeting. But continued professional development will be necessary for the practitioners who devalue care. If they are sent on a training course, a senior practitioner must follow up with links into their practice.

Further problems arise if the more caring practitioners do not get support from the head of centre. A possibility is to talk in confidence with a local adviser: raising the concerns in a professional way and communicating that some active intervention in this setting would be appreciated.

Summary

This chapter has highlighted that a child's well being and welfare needs to be supported by a holistic approach to their care. They require emotional support as well as physical intervention to promote positive development. Strategies should be put in place to ensure safety but it is also important that children are educated so that they too can put their own strategies in place and protect themselves.

Key texts

If you want to find out more about keeping children safe see:

Cyberspace Research Unit: general advice on www.internetsafetyzone.co.uk

Batmanghelidjh, C. (2006) *Shattered Lives: Children who Live with Courage and Dignity*, London: Jessica Kingsley

Carr, J. (2004) *Child abuse, child pornography and the internet*, London: NCH. Available on: http://uploadi.safe.si/editor/1149589931pornographyreport.pdf

Child Exploitation and Online Protection Centre (CEOP) *Strategic Overview 2009–10*, www.ceop.police.uk/Documents/Strategic_Overview_2009-10_(Unclassified).pdf

Lindon, J. (2011) *Too Safe for Their Own Good? Helping Children Learn about Risk and Life skills*, London: National Children's Bureau

Lovell, E. (2003) *Children and Young People who Display Sexually Harmful Behaviour*, London: NSPCC

NCH (1992) *The Report of the Committee of Enquiry into Children and Young People who Sexually Abuse other Children*, London: NCH

Young Report (2010) *Common Sense – Common Safety* Available on: www.hse.gov.uk/aboutus/commonsense/index.htm

The NSPCC also provide advice on online safety and have tools that can be used to help keep children safe whenever they go online: www.nspcc.org.uk/preventing-abuse/keeping-children-safe/online-safety/?

8 Supporting children and families

Introduction

There is no single pattern of how best to help children or to offer support to their families. A common strand is for practitioners to work in partnership with families, most often parents, with their approach to safeguarding. This chapter also covers practice issues that especially arise when working with families who are involved in the child protection process.

It covers working with parents to support children, child protection and the courts, and families and children under stress

Working with parents to support children

Good contacts between your service and the local child-protection team should include practical discussions about the contribution of your setting and your own skills as an individual practitioner. You might be asked to be especially attentive to a child's regular attendance, their well being, play and conversation, without distorting their experiences with you through obvious extra attention. Children who have been abused or neglected need a place and familiar people with whom everything is as 'normal' as possible.

Working well with other professionals

If concerns have been raised about a child, it is unlikely that early years provision will be the only service involved with the family. The designated safeguarding lead and the manager (if this is a different person) have an important role in maintaining contact with other agencies.

Even when there are no child protection concerns, multi-agency working can bring challenges. Other professionals might bring different priorities, core knowledge and language, and sometimes a different interpretation of issues around confidentiality and information sharing. If you work in a children's centre, then it is possible that other professionals based in the centre will be involved in support of the child or family. Even when you share a building, effective communication does not just happen. The centre head has to take a clear lead in ensuring that any professional differences do not confuse communication. Everyone needs to respect the contribution of other professionals, including the input of early years practitioners, through a child's key person, as this will be crucial for that child's well being (as described on page 107).

What does it mean?

Leading across professional boundaries: the task of effective leadership when a range of different professions are represented within the staff group.

Multi-agency working: the task of drawing on the contribution of different agencies for the well being of children and families.

If other services are not offered on site, it will be important to know whether other specialist input is being provided for the child or family. You are not asking for confidential details of counselling or family support. However, some shared information will help you know the identity of 'Lisa', for example, who apparently talks with this child every week. Counselling for children, including play therapy, is a specialised task and practitioners should not attempt to undertake this kind of work unless they have been trained. But not all children who have been abused want or need special therapy. They can be well supported by what you offer within the ordinary day or session. You will share this understanding and knowledge in your partnership with some families.

Talking and listening with children

The key guideline for practitioners is to treat children as normally as possible, without pretending that nothing has happened. An abusive experience can make children seriously doubt themselves and the trustworthiness of adults. You can help in the following ways, adjusting your words to the age of the child.

- If children say critical things about themselves, you need to offer positive emotional support. Avoid saying simply to the child that 'It's not true' and do not deny the child's feelings with 'You don't think that, really.'
- Acknowledge that the child has expressed a strong feeling with a comment such as 'It must be difficult for you to feel that way.' You do not bluntly disagree with the child's negative remark but reply warmly, 'I'm glad you come here to the club,' or 'I don't think you're a "waste of space"' (a child's own phrase).
- Take the time to encourage a distrustful child and do not feel that your skills are in question. Some children take a long time to open up and you have to be pleased with small successes. Older children may have experienced years of rejection or unpredictability from adults. They may persist in rejecting any help in their turn. Such a relationship is

emotionally very wearing for the practitioner, which is another reason why support for adults is so necessary.

- Children need your support and sympathy, but pity is rarely a helpful emotion to express to a child in distress. Practitioners should avoid talking about children in hushed tones or expressing the message of 'poor little Wesley', whether you communicate through spoken words or your body language.
- It is important to relate to abused children in play as you would to any child: enjoying their satisfaction and looking for opportunities for them to learn. It will not be helpful to seek deep meanings in every drawing they do, or find greater significance in rough physical play than you would for another child.

Children do not forget about distressing events just because adults avoid talking about the topic. It is more likely that children decide that adults are cross with them, that they did something very wrong. The ways in which you offer time and attention will vary according to your work. Ideally, you would respond when a child starts to talk. However, there may also be times when you have to say carefully to a child, 'I really want to hear what you want to tell me, but there is no way for us to have privacy until (give a time). Can we please talk together then?'

A positive approach to behaviour

Children need your understanding of the likely impact of distressing experiences and you may have to adjust the expectations you usually bring to a child of this age.

- Children will not benefit from a tolerance that is without limits. Practitioners may be concerned that keeping to ground rules will add to the burden of an already distressed child. On the contrary, it can reassure a child that these grown-ups take responsibility and act in a predictable manner. They may complain, but this behaviour is within the usual 'job description' for being a child.
- You need to be prepared for individual reactions from children. When children have witnessed bouts of domestic violence, they may become aggressive in their turn and need to be guided towards non-disruptive ways to deal with ordinary conflicts. However, some children become distressed by even mild altercations, or expect fierce words from you for minor problems. They need a great deal of reassurance, such as 'It's all right, Barry, everyone makes mistakes. We'll mop it up together.'
- When one child brings her problems into a group, the other children need to feel reassured that you are aware of what is happening. Children who have been abused should not be allowed to release their misery or anger on their peers through unacceptable behaviour. It is unfair to the other children and will not help the distressed child in the long run. Their actions will undermine their peers' inclination to offer the friendly support that could be available from this age group.

- Even younger children can be caring towards each other and react well to simple explanations that do not break confidences. Perhaps you might explain, 'It's okay, Melissa, I know you didn't say anything mean. Paresh gets upset if people shout at him [include Paresh in your glance at this point, so that he does not feel excluded]. Just talk in your indoors voice.'

If a child's abusive experience is emerging through behaviour in the group, you may have to give an explanation to other parents that does not breach confidences about the other family. Explanations should never become excuses and parents should not be expected to tolerate their own children's pinch marks or emotional distress because another child is experiencing family problems. Explain simply to concerned parents those steps you are taking in your provision to deal with the situation that their child has faced. In a small community, some parents may be fully aware of the stresses in a particular family. You take a professional stance by listening to any concerns expressed by other parents, or information about a household. However, you do not allow such exchanges to slip into an ordinary conversation.

Supporting parents involved in child protection

In most cases children will stay in the setting they are already attending or with their childminder. The exception would be if safeguarding issues have arisen about the setting or childminder. Although relationships with the parent may not be easy, partnership can still be possible. Parents do not necessarily turn against their child's key person or childminder, even if it was you who first raised the concerns. Parents may feel that, despite mixed emotions, this familiar professional is basically on their side and cares about their child and family. It is also possible that a parent is looking for support and trusts the practitioner to provide it. Some parents ask for help when they recognise that they are close to ill-treating their child.

Families who feel convinced that a practitioner or entire team has behaved badly may choose to move their child to another nursery or school, or cancel a childcare arrangement. If worries about the child have been fully resolved, the change has to be accepted as the family's choice. However, if any concerns still remain, it is crucial to inform social-care services that the family is no longer in regular contact with your setting or service.

Your partnership with parents or other key family carers such as a grandparent may take several forms as you:

- continue a working relationship with parents who are alleged to have abused or who have admitted ill-treating their child;
- support a non-abusing parent who is distressed and confused that their partner has abused the child(ren);
- work with parents whose child has been abused by somebody else, either within the family, a trusted person allowed contact with the child, or, less usually, a stranger.

Even when children are taken into care, it is good practice that every effort is made for a young child to continue at a familiar nursery, or for an older child not to have to change school. In this situation, practitioners in nursery, school or club establish a partnership with the child's foster carer or with a slightly older child's key person from the residential home. You need to work closely with these fellow professionals. They and the child will have suggestions about how you will refer, in conversation, to someone who is in a parental role but is not a carer from the birth family.

Only practitioners in more specialist settings, and those with additional training, would undertake counselling or other therapeutic work with fellow adults. But a very great deal of support can be offered through daily communication with parents and other carers. A friendly face and a continued welcome to your setting may be exactly what some parents need. Their life has been turned upside down and their child's nursery, school or out-of-school club might be the only element that is constant. Non-abusing parents may really appreciate a place where they and their child are well known from before the current crisis. You are available to talk about difficulties if they wish, but you still show, for example, the collage their daughter completed or tell how their son had such good ideas about the garden makeover.

Sharing the support for an abused child

The confidence of non-abusing parents in their own skills can be severely shaken. They may try to make everything up to the child with treats or by abandoning normal family rules. Or perhaps a parent feels that the child needs the security of positive family boundaries, but is over-ruled by someone else in the family. You can listen to this parent's dilemma and explain how you are dealing with similar choices and concerns during your time with the child.

Parents may need to be encouraged to respond to their child's overtures in conversation. Non-abusing parents and other carers may feel, or may even be told, that it is better not to talk about a distressing experience with their child on the 'least said, soonest mended' principle. You can reassure them that although children should not be pressed to talk, parents should show that they are responsive and will listen.

A child who has been sexually abused may make inappropriate physical approaches to other children or to adults. Parents may not realise that such consequences could follow from their child's experience. You can offer support by acknowledging the seriousness of this kind of behaviour, but explain that it is not unusual in these circumstances. Explain to the parents how you deal with this situation through the twin messages of 'I like you and I am happy to have you close to me' and 'The way you want to touch me is not the right way to show we care about each other.'

Talking and listening with parents

Some parents may wish to talk with you about what has happened and what is yet to come. These supportive conversations should be private. Parents may have deep and confused feelings; they may become distressed or angry (not necessarily with you) and they may talk about their child(ren) in the hearing of other children or parents. Perhaps what seemed to be a quick question about basic information is turning into what ought to be a longer and private conversation. Then you should attempt to halt the parent at this point. Explain by saying, for example, 'I want to give you some proper time, but it's impossible now. Can you can come back at ... ?'

There is no single blueprint for how parents will feel. They may express any of the following emotions, and feelings often change over time. They may feel:

- Shocked and unable to take in what has happened. A non-abusing parent may still find it hard to believe what has occurred. An abusing parent may feel stunned that matters got this much out of hand.
- Angry that someone else has abused their child. Or an abusing parent may feel aggrieved that what they consider to have been justifiable discipline has been called abuse, or that a child's word is believed over an adult's counterclaim. Parents feel anger towards the person(s) who first raised the concerns, even if they also feel a sense of relief.
- Guilty about not realising earlier or not facing nagging worries about a child's physical or emotional state. A non-abusing parent may fret over why the child did not tell. An abusing parent may feel very guilty about what has been done and may be willing to accept help – or not, of course.
- Relieved that the abuse has been discovered and is being challenged. A neglectful parent may feel many other emotions, but still feel that it is better to get help than to struggle.
- A conflict of loyalties between commitment to the child and to the alleged abuser, when this person is a previously trusted partner or friend. Sometimes this conflict is resolved, at least initially, by doubting or blaming the child who disclosed the abuse.
- Shame and embarrassment about what has happened and that family life has become public. Once a child abuse investigation starts, professionals have the right and obligation to ask many questions that intrude into what are otherwise private family matters.
- Distress and pressure from other family members, or local people, who are not being supportive. Non-abusing parents may have to deal with relatives and neighbours who want to disbelieve the child. There may be criticism that the whole matter should have been handled within the family, immediate community or faith group.

Parents can doubt their ability to protect their own children. Non-abusing parents whose child has been ill-treated by a relative or close friend feel a serious loss of confidence about their own judgement. In cases of sexual abuse, for instance, children may have been abused for some time and have said nothing. Alternatively, what they did say earlier was not recognised as a serious cry for help. When the facts emerge, the non-abusing parents are faced with the fact that for a time of weeks, months, or even years their perception of events was completely wrong. This kind of discovery of abuse has been likened to bereavement or loss.

You will support parents if you acknowledge their feelings and recognise their mixed and changing emotions. You are not saying that they are right to feel that way – for instance, in almost blaming a child for keeping the abuse a secret – but you show that you have heard what they said. You may be able to present an alternative perspective: for example, explaining why children can have such difficulty in telling. It is also important to recognise that, once an abuser has been removed from a family or denied any more access to a child, the situation does not suddenly revert back to what was normal before the crisis. Children have distress to work through and so, too, will the non-abusing adults of the family.

Safety and risk assessment

If parents are angry with you, or with your team as a whole, you need to acknowledge that anger rather than try to argue or get cross in return. There is no sure way to deal with anger and defuse the power of that emotion, but the following guidelines will help:

- Stay calm and do not answer the parent's anger with your own angry or hurt replies, or counterclaims that the parent is being unfair. When emotions run high, there is little point in trying for rational discussion at that point.
- Show that you recognise the feelings. You are not saying a parent is right to be angry, nor agreeing, perhaps, that all social workers are interfering busybodies.
- Explore if a parent is ready to listen. You might try, 'I appreciate that you're really fed up with what has happened. You feel the social worker won't answer your questions. Do you want me to explain what happens next?'

You still have a responsibility for children in the setting, who can become distressed by adults who lose control. A furious adult or one who is using offensive language needs to be told firmly, 'This isn't the time and place to be this angry. You're frightening the children.' All practitioners have a right to their own safety and any setting should have clear procedures on how staff come to a colleague's aid when an altercation risks getting out of hand.

When your setting or service is involved in child protection, it is appropriate to make a risk assessment about the behaviour of adults who are alleged to have abused or neglected their children, or who may already have admitted to their actions. Adults cannot neglect children unless they are responsible for them, so this pattern of maltreatment would not usually have a direct impact on other children in your setting. Nevertheless, physical, emotional or sexual abuse could be a potential risk issue while a parent was present legitimately, for instance, to pick up their child. However, this risk could only become real if a parent were left alone with a group, which should not happen in any case.

It is appropriate to remain alert to the actions or words of an alleged or identified abuser, without over-reacting. Practitioners have to deal immediately with unacceptable behaviour from any adult that occurs within the boundaries of the setting, regardless of whether words or actions are directed at a parent's own child or another. Perhaps an accused parent or other family member is involved directly in your setting, for instance, as a volunteer. Then it is necessary to take appropriate action that is proportionate, and does not assume guilt when none is certain – see page 183 about allegations.

Information about the child protection process

If an investigation is ongoing, then parents should definitely be kept informed of what is happening. The assigned social worker should be ready to explain to parents, but they may prefer to talk with you. Practitioners should understand the child protection process, so they can explain what will happen next and that some events (for instance, taking children into care) are definitely not inevitable. You can ensure that parents know about case conferences and their right to attend. Explain your role in such events and that although the parent may appreciate a familiar face, you have to give your setting's impartial report as a contribution to the meeting.

Normal practice is that parents are invited to case conferences on their child unless there is good reason to exclude them. Parents can see the process for themselves and, at least sometimes, will feel reassured that people are not simply condemning them. Parents should also see that different professionals work together so they can understand how far family members are motivated to take an active part in the child protection plan for this child.

The focus within the case conference must be on the child. The professionals present have to be ready to express the more difficult issues about the family situation. As the practitioner who will give a report, you should not make comments that will surprise a parent. You should have had any difficult discussions with the parent prior to the case conference. Nevertheless, it can be hard for any professionals to listen to parents' distress or fear about what is happening. You may be discomforted by an articulate defence by parents of their actions, or a verbal attack about professional assumptions or attitudes.

Child protection and the courts

All the professionals involved in a child protection case will work to achieve a plan to protect children without court proceedings (unless there is no option) in order to keep a child safe from harm. Practitioners are therefore unlikely to have to go to court, especially if you do not work in specialised services for vulnerable children and families. However, you could be involved as a witness yourself, or in supporting children who have to go into the witness box. This section provides information that will help you understand how the court process works. The two broad types of courts are civil and criminal, and there are significant differences in how they operate.

Civil proceedings

Civil courts are less formal than the criminal courts and the standard of proof is different. In civil proceedings for child protection, there has to be evidence that suggests on the balance of probabilities that a child has been abused and that a named person (or persons) is the likely abuser. In criminal proceedings, the evidence has to be on the basis of beyond reasonable doubt, which is a tougher test of any evidence. However, child protection legislation across the UK allows for some strong legal steps to be taken to protect children that do not require a criminal court case and prosecution of the alleged abuser.

Civil proceedings in court can lead to rulings that the named alleged abuser stays away from the child, or can only have supervised contact. A social worker might be involved in such contact, or a clearly described arrangement might be made with a daily setting that supported vulnerable children and their families. Alternatively, a ruling might be made that children should be removed from the family home as the only way to ensure their safety. Foster parents or the staff of a residential children's home might then be supervising the agreed contact. Civil proceedings allow for a range of serious steps to protect children but which do not involve any prosecution against the alleged abuser(s).

Civil proceedings are not only less formal, but tend to be less confrontational than the legal process in a criminal court. Yet there can still be disagreements and arguments. If an acceptable solution had been found between social workers and the family, the case would have been resolved outside the courtroom. Civil proceedings are more likely to occur when:

- The local-authority social workers cannot reach an agreement with the family about what has happened, or is continuing to happen, to the child, and the family's response to the situation.
- The child protection team judges that children need to be removed from the family and no voluntary arrangement has successfully been made with the parents or other relatives. Family group conferences (see page 124) are sometimes the way that a successful arrangement has been reached.

● Custody and access issues in a matrimonial dispute hinge on an allegation of abuse by a parent of the children.

Children do not have to appear in civil proceedings (whereas they may be a witness for the prosecution in a criminal case). Children in civil proceedings have an independent legal representative, different from the solicitor for the local authority and another solicitor representing the parent(s). The court also appoints a guardian *ad litem* (GAL): a specially trained person, usually a social worker, who represents the child's best interests and wishes for the duration of this legal case. GALs are advocates on behalf of the child and operate independently from anyone else from the local authority. In Scotland, the independent representative for the child is known as a 'safeguarder'. Scottish law is especially strong on providing ways for children's views to be heard.

It is possible that early years, school and out-of-school practitioners might be called to civil proceedings to give evidence about a child. You might have knowledge and records of a child's physical health, development or behaviour that had a bearing on the child's need for protection. You may have observed important incidents between a parent and child, or the child may have chosen to disclose an experience of abuse to you. The procedure in civil courts is not as adversarial as criminal proceedings, but many of the key issues (raised on pages 237–9) about being a reliable and credible witness are equally important.

Criminal proceedings

Only a minority of child abuse cases reach the courts as part of a criminal case. A prosecution will only be undertaken when the abuse, if proven, falls into the category of a crime and there is sufficient evidence to support the case. So, most practitioners will not experience court process as part of their work. However, it is crucial that no practitioner finds themselves in the witness box without prior support. Practitioners who work with vulnerable families, and certainly those in services for looked-after children and young people, should have training for the court experience as an early part of their continued professional development.

Appearing as a witness

In terms of a specific case, the local authority lawyer should find time to meet before your appearance as a witness. He or she should explain what will happen and go through any practical issues about your evidence. The lawyer can alert you to the kind of questions that she or he will ask you as the case is developed. Other people in court will not necessarily be experienced with children. So you will need to explain any specialist terms or preferably use ordinary language. The local authority lawyer should help you prepare in this way.

If you are uncertain about anything or have new information, speak up within this meeting. Lawyers' nightmares are court scenes in which their witness suddenly reveals new facts or voices doubts. You should raise, if the lawyer does not, any potential problems of inconsistency in your account, gaps in your written record, or likely disagreement over interpretation between you and other witnesses in the case. The lawyer may also offer good guesses about the questions likely to be put to you by the defence lawyer. If there seems to be a delay in your being contacted, then phone the local authority lawyer yourself, especially if you are facing your first time as a witness. You might also welcome a prior visit to the courtroom. Unless you have been on jury service, you will have little idea of what to expect.

The experience of being a witness

Smart clothes are appropriate dress for attendance at court; on the day of the hearing avoid wearing very casual clothing, even if this style is usual for your work. If you are going to use your notes in the witness box, ensure everything is in your bag or briefcase. You should arrive at the court with time to spare, so that you do not feel rushed. Do not let yourself be drawn into discussions or disagreements with other parties outside the court – for instance, parents or other relatives who dispute the events.

Once you are in the witness box there are practical guidelines to bear in mind:

- You will be asked to take an oath on a holy book relevant to your faith, or make an affirmation that you will speak the truth. Then you are guided through your evidence by questions from the prosecution lawyer.
- Speak steadily and clearly. Look up and not down at the floor. Although the lawyer asks you the questions, you should direct your reply to the magistrate or judge sitting at the bench.
- You probably need to talk slightly slower than a normal conversational pace. The clerk of the court takes notes and magistrates or judges usually make their own notes as well.
- If you could not hear all or part of a question, ask for it to be repeated. If you do not understand the question, then say so.
- Witnesses are not expected to remember everything when they are going to be asked for many details, as you could be. It is therefore acceptable to take notes into the witness box and to consult them to ensure the accuracy of your answers – for instance, about dates or what a child said.
- However, as soon as you use notes you can legitimately be asked when you made this written record; this is another reason why you should be prompt in your record keeping. Your notes can also be copied as evidence and made available to the defence lawyer in criminal proceedings.
- Your evidence should be limited to what you personally observed, what you can honestly say 'I saw' or 'I heard'. Quote a parent's or child's actual words only if you are certain that those were the exact words used. Otherwise give the gist of the communication.
- Answer the question and do not move onto other topics, unless what you have to say is a relevant explanation. You would normally reply more

than 'Yes' or 'No' to a question, although this simple answer is sometimes appropriate.

- In some cases, your evidence may include positive points about a parent or other adult. Express these as honestly as you would any negative evidence.
- Part of your legitimate evidence may be second-hand, in that you were told something by another person. Express this accurately – for example, 'Mrs Jones asked to speak with me on the 25th May. She told me she had seen Lena's mother hit the child and Lena had fallen against the concrete post.' You know what you were told, but you did not directly observe that Lena was hit by her mother.
- You may be asked to express an opinion based on your knowledge of the child or of children in general. Support your opinion with 'because ...' or 'My experience has been ... '. Do not go beyond issues on which you can reasonably express a professional opinion.
- If you do not know the answer to a question, then it is better to say, 'I don't know' or perhaps 'I wasn't able to hear what Teddy's father said to him. I could see that Teddy was crying and pulling away from his father.'

In criminal proceedings, witnesses are first questioned by the prosecution lawyer. There should be no surprises in this part of your evidence, since your answers are part of the local authority and police case for the prosecution. You will then be cross-examined by the defence lawyer. In civil proceedings the parents' lawyer may ask you questions. The job of defence lawyers is to defend their client, so their responsibility is to challenge the reliability of any evidence. Lawyers use a number of adversarial tactics in order to achieve this aim. The end result for witnesses can be anything from slightly uncomfortable to feeling under attack for your credibility.

Defence lawyers are not being personally vindictive, although some tactics are very unpleasant. Their job is to express public doubt about your observations or professional experience; your role is to remain focused and calm.

- Avoid getting either annoyed or distressed. Do not relax, even if the approach is initially friendly. You are not having a conversation together; the defence lawyer is cross-questioning you on behalf of the accused.
- Take no notice of theatrical tactics used by some lawyers, such as looking contemptuously at bits of paper and throwing them onto the table. Ignore doubtful expressions, shrugs or other dismissive body language and concentrate on the questions.
- Answer only the question that is asked and reply with what you can contribute from your direct observations and professional experience. If you are asked questions to which you cannot honestly give an answer or opinion, then do not guess. For instance, you might be asked, 'What did Steven's uncle think about the child's claims?' and you may have to reply, 'I don't know. Mr O'Hare didn't say anything to me.'

- If you are asked the same or very similar questions again, do not feel provoked into giving an extended or different answer, as though you were wrong the first time. If a lawyer uses this tactic, you could say courteously, 'I have already answered that question.' The magistrate, judge or the prosecution lawyer should also step in to prevent your being harassed.

- Take each question on its own and do not be afraid to think for a moment before replying. You may experience the defence tactic of asking you a series of quick questions to which you can honestly reply 'Yes', followed by a question to which your answer should be 'No', but the lawyer hopes to establish a pattern of your agreement.

- If you have inadvertently said something that is inaccurate, or not what you meant, then correct yourself straightaway.

If you are called as a witness, it is unlikely that all the practical issues about evidence outlined in this section will arise. But some of them will be part of your court experience. Be prepared and remember that your time in court is a particular kind of exchange. Concentrate on the task in hand; do not relax until you have left the witness box. This section assumes you will be called as a witness for the prosecution. It is possible the defence team may call you. Most of the practical points are still relevant; certainly do not be tempted to go beyond what you know, however much you like a parent.

Pause for reflection

After you emerge from court, it is important to give yourself a short time to readjust and later to reflect on your experience in the witness box.

Avoid reworking the details and certainly do not spend ages on regrets. Take the opportunity to talk with someone in your team if the experience has actually caused you distress.

Otherwise, reflect on what you have learned – for yourself and to share with colleagues:

- In what ways was your experience more or less what you expected and in what ways different?
- In what ways did your preparation, which may have included a training workshop or support from the local authority lawyer, help you to be ready?
- What would you add in terms of advice to other practitioners?
- What might you do differently next time? But realise that each experience as a witness will vary in the details.

Children in court

Children and young people can be directly involved in court proceedings because they are called as a witness. The alternative reason is that an older child or adolescent is accused of a crime. The age of criminal responsibility is ten years of age in England, Wales and Northern Ireland and eight years of age in Scotland. Practitioners who work with vulnerable older children may support them because they are involved with the police owing to the child's own behaviour. The resources on page 252 are also helpful for this situation. But the main focus here is for the support of children who give evidence against their abuser.

Young witnesses

If a child protection case involves a criminal prosecution, then children or young people could be called as a witness. If the alleged abuser pleads guilty, then children do not have to go to court. But if the plea is not guilty, then children's evidence has to be heard in court and they have to undergo cross-examination. Adult witnesses can find the experience daunting and need to be prepared. The situation can be even more distressing for children, especially since in these legal cases where they are the person who has been ill-treated.

Children are in a particularly vulnerable position when there have been no adult witnesses to the abuse and there is no clear physical evidence of maltreatment. This situation often applies over allegations of sexual abuse, since abusers put immense effort into ensuring secrecy and are not necessarily violent. The evidence of a young witness, or more than one, may be the only strand of the prosecution's case. The evidence of children has become more acceptable in court, partly as a general recognition in child protection that children can understand the difference between truth and lies.

There is no fixed lower age limit for a child witness. The two key issues are whether children will be able to understand the questions asked of them in the courtroom and whether they will be able to answer in ways that can be understood. In practice, prosecutions over child abuse are rarely taken forward when crucial child witnesses are younger than six or seven years of age. If your professional role is within early childhood, then it is highly unlikely that you will support a child witness. This section offers information that will be helpful in that unlikely situation, but also reflects the fact that some readers may work with children into middle childhood.

Apart from considerations of the weight of the evidence, police and social workers are also concerned about a child's well being. They have to make a balanced decision about the likely distress for a child of being a witness, against the public interest that an abuser be prosecuted and punished in law. This decision should be taken in partnership with the family, unless they are involved in the abuse. Older children and adolescents should be enabled to understand what is involved and give their informed consent or refusal.

The court process in a prosecution is confrontational and can be distressing for any witness. The defendant must be presumed innocent until proven guilty and it is the job of the defence lawyer to question and undermine the evidence against their client. The judge should control inappropriate tactics, especially when children and adolescents are involved. However, it is still difficult to decide whether individual children and young people will be able to cope with cross-examination and having their word doubted in public. Young witnesses state from experience that you have to be ready for accusations of lying. They also recount that the prosecution lawyer will make it difficult for you to tell your story: by interrupting and talking over your replies and using complicated words that you do not understand.

There are strict guidelines that govern how children and young adolescents give evidence in any court case, not only one about child protection. If guidance is followed, then it should be possible to reduce potential distress for children, as well as to ensure a good quality of evidence.

- Children can be interviewed for their evidence before the court hearing. The child is interviewed in a special police suite that looks like a living room and the whole interview is video recorded.
- Children must not be prepared for the interview and there must be no leading questions from the adult. In other words, there must be reassurance that children's evidence has not been shaped by anyone, including the police.
- A video link between the courtroom and a separate room can be used so that children do not have to be in court, and they do not have to face their alleged abuser. Alternatively, some courtrooms have a screen that shields the child or young person from the majority of the court. However, some courts do not offer this facility.
- Each court should have a child witness officer who supports the familiarisation process for a child or young person and ensures that, on the day, they are able to access the court and a waiting area without risk of contact with the alleged abuser, their family or other supporters.
- Young people older than 14 years will usually be asked to take an oath or make an affirmation: the same commitment to speak the whole truth that is required of adult witnesses.
- Children will still be cross-examined by the defence lawyer, whether in open court or via the video link, and have to answer questions about their evidence, including details of the abusive experiences. In sexual abuse cases, in particular, young witnesses find this experience embarrassing and intimidating.

- The main thrust of the defence is likely to be that the young witness is lying or, at the very least, confused and mistaken. Some lawyers have insinuated that children have been complicit in their own sexual abuse.

It is important to know about local support facilities for young witnesses. Apart from the child witness officer of the court, Victim Support often have someone who can support in a similar way. Additionally, the NSPCC has several witness support projects around the country. If there is a programme in your area, they may be able to provide a trained supporter for a young witness.

A practitioner who is closely involved with the family can have an important role in supporting a child and non-abusing members of their family. However, everyone needs to have realistic expectations of what may happen. The more you understand court process, the better you can prepare the child, as well as offering support after an unpleasant court experience. You may need to work hard to reassure children that you believe them and help rebuild their confidence.

Children and young people who are deeply distressed by their abuse may need the support of specialised therapy or other forms of counselling. Such support used to be postponed until the criminal trial was complete. This process could take months and it has now been accepted that it cannot be in children's best interests to have this necessary help delayed.

Families and children under stress

All the key laws about child protection across the UK include the option to use family support services in order to ensure the welfare of children judged to be 'in need', as well as sometimes considering the best way to protect individual children. Some of the low-key support will be offered by practitioners who are already involved with families through their child. Families under serious stress, or those who have put their children at significant risk, will need more specialised services. Practitioners in early years, school and out-of-school services still need to know about those possibilities.

Support in childcare and parenting skills

Parents whose neglect or abuse has largely arisen through ignorance of their child's basic needs may accept help within your setting. However, any team needs to be clear about the boundaries to what you can offer, as well as being well informed about other local services. Children's centres aim to offer informal support, as well as easy links with local family support services. Some early years provision may be part of the child protection plan, in that a firm agreement (maybe called 'a contract') has been made with parents for their attendance, as well as that of their child.

Some parents may genuinely have very little idea about children's physical and emotional needs. The problem may have arisen because the parents are very young themselves. Some adults might have had a disrupted childhood from which they have no useful memories of how to treat children well. In other families, serious stress may have overwhelmed the parents and blotted out concerns for their children.

As the key person, you may be able to offer advice on basic childcare, usual patterns of development and ordinary 'problems'. However, it is professional that you remain aware of the full range of your responsibilities. In many early years settings it is not possible for the key person to give very generous time to one family without seriously reducing time and attention for other parents and children. Children's centres are more likely to have a family support worker on site, or a clear channel for referral.

Family support services are offered in different forms, and their extent and availability vary considerably between different areas of the UK:

- Home visiting schemes can be a great support to families under stress and those who would welcome some advice about play and dealing with their children's behaviour. Home visitors from schemes such as Home Start are part of a broad-based family support service. They do not only visit families about whom there are child protection concerns.
- Some early years and school settings are able to offer supportive parents' groups that can cover a range of issues and, again, these are not only for families about whom there are worries. Some groups and sessions follow one of the parenting programmes that are widely available.
- Some schools have organised the funding for home–school link workers, whose role is to help families who are struggling. If schools are successful in creating a welcoming atmosphere, many families may regard them as the best first contact point for seeking help.
- Specialist family-support workers may be assigned as a response to child protection concerns. In that case, the family can be well aware that noticeable improvement in the well being of their children is essential, or else more serious intervention will be the next option.

A consistent theme is encouraging and enabling parents to put their child's needs to the forefront. It is not only families in poor or deprived neighbourhoods who put their children at risk. Some two-parent families with substantial incomes place such a high priority on their careers that children struggle with a patchwork of different carers or inadequate supervision. Different issues arise when older children and young adolescents are at potential risk. In this case, family support may be more about setting boundaries for an older child who is allowed inappropriate levels of freedom or who is expected to take significant domestic responsibility to enable adults to continue with their life.

Winston, Janice and Clement

Imagine you are the practitioner facing each of these situations. Consider the following questions:

- What do you feel are the main issues here?
- What would be your next steps?

You will find a commentary for each scenario on pages 251–2.

Winston

Fifteen-month-old Winston often seems to be grumpy in the morning but today he was very out of sorts and wandered around in a daze until lunchtime. When his mother picks him up you ask whether Winston has been unwell. She replies, 'I think we overdid the sleeping medicine.' You look puzzled and she continues, 'Winston is an awful sleeper. My mum said to give him a tot of sherry. She said that was what she used to do and it didn't do us any harm. I was having a terrible time and one night I started to shake him. So I thought the sherry would be safer.'

Janice

Janice is three years old and has attended the pre-school for several months. She started when her mother, Ruth, had not long given birth to a baby boy, Sachin. Janice's brother is very unwell. He has been in hospital several times, but as yet with no definite diagnosis of what is wrong. His illness has caused Ruth to become distraught; she has told you that she is getting very little sleep because of Sachin's screaming and Janice wanting to get into bed with her and her husband.

When she started pre-school, Janice was a relatively quiet child but made friends and joined in the play activities. But over the last few weeks you have noticed a significant change in Janice and she spends a lot of time rocking and hugging herself. She has complained to you of stomach aches and one day says that her bottom is 'so sore'. You tried to speak with Ruth, but she rushed off the premises, taking Janice with her to a hospital appointment for Sachin. The next morning Janice comes to pre-school with a long scratch mark over one cheek. Her mother asks to speak with you in private and as soon as you are alone together, she bursts into tears.

Janice's mother admits that she hit her daughter the previous afternoon. She had found Janice trying to put Sachin in the dustbin. Janice said, 'I just snapped. I hit out at her and my ring scratched her cheek. It's terrible. I said I would never, ever hit one of my children. My father used to hit us. I can't believe I did it.' You take the opportunity to ask about Janice's remark of having a sore bottom. Ruth replies straightaway, 'It's the constipation. Janice won't go to the loo for days. Then of course she's in pain when she finally does go. And then she has stomach aches as well. We've taken her to the doctor and he just says Janice is obviously jealous of all the attention for Sachin and she'll get over it. I'm at my wits' end!'

$\Rightarrow$

Clement

You work in a children's centre. Clement, who is two years old, has started in your group this week. Clement seems happy and he talks with single words and a few two-word phrases. But he has very little idea about what to do with the play materials that you would usually give to his age group and is keener to handle the baby toys. He cannot walk but stands steadily holding onto a firm surface and cruises along by hand holds.

The health visitor has told you that Clement was found a place in the centre because she realised that the boy's mother and grandmother did not let him out of his cot. They both expressed great worries about the potential dangers to Clement if they let him roam around their flat, or if they took him out into the local neighbourhood. Both women seem caring towards Clement. However, the settling-in time at the centre has been hard, as his grandmother has been especially concerned about Clement's safety in the playroom and the centre garden.

Domestic violence and abuse

What does it mean?

Domestic violence: threatening behaviour, or actual aggression, in the home between relatives, or adults of either sex or any sexual orientation, who are (or have been) intimate partners of family members.

Domestic violence and abuse are harmful to children and will affect their emotional well being, as well as physical well being, should they be caught in the crossfire of domestic violence.

Domestic violence and abuse is not only linked with poverty or stressful living conditions. The situation can arise in any social class or ethnic group. The term covers any kind of threatening behaviour, or actual violence, between adults of either sex or any sexual orientation, who are related or are (or have been) intimate partners of family members.

Domestic abuse is defined by the Government as:

'Any incident or pattern of incidences of controlling, coercive, threatening behaviours, violence or abuse between those aged 16 or over who are or have been intimate partners or family members regardless of gender or sexuality. The abuse can encompass but is not limited to the following types of abuse:

- *psychological*
- *physical*
- *sexual*

- *financial*
- *emotional.*

  'Controlling behaviour is: a range of acts designed to make a person subordinate and/or dependent by isolating them from sources of support, exploiting their resources and capacities for personal gain, depriving them of the means needed for independence, resistance and escape and regulating their everyday behaviour.

  'Coercive behaviour is: an act or a pattern of acts of assault, threats, humiliation and intimidation or other abuse that is used to harm, punish, or frighten their victim.'

(Home Office, 2013)

This definition includes so-called 'honour' based violence, female genital mutilation (FGM) and forced marriage, and is clear that victims are not confined to one gender or ethic group.

Children are adversely affected by living in a home where there are regular violent disputes. Their emotional well being and psychological development are poorly affected, even if they do not suffer any physical abuse themselves. The problems of domestic violence have been brought into a more central position within safeguarding, with the recognition that the situation always affects children; the only question is by how much. The likely risks are that:

- Children are distressed by continuing arguments in their home and by the threat of possible violence. They may be torn by conflicting loyalties between their parents or other family members. They can also be pulled into the damaging secret that nobody outside the family must know how bad matters have become. It has been accepted that significant harm can be experienced by children when they frequently see and hear the ill-treatment of someone else.
- Children may fail to be protected in a home full of violence. Conflicts between the adults may erupt into physical attack and the children are caught in the middle. The adults may not intend that the children are injured and they do not directly attack them, but adult violence can injure children as bystanders.
- Parents who are prone to violence sometimes also attack their children or stepchildren, or threaten to do so in order to control their partner. Domestic violence directed at adults is sometimes part of a more general abusive pattern in which children are directly abused, physically or sexually, and family pets are also cruelly treated.
- Parents under extreme stress are not in a position to offer their children the kind of support that is necessary for healthy development. Additionally, some mothers or fathers divert their frustration and anger onto the children. Children in their turn may become aggressive to other children, or turn in on themselves to become distressed and withdrawn.

In order to help parents, you need to understand the complex situation that they face. People who have very little experience of the problem often say,

'But surely, she could just leave.' Yet women, or the more hidden number of men, who are on the receiving end of domestic violence often have very few options of where to go; and the extended family is not always supportive. Despite the violence, abused adults may still be attached to their partner and continue to hope the violent person will eventually change or hold to their promise to do so. They may excuse violent actions as explained by drink or stress, or feel that they somehow provoke outbursts. Parents in violent homes may be afraid their children will be taken into care unless the violence remains a family secret, into which the children are inevitably drawn.

You may not be the person to help directly but you could be invaluable in alerting a parent to other sources of help and support.

- You may be able to reassure parents that they do have resources for the children, when failure to protect them from a violent partner has seriously undermined this confidence. Parents sometimes also have mixed feelings, seeing echoes of the violent partner in the actions of one or more of their children.
- It is a practitioner's responsibility to alert parents to the fact that children are affected by violence in the home. Sons and daughters can suffer serious emotional distress, even when they are not physically harmed. Parents may feel that they are protecting children, perhaps by tolerating the violence. In the case of the younger age range, perhaps the non-violent parent is convinced that the children are ignorant of what happens after they have gone to bed. You may also support a parent who needs to be honest with children about what is happening or the steps their non-violent parent has taken to protect them.

Take another perspective

The early years' workforce is overwhelmingly female, so children whose mother or grandmother is violent should not lack experience of kind women if they attend a setting. However, children whose fathers are the violent partner may lack any experience of caring, non-aggressive men. An alternative and positive image may be offered if you have male practitioners or volunteers. You can also present positive male role-models using stories, images and toys in your setting.

Keep the child in mind

If it comes to light that a child is living within the context of domestic abuse, which may or may not include physical abuse, a child protection referral must be made to children's social care. Investigation and assessment is required to determine whether or not the child is at risk of, or is suffering, significant harm, and multi-agency interventions will be required to support the child and family.

Serious health problems in the family

Despite years of guidance about inter-agency working, some local authorities still need to make progress in ensuring that all services know they should work together for effective safeguarding.

Professionals involved with addicted adults should always be alert as to whether individuals who can scarcely take care of themselves are (theoretically) responsible for the well being of children or young adolescents. The same principle of practice applies to adult mental-health services. It is important not to stigmatise adults who seek help for any kind of problem. However, any professional directly involved may need to alert other services to possible risks for children in the family. Depression is a serious mental-health issue for the adult involved, but it is equally a potential safeguarding issue when this adult is the primary carer for a baby or child.

A significant number of children and adolescents live in families where life is utterly disrupted because of their parents' alcohol consumption or use of drugs – illegal or abuse of prescription medication. A noticeable proportion – some sources estimate this to be as much as a quarter – of children with a child protection plan have reached that position because of their parents' use of drugs or alcohol. Drug users and alcoholics are not necessarily bad parents, at least not deliberately. However, it is irresponsible of any service team to ignore the fact that the capacity of addicted adults to be a safe parent has been seriously compromised.

Some adults who are addicted to alcohol or drugs make significant efforts to take care of their children and get help for themselves. However, any kind of addictive behaviour absorbs an adult's attention and will often affect parents to the extent that they cannot possibly ensure the well being or direct safety of their children. Carelessness about bottles of alcohol, drugs and the paraphernalia that accompanies drug addiction inevitably places young children at risk. Parents who are regularly drunk or incapacitated by drug usage have also opted out of keeping their children or young adolescents safe from dubious behaviour of the adult's friends or acquaintances.

Any early years provision, school or club should have clear procedures to follow if a parent or other known adult arrives at the end of your day or session and is clearly not in a fit state to take responsibility for this baby or child. In brief, these procedures should outline how you express your concern and that you do not release a child into unsafe care. It would be usual practice that two staff members will remain until the end of a day or session. So one person can take care of the child and the other monitor the adult. It will be necessary to wait until a safe adult, a family member or known friend, has arrived. If a seriously ill, drunk or otherwise incapacitated adult refuses to co-operate or insists on leaving with the child, then your procedures should make clear who to call. Childminders are unlikely to have a colleague, but should otherwise follow a similar procedure.

In some families, one parent may work hard to protect children from the impact of the other parent's addictive behaviour. However, in some households both parents are involved and children are unsafe in what operates as an open house. An unknown number of grandparents have taken on primary responsibility for their grandchildren because the parents are unable to cope as the result of their addiction. Sometimes addictions remain a family secret or older children step up to the parental responsibility. These young carers (see below) often still care deeply about their parent(s). They want help, but are blocked by not knowing who to ask. They also fear that telling a teacher, for example, will result in the break-up of their family by social care services.

Children and young adolescents should be seen as 'in need' whenever drug use affects family life. They are also affected when older siblings have a drug problem and parents are struggling to deal with that situation. Family life is disrupted by the continuing anxiety and the actions of young addicts, such as stealing from family members. The presence of drugs increases the risk that siblings may try them, and some addicted young people have deliberately introduced their siblings to drugs.

Pause for reflection

Unless you work in a specialist centre, it will not be appropriate to attempt direct work with parents on complex problems, such as severe depression or alcoholism. Your support will be through knowing about local facilities and sharing this information. It is not your role to push parents into using helplines or support groups; such decisions remain their choice.

Develop a file or folder, updated at regular intervals, containing details on local services and special units. You can add national organisations that offer advice on reliable websites, telephone helplines or practical leaflets. If you already have such a resource, then check it covers these safeguarding issues.

Young carers

A considerable number of daughters and sons are responsible for much of their own family life: taking care of their parent(s) and sometimes also younger siblings. Their situation is still often overlooked, despite more public awareness of the extent of the problem since the 1990s. These young carers are in a different situation from children and young adolescents who are effectively raising themselves because their parents are neglectful or abusive. Many young carers have loving parents who do not in any way ill-treat them but these adults are unable to be as fully an active parent as they might wish, as the consequence of chronic physical or mental ill-health, or the impact of disability. If your professional work is within early childhood, then the main issue about young carers is that they could take significant family responsibility for the young children who attend your provision. You may have a lower age limit for any person who is judged appropriate to take responsibility for a young child at the end of your day or session.

What does it mean?

Young carer: older children or young people who take on a parental role within their family, looking after themselves, one or both parents and younger siblings.

From available statistics it seems that most young carers are adolescents, but some older children carry similar levels of family responsibility. The problem is long-standing and often hidden. Young carers, together with their parents and young siblings, can be very anxious about the family situation becoming public, out of fear that a blunt social-care response will be to take children into care. Such a response is unlikely unless there is significant risk, and family support services should be the chosen option. However, young carers frequently say that help is delayed, sporadic and sometimes a poor fit, given the family's needs.

Young carers share all the stresses that are experienced by adults who care for an incapacitated family member. They carry out normal household duties, worry about money, deal with a range of health and other professionals, can be responsible for medication, have disrupted sleep and try to take good care of younger siblings. It is hardly surprising that young carers, whether an only child, the eldest or most responsible of a sibling group, feel tired and worried much of the time. Older children and young people can also be troubled by health problems like back troubles, arising from lifting or helping to support the full weight of an adult.

The plight of a young carer often comes to light because the school takes action about unauthorised absence or frequent late arrival. Sometimes a sympathetic teacher finds out about the young person's domestic burden when following up the lack of homework. However, many of the signs that should concern practitioners could indicate other problems, including neglect by an able parent. It is another reminder about recognising a serious concern, but keeping an open mind about the origin of the problem. If you work with younger children, then a young carer's situation may become clear because of your efforts to understand why you never get to see the parent or your concerns about the standard of care at home for a young boy or girl. If you work with older children, then you can find out more from the suggested further resources.

Practitioners can support young carers by keeping confidences appropriately, but clearly not joining in a secret that blocks appropriate help. Young carer support services will often work with schools, to extend knowledge and find ways for young carers to cope with the long list of responsibilities in their daily life. Like any other aspect of support, it is important that you find out more in general, as well as aim to locate services in your area.

Make the connection with ...

Regular attendance

Unexplained absence of a child should always be followed up in nursery, club, school or your home as a childminder. Practitioners in any setting have a responsibility to check when this child should have arrived today, or when they should have been seen by now, even on an irregular pattern of attendance.

It is good practice that parents realise that you are concerned to know they are all right. Most times, such follow-up will prompt an apology that you were not told about a planned absence or unexpected illness. However, there have been cases where a nursery or other setting has sounded the alarm and young children have been found with a desperately sick parent, or children have been abandoned in their home.

Commentary on the scenarios

Here are some ideas. You and your colleagues or fellow students may have brought other perspectives.

Winston (page 244)

Some parents have resorted in desperation to using alcohol to deal with night-waking children. It is not a safe option, since young children can easily be made ill by alcohol. It is, additionally, against the law, since they are younger than the legal age at which children can be given alcohol (five years of age under the Children and Young Persons Act 1933).

Winston's mother needs empathy for this very tiring period and advice for coping with the sleep disruption. The nursery may be able to give suggestions within friendly conversation. Additionally, the local clinic or health visitor team should offer constructive support on this common problem. The next step would be to check with Winston's mother if she has asked for help and let her know about local facilities. You would not speak with these professionals without asking her.

His key person should monitor Winston's behaviour each day. As long as it seems very likely that Winston's mother has stopped dosing him with alcohol, then the incident may not need to go further than support and advice. This kind of example is one in which it is very helpful if a designated safeguarding lead can talk in confidence to a local authority adviser.

Janice (page 244)

The pre-school team are right to be concerned about the changes in Janice's behaviour, since she sounds like a very unhappy child. The family seems to be under heavy stress and Janice's mother (Ruth) is scarcely coping with all the problems. Her explanation about the constipation is feasible and she is open, and distressed, about having hit Janice.

If this pattern of behaviour is consistent, the pre-school team could feel confident to monitor and support Janice. They need, through a relationship with Ruth, to communicate their awareness that the situation is very stressful and it is not acceptable for Janice to be hit. The situation needs to be written up in the notes and monitored with care. It would be very helpful for Janice's key person or the designated safeguarding lead to talk with someone in confidence for a second opinion. However, if the explanation from Janice's mother seems feasible, the next step would be to support her in contacting a local source of family support. If Ruth is willing to accept this option, it reduces the immediate level of concern for the pre-school team.

Clement (page 245)

Young children who have had a caring but restricted early experience can develop quite quickly when their horizons are stretched, but this change cannot be assumed. It is important to monitor Clement and ensure that his development progresses well.

Clement's mother and grandmother sound caring yet seriously anxious. Family support could be a great help to guide them in more positive childcare and play for Clement. It would be worth exploring whether the family would accept, even maybe welcome, someone from a local home-visiting service. Supportive conversations may also help to determine whether there are genuine dangers within the family home or the local neighbourhood, and what needs to be done.

The key person needs to welcome Clement's grandmother, but cannot agree to inappropriate restrictions on his movement, either indoors or out in the garden. A positive approach on partnership means that the key person, and other staff, are ready to explain and show how they keep young children safe.

Find out more

www.nagalro.com/about-nagalro/aims-and-structure.aspx
Look at the Nagalro website under the 'Information for children and families' section to understand more about the role of a guardian *ad litem*.

www.victimsupport.com/Help for witnesses/Help for young witnesses
Victim Support.

Plotnikoff, J. and Woolfson, R. (2004) *In their own Words: the Experiences of 59 Young Witnesses in Criminal Proceedings*, London: NSPCC

Summary

This chapter has addressed how practitioners can work together in partnership with the child and their family. Support to parents is essential if they are 'struggling' to meet the needs of their child(ren) or there are factors that impact on parenting capacity. The chapter has considered some of the stressors that impact on parenting and the family as whole. Factors such as domestic violence and abuse, and parental mental illness, can impact adversely on parenting capacity and affect the well being and welfare of the child(ren) in the family. These phenomena were discussed in Chapters 1 and 2, highlighting the vulnerability of the child in such contexts. This chapter has, however, discussed support that can be given by practitioners to help prevent further harm. Young carers have also been discussed.

What is important is that vulnerable families are provided with appropriate support, and that interventions are put in place early so harm is reduced or prevented. Chapter 9 discusses contemporary policy perspectives on early help.

Key texts

Bibby, A. and Becker, S. (2000) *Young Carers in Their Own Words*, London: Calouste Gulbenkian Foundation

The Princess Royal Trust for Carers www.carers.org

Advisory Council on the Misuse of Drugs (2003) *Hidden Harm: Responding to the Needs of Children of Problem Drug Users*. Available online at: www.gov. uk/government/publications/amcd-inquiry-hidden-harm-report-on-children-of-drug-users

Barnard, M. (2005*) Drugs in the Family: The Impact on Parents and Siblings*, York: Joseph Rowntree Foundation. Available online at: www.jrf.org.uk/ report/drugs-family-impact-parents-and-siblings

Davies, C. and Ward, H. (2011) *Safeguarding Children across Services: Messages from Research on Identifying and Responding to Child Maltreatment*. Available online at: www.gov.uk/government/uploads/system/ uploads/attachment_data/file/184882/DFE-RBX-10-09.pdf

Devaney, J. (2010) *The Impact of Domestic Violence on Children, Highlight No 259*, London: National Children's Bureau

Gorin, S. (2004) *Understanding What Children Say about Living with Domestic Violence, Parental Substance Abuse or Parental Health Problems*, London: National Children's Bureau. Available online at: www.jrf.org.uk/ report/understanding-what-children-say-about-living-domestic-violence-parental-substance-misuse-or

See the guidance issued by the Home Office: Home Office (2013) *Definition of Domestic Violence and Abuse: Guide for Local Areas*, London: Home Office. Available online at: www.gov.uk/government/publications/definition-of-domestic-violence-and-abuse-guide-for-local-areas

Department of Health (2005) *Responding to Domestic Abuse: A Handbook for Health Professionals.* London: Department of Health. Available online at: www.domesticviolencelondon.nhs.uk/uploads/downloads/DH_4126619.pdf

Radford, L., Aitkin, R., Miller, P., Ellis, J., Roberts, J. and Firkic, A. (2011) *Meeting the Needs of Children Living with Domestic Violence in London,* Refuge/NSPCC research project funded by the City Bridge Trust.

Cleaver, H., Unell, I. and Aldgate, J. (2011) *Children's Needs – Parenting Capacity. Child Abuse: Parental Mental Illness, Learning Disability, Substance Misuse and Domestic Violence,* 2nd edn. London: The Stationery Office

9 Concluding chapter

Introduction

This short concluding chapter discusses the importance of early help and summarises the key principles for practice.

Early help

It is everyone's responsibility to safeguard children and young people. As highlighted in Chapter 1, while local authorities play a lead role in child protection, everyone who comes into contact with children and families has a role to play (HM Government, 2015). Furthermore, Section 11 of the Children Act 2004 places duties on a range of organisations and individuals to make arrangements for ensuring that their functions, and any services that they contract out to others, are discharged with regard to the need to safeguard and promote the welfare of children (HM Government, 2015a).

Additionally, under section 10 of the same Act, a similar range of agencies are required to co-operate with local authorities to promote the well being of children in each local authority area. This co-operation should exist and be effective at all levels of the organisation, from strategic level through to operational delivery, and those working in agencies with these duties are responsible for ensuring that they fulfil their role and responsibilities in a manner consistent with the statutory duties of their employer (HM Government, 2015a).

It is also important to note that section 175(4) of the Education Act 2002 states that governing bodies of maintained schools (including maintained nursery schools), further education institutions and management committees of pupil referral units must have regard to any guidance given by the Secretary of State.

It is, however, those practitioners who work with children on a daily basis who are well placed to identify early when a child's welfare is at risk. Not only do they have a responsibility for keeping them safe, but they have a key role to play in identifying concerns, sharing information and taking prompt action. The actions taken to meet the needs of vulnerable children as early as possible are crucial to a child's future health and development. It is therefore important to recognise vulnerability as well as respond to signs of abuse and neglect.

HM Government (2015a) makes it clear in contemporary policy that the provision of early help is more effective in safeguarding the welfare of children than is reacting later.

What does it mean?

'**Early help** means providing support as soon as a problem emerges, at any point in a child's life, from the foundation years through to the teenage years. Early help can also prevent further problems arising, for example, if it is provided as part of a support plan where a child has returned home to their family from care.'

However, 'Effective early help relies upon local agencies working together to:

- identify children and families who would benefit from early help;
- undertake an assessment of the need for early help; and
- provide targeted early help services to address the assessed needs of a child and their family which focuses on activity to significantly improve the outcomes for the child.

Local authorities, under section 10 of the Children Act 2004, have a responsibility to promote inter-agency co-operation to improve the welfare of children'.

(HM Government, 2015a)

It is therefore important that children's vulnerabilities and families in crisis are identified and referrals made early to appropriate social care or universal services to enable the child and family to access appropriate help. It is important to identify emerging problems and to share information with other agencies and professionals to support early identification and assessment.

However, it is important to note that consent should be obtained from the parents if information is to be shared with another agency.

Practice point: key messages

A practitioner working with children of 0–8 years and their families should be particularly alert to the potential need for early help for a child who:

- is disabled and has specific additional needs;
- has special educational needs;
- is a young carer;
- is showing signs of engaging in anti-social or criminal behaviour;
- is in a family circumstance presenting challenges for the child, such as substance abuse, adult mental-health problems and domestic violence;
- has returned home to their family from care; and/or
- is showing early signs of abuse and/or neglect.

Additionally, 'professionals working in universal services have a responsibility to identify the symptoms and triggers of abuse and neglect, to share that information and work together to provide children and young people with the help they need. Practitioners need to continue to develop their knowledge and skills in this area. They should have access to training to identify and respond early to abuse and neglect, and to the latest research showing which types of interventions are the most effective'.

(HM Government, 2015a)

It is also important to note that early years providers have a duty under section 40 of the Childcare Act 2006 to comply with the welfare requirements of the Early Years Foundation Stage. Early years providers should ensure that:

- staff complete safeguarding training that enables them to recognise signs of potential abuse and neglect; and
- they have a practitioner who is designated to take lead responsibility for safeguarding children within each early years setting and who should liaise with local statutory children's services agencies as appropriate. This lead practitioner should also complete child protection training.

Key principles for practice

It is important to recognise and respond to concerns about a vulnerable child, a child in need and a child in need of protection from harm:

- Do not dismiss concerns – make sense of those 'gut feelings' and why you are concerned.
- Concerns must be shared with other professionals according to national and local policy.
- A designated safeguarding lead, named professional or adviser is available to offer guidance.
- All concerns and actions must be recorded, factually and in a timely way, even if no further action is taken. Decisions must be justified. Records must be contemporaneous.
- Guidance must be sought through the local policies and procedures and in accordance with national guidelines.
- Work together and in collaboration with other agencies as required in accordance with the legislation and policy.
- Refer to the Multi-Agency Safeguarding handbook/policy and other guidelines.
- Seek personal support.
- Access supervision and opportunities for reflection on practice.
- Keep up to date.

Summary

The safeguarding and protection of children is the responsibility of every professional who comes into contact with children and their families. Those working with children 0–8 years have an important role to play in this.

This book has covered the key issues in relation to recognising concerns, what to do and the referral process. It has addressed the contemporary issues for practice within the legislative and policy framework for practice. Ways of working to promote best practice to ensure that vulnerable children are recognised and that future harm is prevented are described. Means of supporting families have also been identified within the wider remit of safeguarding work.

However, it is vital that practitioners receive education and training about safeguarding children and child protection in order to keep them up to date and in line with national contemporary legislation and policy (and evidence that guides and underpins practice). Furthermore, it is important that practitioners are conversant with both national and local policy and procedures for safeguarding children. Responding to concerns and sharing information are vital to improve outcomes for children who may be at risk or are in need of protection. Indeed, everybody who works with children, parents and their families should be able to recognise, and know how to act upon, indicators that a child's welfare or safety may be at risk. Practitioners across all sectors of the children's workforce, including foster carers, child minders, early years and education professionals, healthcare professionals and managers should always be mindful of the welfare and safety of children – including unborn children and older children who they may come across in their work.

Remember: the child and their individual needs should be central to policy and practice. While it is important to 'think family' the child's needs should be central to this and should be the focus when making decisions as to how to best support the child and their family as a whole.

Further resources

References to key suggested texts are placed with the relevant section in each chapter. This section suggests organisations whose websites are useful sources of information, in addition to those already referred to within the book.

Action for Children – www.actionforchildren.org.uk
Barnardo's – www.barnardos.org.uk
ChildLine – www.childline.org.uk
Children in Wales (Plant yng Nghymru) – www.childreninwales.org.uk
Children in Scotland (Clann An Alba) – www.childreninscotland.org.uk
Children's Law Centre, the law in Northern Ireland – www.childrenslawcentre.org.uk
Children's Legal Centre, the law in England and Wales – www.childrenslegalcentre.com
Council for Disabled Children – www.ncb.org.uk/cdc
Children's Rights Alliance England – www.crae.org.uk/about-us
Early Years, the organisation for young children in Northern Ireland – www.early-years.org
Kidscape, information about child protection, personal safety and bullying – www.kidscape.org.uk
Legislation.gov.uk, legislation and bills in progress – www.legislation.gov.uk
NSPCC, research and statistics accessed through: www.nspcc.org.uk
National Children's Bureau, research and information about children and families – www.ncb.org.uk
Save the Children – www.savethechildren.org.uk
Scottish Child Law Centre, the law in Scotland – www.sclc.org.uk
The Children's Society, provides information and resources related to addressing child poverty and neglect – www.childrenssociety.org.uk

Key texts for safeguarding information

Action for Children (2012) *In the Eye of The Storm: Britain's Forgotten Children and Families, A Research Report for Action for Children*, London: The Children's Society and NSPCC

Coffey, A. (2014) *Real Voices: Child Sexual Exploitation in Greater Manchester, An Independent Report*

Daniel, B., Wassell, S and Gilligan, R (2010) *Child Development for ChildCare and Protection Workers*, 2nd edn, Jessica Kingsley

Davies, C. and Ward, H. (2011) *Safeguarding Children across Services: Messages from Research on Identifying and Responding to Child Maltreatment*. Available online at: www.gov.uk/government/uploads/system/uploads/attachment_data/file/184882/DFE-RBX-10-09.pdf

Harker, L. *et al.* (2013) *How Safe are Our Children?* London: NSPCC.

HM Government (2015a) *Working Together to Safeguard Children: A Guide to Inter-agency Working to Safeguard and Promote the Welfare of Children*, London: Department for Education

HM Government (2015b) *Keeping Children Safe in Education*, London: Department for Education

HM Government (2015c) *What to Do if You're Worried a Child is Being Abused*, London: Department for Education

Laming (2009) *The Protection of Children in England: A Progress Report*, London: House of Commons. Available online at: http://dera.ioe.ac.uk/8646/1/12_03_09_children.pdf

Lindon, J. (2011) *Too Safe for Their Own Good? Helping Children Learn about Risk and Lifeskills*, London: National Children's Bureau

Lindon, J. (2012) *Equality and Inclusion for Children and Families: Linking Theory and Practice*, London: Hodder Education

Miller, D. and Brown, J. (2014) *Protecting Disabled Children from Abuse*. NSPCC. Available online at: www.nspcc.org.uk/services-and-resources/research-and-resources/right-to-be-safe/

National Institute for Health and Care Excellence (2009) *When to Suspect Child Maltreatment*, NICE

NCH (2007) *Literature Review: the Emotional Harm and Well being of Children*. Available online at: www.actionforchildren.org.uk/media/145524/emotional_harm_and_well being_of_children.pdf

NSPCC (2014) *Assessing Parenting Capacity: An NSPCC Factsheet*, London: NSPCC

NSPCC (2014) *Culture and Faith: Learning from Case Reviews. Summary of Risk Factors and Learning for Improved Practice around Culture and Faith*, London: NSPCC. Available online at: www.nspcc.org.uk/preventing-abuse/child-protection-system/case-reviews/learning/culture-faith

NSPCC (2015) *Statistics on Child Abuse: Incidence and Prevalence*, London: NSPCC. Available online at: www.nspcc.org.uk/services-and-resources/research-and-resources/statistics/incidence-prevalence/#tab-registers

Powell, C. (2011) *Safeguarding and Child Protection for Nurses, Midwives and Health Visitors: A Practical Guide*, London: Open University Press

Rose, J. (2010) *How Nurture Protects Children. Nurture and Narrative Work with Children, Young People and Families*, RS

Wilkins, D., Shemmings, D. and Shemmings, Y. (2015) *A–Z of Attachment*, London: Palgrave Macmillan

References

Action for Children (2012) *In the Eye of The Storm: Britain's Forgotten Children and Families, A Research Report for Action for Children*, The Children's Society and NSPCC

Alford, N. and Bullock, R. (2005) *Insight 19: Child Death and Significant Case Reviews*, www.gov.scot/resource/doc/55971/0015630.pdf

Alternative Family Law (2015) *Children ("Custody")*, London: Alternative Family Law. Available online at: www.alternativefamilylaw.co.uk/en/children/index.html

Barnardo's (2011) *Reducing the Risk, Cutting the Cost: An assessment of the potential savings from Barnardo's interventions for young people who have been sexually exploited*, Ilford: Barnardo's. Available online at: www.barnardos.org.uk/reducing_the_risk_cutting_the_cost__final_.pdf

Bichard, M. (2004) *The Bichard Inquiry Report*, London: The Stationery Office. Available online at: http://dera.ioe.ac.uk/6394/1/report.pdf

Bradford, S. (2004) 'Management of growing up' in J. Roche, S. Tucker, R. Thompson and R. Flynn, Youth in Society: Contemporary Theory, Policy and Practice, 2nd edn, London: Sage/Open University Press

Brandon, M., Bailey, S. and Belderson, P. (2010) *Building on the Learning from Serious Case Reviews: A Two-year Analysis of Child Protection Database Notifications 2007–2009*, London: Department for Education

Brandon, M., Bailey, S., Belderson, P., Gardner, R., Sidebotham, P., Dodsworth, J., Warren, C. and Black, J. (2009) *Understanding Serious Case Reviews and their Impact: A Biennial*

Analysis of Serious Case Reviews 2005–07, London: Department for Children, Schools and Families, DCSF-RR129. Available online at: www.uea.ac.uk/centre-research-child-family/child-protection-and-family-support/understanding-scr-s-and-their-impact

Brandon, M., Sidebotham, P., Bailey, S., Belderson, P., Hawley, C., Ellis, C. and Megson, M. (2012) *New Learning from Serious Case Reviews*, London: Department for Education, DFE-RR226

Brodie, I. and Shaw, C. (2010) *Private Foster Care Highlight No 260*, London: National Children's Bureau

Bunting, L., Webb, M.A. and Healy, J. (2008) *The 'Smacking Debate' in Northern Ireland: Messages from Research*. Available online at: www.nspcc.org.uk/globalassets/documents/research-reports/smacking-debate-northern-ireland-report.pdf

Carlile Report (2003) *The Review of Safeguards for Children and Young People Treated and Cared for by the NHS in Wales*, Cardiff: National Assembly for Wales. Available online at: www.wales.nhs.uk/publications/English_text.pdf

Casey, L. (2015) Report of Inspection of Rotherham Metropolitan Borough Council. London: Department for Communities and Local Government. Available online at: www.gov.uk/government/uploads/system/uploads/attachment_data/file/401119/46966_Rotherham_Report_PRINT.pdf

Cawson, P., Wattam, C., Brooker, S. and Kelly, G. (2000) *Child Maltreatment in the United Kingdom: A Study of the Prevalence of Child Abuse and Neglect*, London: NSPCC

CEOP (2013) *Threat Assessment of Child Sexual Exploitation and Abuse*, London: CEOP. Available online at: www.ceop.police.uk/Documents/ceopdocs/CEOP_TACSEA2013_240613%20FINAL.pdf

Chase, E. and Statham, J. (2005) Commercial sexual exploitation of children and young people in the UK – a review', *Child Abuse Review* 14: 4-25

Coffey, A. (2014) *Real Voices: Child Sexual Exploitation in Greater Manchester*. An Independent Report

Corby, B., Shemmings, D. and Wilkins, D. (2012) *Child Abuse: An Evidence Base for Confident Practice, 4th edn*, London: Open University Press

Daniel, B., Wassell, S. and Gilligan, R. (1999) *Child Development for Child Care and Protection Workers*, London: Jessica Kingsley Publishers

Davies, C. and Ward, H. (2011) *Safeguarding Children Across Services: Messages from Research*, London: Jessica Kingsley

Department for Education (2012) *National Action Plan to Tackle Child Abuse Linked to Faith or Belief*, London: Department for Education. Available online at: www.gov.uk/government/publications/national-action-plan-to-tackle-childabuse-linked-to-faith-or-belief

Department for Education (2013) Tables D2 and D4 in: *Characteristics of Children in Need in England: 2012 to 2013*, London: Department for Education

Department for Education (2014) *Statutory Guidance on Children who Run Away or Go Missing from Home or Care*, London: Department for Education. Available online at: www.gov.uk/government/uploads/system/uploads/attachment_data/file/307867/Statutory_Guidance_-_Missing_from_care__3_.pdf

Department for Education and DHSSPS (2012) *Regulated Activity in Relation to Children: Scope*. Available online at: www.gov.uk/government/uploads/system/uploads/attachment_data/file/316179/Regulated_Activity_in_relation_to_Children__DfE_.pdf

Department of Health (2009) *Healthy Child Programme. Pregnancy and the First Five Years of Life*, London: Department of Health

DHSSPS (2006) *Our Children and Young People – Our Shared Responsibilities. Overview Report*, Belfast: Department of Health, Social Services and Public Safety. Available online at: www.dhsspsni.gov.uk/osschild-protection.htm

DHSSPS (2011) *Understanding the Needs of Children in Northern Ireland*, Belfast: Department of Health, Social Services and Public Safety. Available online at: www.dhsspsni. gov.uk/publications/understanding-needs-children-northern-ireland-unocini-guidance

Elliott, M. (ed.) (1993) Chapter 5 in *Female Sexual Abuse of Children*, London: Longman

Elliott, M. (ed.) (2002) *Bullying: a Practical Guide to Coping for Schools*, Harlow: Pearson Education

Ferguson, H. (2011) *Child Protection Practice*, Basingstoke: Palgrave Macmillan

Gill, T. (2007) *No Fear: Growing up in a Risk-Averse Society*, London: Calouste Gulbenkian Foundation, www.gulbenkian.org.uk

Great Britain (1989) *The Children Act 1989: Elizabeth II*, London: The Stationery Office

Great Britain (2004) *The Children Act 2004: Elizabeth II*, London: The Stationery Office

Green, R., Rodger, H., Cappleman, S. and Dale, R. (2014) *Learning from Cafcass Submissions to SCRs*, London: Children and Family Court Advisory and Support Service. Available online at: www.cafcass.gov.uk/media/224016/learning_from_cafcass_submissions_to_scrs.pdf

Hanson, E. and Holmes, D. (2014) *That Difficult Age: Developing a More Effective Response to Risks in Adolescence: Evidence Scope*, Totnes: Research in Practice. Available online at: www.rip.org.uk/resources/publications/evidence-scopes/evidence-scope-that-difficult-age-developing-a-more-effective-response-to-risks-in-adolescence/

Haringey LSCB (2009) *Serious Case Review: Baby Peter. Executive Summary*, London: Haringey Local Safeguarding Children Board. Available online at: www.haringeylscb.org/sites/haringeylscb/files/executive_summary_peter_final.pdf

Harker, L. et al. (2013) *How Safe are our Children?* London: NSPCC

HM Government (2014) *Female Genital Mutilation: Multi-Agency Practice Guidelines*, London: Home Office and Department for Education. Available online at: www.gov.uk/government/publications/female-genital-mutilation-guidelines

HM Government (2015a) *Working Together to Safeguard Children: A Guide to Inter-agency Working to Safeguard and Promote the Welfare of Children*, London: Department for Education. Available online at: www.gov.uk/government/uploads/system/uploads/attachment_data/file/419595/Working_Together_to_Safeguard_Children.pdf

HM Government (2015b) *Keeping Children Safe in Education*, London: Department for Education. Available online at: www.gov.uk/government/uploads/system/uploads/attachment_data/file/447595/KCSIE_July_2015.pdf

HM Government (2015c) *What to Do if You're Worried a Child is Being Abused*, London: Department for Education. Available online at: www.gov.uk/government/uploads/system/uploads/attachment_data/file/419604/What_to_do_if_you_re_worried_a_child_is_being_abused.pdf

HM Government (2015d) *Information Sharing*, London: Department for Education. Available online at: www.gov.uk/government/uploads/system/uploads/attachment_data/file/419628/Information_sharing_advice_safeguarding_practitioners.pdf

Horvath, M., Alys, L., Massey, K., Pina, A., Scally, M. and Adler, J. (2013) *"Basically… porn is everywhere" A Rapid Evidence Assessment on the effect that access and exposure to pornography has on children and young people*, London: Office of the Children's Commissioner. Available online at: www.childrenscommissioner.gov.uk/sites/default/files/publications/Basically_porn_is_everywhere.pdf

Home Office (2013) *Definition of Domestic Violence and Abuse: Guide for Local Areas*, London: Home Office. Available online at: www.gov.uk/government/publications/definition-of-domestic-violence-and-abuse-guide-for-local-areas

Home Office (2015) *Mandatory Reporting of Female Genital Mutilation: Procedural Information*, London: Home Office. Available online at: www.gov.uk/government/uploads/system/uploads/attachment_data/file/469448/FGM-Mandatory-Reporting-procedural-info-FINAL.pdf

Jay, A. (2014) *Independent Inquiry into Child Sexual Exploitation in Rotherham: 1997–2013*, Rotherham: Rotherham Metropolitan Borough Council. Available at: www.rotherham.gov.uk/download/downloads/id/1407/independent_inquiry_cse_in_rotherham

Kellet, J. and Apps, J. (2009) *Assessments of Parenting and Parenting Support Need: A Study of Four Professional Groups*, York: Joseph Rowntree Foundation. Available online at: www.jrf.org.uk/sites/default/files/jrf/migrated/files/parenting-support-need-full.pdf

Lalor, K. and McElvaney, R. (2010) 'Child sexual abuse, links to later sexual exploitation/high-risk sexual behaviour, and prevention/treatment programs', *Trauma, Violence, & Abuse* 11(4) 159-177

Laming (2003) *The Victoria Climbié Enquiry: Report*, London: House of Commons

Laming (2009) *The Protection of Children in England: A Progress Report*, London: House of Commons. Available online at: http://dera.ioe.ac.uk/8646/1/12_03_09_children.pdf

Lindon, J. (1999) *Understanding World Religions in Early Years Practice*, London: Hodder and Stoughton

Lindon, J. (2008) *Safeguarding Children and Young People 0–18 Years, 3rd edn*, London: Hodder Education

Lindon, J. (2009) *Guiding the Behaviour of Children and Young People: Linking Theory and Practice*, London: Hodder Education

Lindon, J. (2010) *The Key Person Approach: Positive Relationships in the Early Years*, London: Practical Pre-School Books

Lindon, J. (2011) *Too Safe for Their Own Good? Helping Children Learn about Risk and Life Skills*, London: National Children's Bureau

Lindon, J. (2012a) *Safeguarding and Child Protection 0–8 Years, 4th edn, Linking Theory and Practice*, London: Hodder Education

Lindon, J. (2012b) *Equality and Inclusion for Children and Families: Linking Theory and Practice*, London: Hodder Education

Lock, R. (2013) *Serious Case Review re Daniel Pelka: born 15th July 2007 died 3rd March 2012* [full overview report]. Coventry: Coventry Safeguarding Children Board. Available online at: https://library.nspcc.org.uk/HeritageScripts/Hapi.dll/retrieve2?SetID=C85A0FDF-0A1E-4612-AEFE-6C0DF95FCF10&searchterm=Daniel%20Pelka&Fields=%40&Media=%23&Bool=AND&SearchPrecision=20&SortOrder=Y1&Offset=7&Direction=%2E&Dispfmt=F&Dispfmt_b=B27&Dispfmt_f=F13&DataSetName=LIVEDATA

Miller, D and Brown, J (2014) *Protecting Disabled Children from Abuse*, London: NSPCC. Available online at: www.nspcc.org.uk/services-and-resources/research-and-resources/right-to-be-safe/

Munro, E. (2011) *The Munro Review of Child Protection: Final Report. A Child-Centred System*, London: Department for Education. Available online at: www.gov.uk/government/uploads/system/uploads/attachment_data/file/175391/Munro-Review.pdf

National Institute for Health and Care Excellence (NICE) (2009) *When to Suspect Child Maltreatment*, London: NICE

National Institute for Health and Care Excellence (NICE) (2015) *Obesity in Children and Young People: Prevention and Lifestyle Weight Management Programmes. NICE Quality Standard*, London: NICE. Available online at: www.nice.org.uk/guidance/qs94

National Working Group (2008) *What is Child Sexual Exploitation?* Derby: NWG Network

NMC (2015) *Raising Concerns: Guidance for Nurses and Midwives*, London: Nursing and Midwifery Council. Available online at: www.nmc.org.uk/standards/guidance/raising-concerns-guidance-for-nurses-and-midwives/

NSPCC (2012) Written evidence to the Joint Committee on Human Rights inquiry into the human rights of unaccompanied migrant children and young people in the UK, London: NSPCC

NSPCC (2013a) *Child Sexual Exploitation: Learning from Case Reviews. Summary of Risk Factors and Learning for Improved Practice around CSE*, London: NSPCC

NSPCC (2013b) *Child Sexual Abuse: An NSPCC Research Briefing: An Overview of the Current Literature on Child Sexual Abuse*, London: NSPCC. Available online at: www.nspcc.org.uk/globalassets/documents/information-service/research-briefing-child-sexual-abuse.pdf

NSPCC (2014a) *Assessing Parenting Capacity: An NSPCC Factsheet*, London: NSPCC

NSPCC (2014b) *Culture and Faith: Learning from Case Reviews. Summary of Risk Factors and Learning for Improved Practice around Culture and Faith*, London: NSPCC. Available online at: www.nspcc.org.uk/preventing-abuse/child-protection-system/case-reviews/learning/culture-faith/

NSPCC (2015) *Statistics on Child Abuse: Incidence and Prevalence*, London: NSPCC. Available online at: www.nspcc.org.uk/services-and-resources/research-and-resources/statistics/incidence-prevalence/#tab-registers

Parton, N. (2015) *The Politics of Child Protection: Contemporary Developments and Future Directions*. London: Palgrave Macmillan

Piper, H. and Stronach, I. (2008) *Don't Touch! The Educational Story of a Panic*, Abingdon: Routledge

Plymouth Safeguarding Children Board (2010) *Serious Case Review. Overview Report. Executive Summary in Respect of Nursery Z*, Plymouth: Plymouth SCB. Available online at: www.plymouth.gov.uk/serious_case_review_nursery_z.pdf

Powell, C. (2011) *Safeguarding and Child Protection for Nurses, Midwives and Health Visitors: A Practical Guide*, London: Open University Press

Radford, L., Corral, S., Bradley, C., Fisher, H., Bassett, C., Howat, N. and Collishaw, S. (2011) *Child Abuse and Neglect in the UK Today*, London: NSPCC

Reeves, J. (ed.) (2008) *Inter-Professional Approaches to Young Fathers*, Keswick: M&K Update

Rose, J. (2010) *How Nurture Protects Children. Nurture and Narrative Work with Children, Young People and Families*, London: Responsive Solutions UK

Royal College of Paediatrics and Child Health (2012), *Position Statement: Childhood Obesity*, London: RCPCH. Available online at: www.rcpch.ac.uk/sites/default/files/page/obesitypositionstatement.pdf

Royal College of Paediatrics and Child Health (2015), 'New standards and guidelines endorsed June–July 2015', London: RCPCH. Available online at: ww.rcpch.ac.uk/news/new-standards-and-guidelines-endorsed-june-july-2015

Rudolf, M. (2009) *Tackling Obesity through the Healthy Child Programme: A Framework for Action*. Available online at: www.noo.org.uk/uploads/doc/vid_4865_rudolf_TacklingObesity1_210110.pdf

Scottish Executive (2002) *It's Everyone's Job to Make Sure I'm Alright*, Edinburgh: Scottish Executive. Available online at: www.gov.scot/Resource/Doc/47095/0025590.pdf

Scottish Executive (2003) *The Children's Hearings System in Scotland 2003: Training Resource Manual*. Available online at: www.gov.scot/Publications/2003/12/18611/29851

The Scottish Government (2014) *National Guidance for Child Protection in Scotland*, Edinburgh: The Scottish Government. Available online at: www.gov.scot/Resource/0045/00450733.pdf

United Nations (1989) *United Nation Convention on the Rights of the Child*, UN

Utting, D. (ed.) (2007) *Parenting and the Different Ways it can Affect Children's Lives: Research Evidence*. Available online at: www.jrf.org.uk/report/parenting-and-different-ways-it-can-affect-childrens-lives-research-evidence

Waterhouse Inquiry (2000) *Lost in Care*. Available online at: http://tna.europarchive.org/20040216040105/http://www.doh.gov.uk/lostincare/20102a.htm

Webb, J. (2007) 'Safeguarding and protecting children', in Cleaver, K. and Webb, J. *Emergency Care of Children and Young People*, Oxford: Blackwell Publishing

Webb, J. and Holmes, D. (2015) *Working Effectively to Address Child Sexual Exploitation: Evidence Scope*, Totnes: Research in Practice

Welsh Assembly Government (2002) *Children and Young People: Rights to Action*, Cardiff: Welsh Assembly Government. Available online at: http://gov.wales/docs/caecd/publications/090415rightstoactionen.pdf

Wilkins, D., Shemmings, D. and Shemmings, Y. (2015) *A–Z of Attachment*, Basingstoke: Palgrave Macmillan

Young (2010) *Common Sense – Common Safety*, London: Cabinet Office. Available online at: www.hse.gov.uk/aboutus/commonsense/index.htm

Index